ACCESS

Building Literacy Through Learning™

English

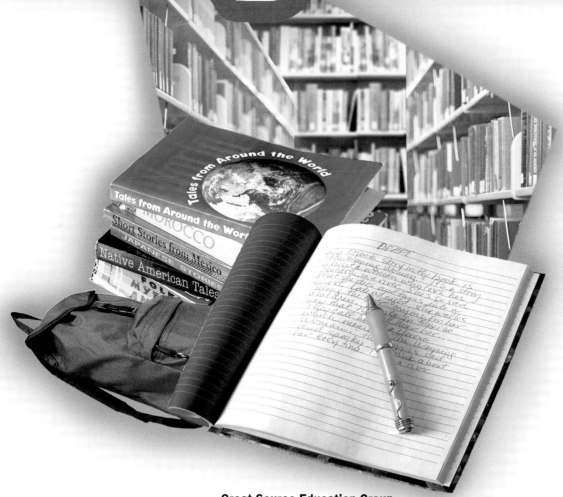

Great Source Education Group

a division of Houghton Mifflin Company

Wilmington, Massachusetts

www.greatsource.com

AUTHORS

Dr. Elva Durán holds a Ph.D. from the University of Oregon in special education and reading disabilities. Durán has been an elementary reading and middle school teacher in Texas and overseas. Currently, she is a professor in the Department of Special Education, Rehabilitation, and School Psychology at California State University, Sacramento, where she teaches beginning reading and language and literacy courses. Durán is co-author of the Leamos Español reading program and has published two textbooks, *Teaching Students with Moderate/Severe Disabilities* and *Systematic Instruction in Reading for Spanish-Speaking Students.*

Jo Gusman grew up in a family of migrants and knows firsthand the complexities surrounding a second-language learner. Gusman's career in bilingual education began in 1974. In 1981, she joined the staff of the Newcomer School in Sacramento. There she developed her brain-based ESL strategies. Her work has garnered national television appearances and awards, including the Presidential Recognition for Excellence in Teaching. Gusman is the author of *Practical Strategies for Accelerating the Literacy Skills and Content Learning of Your ESL Students.* She is a featured video presenter, including "Multiple Intelligences and the Second Language Learner." Currently, she teaches at California State University, Sacramento, and at the Multiple Intelligences Institute at the University of California, Riverside.

Dr. John Shefelbine is a professor in the Department of Teacher Education, California State University, Sacramento. His degrees include a Masters of Arts in Teaching in reading and language arts, K–12, from Harvard University and a Ph.D. in educational psychology from Stanford University. During his 11 years as an elementary and middle school teacher, Shefelbine has worked with students from linguistically and culturally diverse populations in Alaska, Arizona, Idaho, and New Mexico. Shefelbine was a contributor to the California Reading Language Arts Framework, the California Reading Initiative, and the California Reading and Literature Project, and has authored a variety of reading materials and programs for developing fluent, confident readers.

EDITORIAL: Developed by Nieman Inc. with Phil LaLeike
DESIGN: Ronan Design

Printed in the United States of America

International Standard Book Number: 0-669-50892-6

4 5 6 7 8 9–VHG–10 09 08 07

CONSULTANTS

Shane Bassett
Portland, OR

Jeannette Gordon
Senior Educational Consultant
Illinois Resource Center
Des Plaines, IL

Dr. Axia Perez-Prado
College of Education
Florida International University
Miami, FL

Dennis Terdy
Township High School
Arlington Heights, IL

TEACHER GROUP REVIEWERS

Harriet Arons
Lincoln Junior High School
Skokie, IL

Andrea Ghetzler
Old Orchard Junior High
  School
Skokie, IL

Lori Miller
Old Orchard Junior High
  School
Skokie, IL

Marsha Robbins Santelli
Chicago Public Schools
Chicago, IL

Tia Sons
Old Orchard Junior High
  School
Skokie, IL

Mina Zimmerman
Deerpath Middle School
Lake Forest, IL

RESEARCH SITE LEADERS

Carmen Concepcion
Lawton Chiles Middle School
Miami, FL

Andrea Dabbs
Edendale Middle School
San Lorenzo, CA

Daniel Garcia
Public School 130
Bronx, NY

Bobbi Ciriza Houtchens
Arroyo Valley High School
San Bernardino, CA

Portia McFarland
Wendell Phillips High School
Chicago, IL

RESEARCH SITE ENGLISH REVIEWERS

Nicholas Carozza
Bronx, NY

Claudia Estrada
Hialeah Miami Lakes
  Senior High School
Hialeah, FL

Elisabeth Imhof
Edendale Middle School
San Lorenzo, CA

Alice Scruggs
Martin Luther King, Jr.
  Middle School
San Bernadino, CA

ENGLISH TEACHER REVIEWERS

Brenda Custodio
Mifflin Welcome Center
Columbus, OH

Anita Ensmann
J. E. B. Stuart High School
Falls Church, VA

Dianne Grant
Prince George's County
  Public Schools
Capitol Heights, MD

Andy Luu
Sandburg Middle School
New Hope, MN

Nancy Maker
Richfield Middle School
Richfield, MN

Jennifer Moore
Chase Elementary School
Chicago, IL

Vicky Olesky
Harvard Kent School
Charlestown, MA

Kristina Robertson
Minneapolis Public
  Schools
Minneapolis, MN

Jill Wegenstein
La Entrada School
Menlo Park, CA

Karen Zogg
Lincoln Middle School
Berwyn, IL

TABLE OF

STANDARDS Students read and respond to historically and culturally significant works. They know ways in which literature reflects the diverse voices of people from various backgrounds. Students understand imagery and symbolism. Students connect the essential ideas of the text by using their knowledge of text structure, organization, audience, and purpose. Students use the reading process effectively. Students use prewriting strategies to choose a topic, generate ideas, and establish and maintain a focus. They use the writing process to generate ideas, develop drafts, revise, edit, proofread, and publish. Students are able to summarize information.

CONTENTS

STANDARDS Students use a variety of strategies to analyze words and text and draw conclusions. Students connect literature passages to their own lives. Students respond to a text by evaluating key ideas. Students use background knowledge of the subject and text structure to make inferences about the selection. Students understand metaphor. Students use simple, compound, and complex sentences; they use effective coordination and subordination of ideas to express complete thoughts. Students have varied sentence structure and sentences that are complete except when fragments are used purposefully. Students use correct capitalization. They use basic transition words to connect ideas. Students learn how to synthesize information.

STANDARDS Students read and respond to historically or culturally significant works. They know ways in which literature reflects the diverse voices of people from various backgrounds. Students understand tone, mood, and style. Students connect and clarify main ideas. Students focus on stated and implied main ideas. They determine the main idea or essential message in a text and identify relevant details, facts, and patterns of organization. They synthesize key ideas and supporting details to form conclusions. Students analyze characters. Students understand various forms of text structure, including compare and contrast order, cause-effect order, spatial order, order of importance, and chronological order.

CONTENTS

STANDARDS Students understand various elements of authors' craft, including word choice, figurative language, and imagery. Students write descriptive narratives that include sensory details and concrete language to develop plot and character. Students produce final documents that have been edited. Students demonstrate appropriate use of various parts of speech. Students apply the conventions of written language, such as capitalization, punctuation, and spelling, to communicate clearly. Students use literary strategies, such as analyzing, to evaluate texts.

STANDARDS Students read and respond to historically and culturally significant works. Students recognize point of view and identify the details that reveal genre. Students evaluate the evidence for an author's conclusions. Students learn about a variety of reference materials, including magazines, newspapers, and journals. They select varied sources for texts when reading for information or pleasure. Students distinguish fact and opinion. Students determine a text's main ideas and how those ideas are supported with details. Students analyze text that uses chronological and cause-effect order. Students use organizational features of electronic text to locate information. Students use text organizers, including headings, graphic features, and tables of contents, to locate and organize information. Students paraphrase information. Students understand and interpret visual images, messages, and meanings. Students apply survey strategies, such as use of bold print, organization of content, key words, and graphics.

CONTENTS

STANDARDS Students select and use appropriate formats for writing, including persuasive and expository formats, according to the intended audience, purpose, and occasion. They support all claims with anecdotes, descriptions, facts, statistics, and specific examples. Students organize information using chronological order. Students write to inform, such as to explain, describe, and report. Students ensure that verbs agree with compound subjects. Students identify and demonstrate use of various parts of speech. Students produce final documents that have been edited for effective sentence structure and subject-verb agreement, and they use verb tenses, such as present, past, future, perfect, and progressive, appropriately and consistently.

STANDARDS Students read and respond to historically and culturally significant works. They know ways in which literature reflects the diverse voices of people from various backgrounds. Students understand and analyze the differences in structure and purpose between various categories of informational material (for example, textbooks, newspapers, and instructional manuals). They can interpret information from tables, maps, visual aids, and charts to enhance understanding of text. Students use text organizers, including headings, graphic features, and tables of contents, to locate and organize information. They use the reading process effectively. Students analyze text that uses comparison and contrast. Students use study strategies, such as previewing, questioning, and rereading, to learn and recall important ideas from texts. They organize information before writing according to the type and purpose of writing. Students support plausible interpretations with evidence from the texts. Students answer different types and levels of questions.

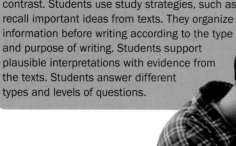

CONTENTS

STANDARDS Students organize information before writing according to the type and purpose of writing. Students engage the interest of the reader and state a clear purpose; they develop the topic with supportive details and conclude with a detailed summary linked to the purpose of composition. Students use organizational features of electronic text to locate information. Students give credit for both quoted and paraphrased information in a bibliography. Students synthesize and evaluate information from a variety of texts. They edit and revise their content. Students identify parts of speech and types and structures of sentences; they identify and use regular and irregular verbs in writing and speaking. Students produce final documents that have been edited for correct common usage. Students use verb tenses appropriately and consistently.

THEME 5

OUR PLACE 240

STANDARDS Students read and respond to historically and culturally significant works. Students identify and analyze features of themes conveyed through characters, actions, and images. Students understand irony and symbolism. Students analyze the effect of the qualities of the character on the plot and the resolution of the conflict. Students identify events that advance the plot. Students use strategies, such as rereading, note-taking, summarizing, and outlining, to clarify meaning. Students identify universal themes and experiences and see how these are communicated across cultures. Students synthesize key ideas and recognize features that distinguish genres. They organize information before writing according to the type and purpose of writing. Students progress through the stages of the writing process and begin to establish a personal voice and style.

CONTENTS

STANDARDS Students analyze the effect of the qualities of the character on the plot and the resolution of the conflict. Students analyze characters as delineated through a character's thoughts, words, and actions; the narrator's description; and the thoughts, words, and actions of other characters. Students generate ideas and plans for writing by using rewriting strategies, such as brainstorming, graphic organizers, notes, and journals. Students use simple, compound, and complex sentences; they use effective coordination and subordination of ideas to express complete thoughts. Students produce final documents that have been edited for effective sentence structure. They should be able to use adjectives, adverbs, and prepositional phrases to enrich written language. Students are able to use adjectives (comparative and superlative forms) and adverbs appropriately to make writing vivid or precise. Students can interpret imagery.

STANDARDS Students read and respond to historically and culturally significant works. They identify and trace the development of an author's point of view or perspective in a text. Students determine meaning from the speaker's denotations and connotations. Students establish and adjust purposes for reading, such as reading to find out, to understand, to interpret, to enjoy, and to solve problems. Students locate, organize, and interpret written information to perform real-world tasks. Students are able to follow multiple-step instructions for preparing applications. Students can apply survey strategies (for example, use of bold print, organization of content, key words, graphics). They use skimming to preview reading materials. Students draw conclusions based on information found in visual information and data. They write to influence, such as to persuade, argue, and request. Students write essays that contain formal introductions, supporting evidence, and conclusions. Students compose writing that supports a topic or thesis statement with evidence. They draft and revise writing that includes support that is substantial, specific, relevant, concrete, and clear.

CONTENTS

STANDARDS Students choose the form of writing (for example, personal letter, letter to the editor) that best suits the intended purpose. Students distinguish between the use of English in formal and informal settings. Students write to influence, such as to persuade, argue, and request, and they collaborate with other writers to compose, organize, and revise various types of text, including letters. Students correspond with peers or others via email or conventional mail. They edit and revise their content. Students identify all parts of speech and types and structure of sentences. Students speak for various occasions, audiences, and purposes, including conversations, discussions, projects, and informational, persuasive, or technical presentations. They identify and apply appropriate word analysis and vocabulary strategies. Students identify and demonstrate different traits of oral presentations intended to inform, to entertain, and to persuade. Students use oral and written language that follows the accepted conventions of the English language for effective social communication with a wide variety of people. As readers and listeners, they use the social communications of others to enrich their understanding of people and their views.

Theme
1 New Beginnings

Every day people start over and make new beginnings. They meet new people, move to new places, and have new understandings about their lives and who they are.

- What are these people doing?
- Where do you think they are going?
- What new beginnings have you made?

Understanding Imagery

Poets use words in a special way to form pictures in your mind. This is called **imagery.** Poets want you to see, hear, feel, smell, or taste what they are writing about. As you read poetry, try to **visualize** the images described on the page. Make drawings of the **images** in your journal.

Visualize—form a picture in your mind

Images—pictures in your mind

Imagery—words that create pictures in your mind and help you see, hear, feel, smell, or taste something

Before Reading Activities

Hands On

Reading Journal Start a reading journal. On the first page, tell some things about yourself. Add pictures from magazines or drawings of your own to tell who you are, things you like, and what you like to read. Then draw a timeline like this one of your own life. Put 3 to 5 important things that have happened to you on your timeline. Share your journal with a partner.

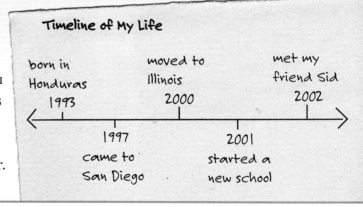

Timeline of My Life

born in Honduras 1993

moved to Illinois 2000

met my friend Sid 2002

1997 came to San Diego

2001 started a new school

Oral Language

Beginnings In a small group, talk about new beginnings in your own life. Where did your life begin? What "new" things have happened to you? When was a time you had to start over?

Poems About New Beginnings

In the poems you are about to read, the poets write about new beginnings in their lives. Pat Mora writes about parents raising children in a new country. Diana Chang explores the new way she sees herself—as both Chinese and American. Joseph Bruchac writes about his grandparents moving to a new country.

As you read the poems, think about how they connect to your own life. Ask yourself how the poems are similar. How are they different? What examples of imagery do the poets use?

IMMIGRANTS
by Pat Mora

wrap their babies in the American flag,
feed them mashed hot dogs and apple pie,
name them Bill and Daisy,
buy them blonde dolls that blink blue
eyes or a football and tiny **cleats**
before the baby can even walk,
speak to them in thick English,
      hallo, babee, hallo,
whisper in Spanish or Polish
when the babies sleep, whisper
in a dark parent bed, that dark
parent fear, "Will they like
our boy, our girl, our fine american
boy, our fine american girl?"

> **VOCABULARY**
>
> **cleats**—metal pieces on the bottom of sports shoes. They keep players from slipping.
> **hallo, babee, hallo**—"hello, baby, hello"

The Statue of Liberty stands in New York Harbor and welcomes immigrants to America. ▶

Saying Yes 是

by Diana Chang

"Are you Chinese?"
"Yes."

"American?"
"Yes."

"*Really* Chinese?"
"No . . . not quite."

"*Really* American?"
"Well, actually, you see . . ."

But I would rather say
yes

Not **neither-nor,**
not maybe,
but both, and not only

The homes I've had,
the ways I am

I'd rather say it
twice,
yes

(**TALK AND SHARE**) **With a partner, draw
the images you see in the poems.**

VOCABULARY

neither-nor—not one or the other

ELLIS ISLAND

by Joseph Bruchac

Beyond the red brick of **Ellis Island**
where the two Slovak children
who became my grandparents
waited the long days of **quarantine,**
after leaving the sickness,
the old **Empires** of Europe,
a Circle Line ship slips easily
on its way to the island
of the **tall woman, green**
as dreams of forests and **meadows**
waiting for those who'd worked
a thousand years
yet never owned their own.

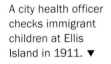

A city health officer checks immigrant children at Ellis Island in 1911. ▼

▲ The Statue of Liberty (upper left) welcomes immigrants to Ellis Island (lower right).

VOCABULARY

Ellis Island—an island near New York City where many immigrants first landed

quarantine—being held apart from everyone else. It is a way of protecting people from getting disease.

empires—lands or countries controlled by one leader

tall woman, green—the Statue of Liberty

meadows—grassy land or ground

from **"Ellis Island"**

Like millions of others,
I too come to this island,
nine **decades** the answerer
of dreams.
Yet only one part of my blood loves
    that memory.
Another voice speaks
of **native** lands
within this nation.
Lands invaded
when the earth became owned.
Lands of those who followed
the changing Moon,
knowledge of the seasons
in their **veins.**

Children wait at
Ellis Island. ▼

TALK AND SHARE **What new beginning does Bruchac write about in "Ellis Island"? Talk with a partner about it.**

Responding to Literature

Explore the Readings

Talk with a partner about each question below.

1. Which poem meant the most to you? Give one or two reasons why you liked it.

2. What did you learn about the idea of new beginnings from "Immigrants"? What did you learn from "Saying Yes"?

3. What beginnings in your own life did these poems remind you of?

4. How do you think these poets felt about their own beginnings?

5. What imagery did you see in "Ellis Island"?

6. How do you think Diana Chang feels about being Chinese in "Saying Yes"?

Learn About Literature

Symbols

A *symbol* is a person, place, or thing that stands for something else. You see and use symbols every day. A red light is a symbol for stop. A dove is a symbol of peace. A plus sign (+) is a symbol for adding.

Poets use symbols to talk about things in a special way. For example, in the poem "Ellis Island," Joseph Bruchac writes:

> "Another voice speaks
> of native lands
> within this nation."

"Another voice" is a symbol for his Native-American ancestors. Bruchac is saying that his Native-American ancestors were in America before anyone else came here.

In a small group, look at the 3 poems again and find more symbols. A few of them are listed below. Work together to figure out what they mean.

American flag   Ellis Island

Statue of Liberty

Activities

Hands On

Make a Poster In small groups, cut out magazine pictures that suggest new beginnings. Add them to a poster and tell how or why you think they are new beginnings.

Oral Language

Give a Reading With a partner, choose one of the short poems, such as "Saying Yes" or "Immigrants," to read aloud. Take turns reading one line at a time. Then read the poem again silently one or more times. Once you know the poem well, read it aloud to your partner.

Partner Practice

Write Your Own New Beginnings Think about the beginnings in your own life. Then choose one of the poem beginnings shown below and write your own poem. Read it aloud to a partner. Here are two ways you could start.

1. Beyond the_____ of _____

2. Are you_____?

Know the Authors

Pat Mora

Pat Mora was born in 1942. She is a mother and teacher in addition to being a well-known writer of such books as *Tomas and the Library Lady*, *Pablo's Tree*, and *Listen to the Desert*.

Diana Chang

Diana Chang was born in San Francisco in 1934. She is both a novelist and a poet. In "Saying Yes," Chang explores what it means to be both Chinese and American.

Joseph Bruchac

Joseph Bruchac was born in New York. He writes in "Ellis Island" about one of the country's greatest symbols of immigration. Bruchac is English, Slovak, and Native American. He is both a teacher and a writer.

The
Reading Process

Here you'll learn about how to better understand what you read. You'll also learn how to take notes and practice explaining the steps in the reading process.

Building Background

▲ My favorite place to read is under the tree in my back yard.

■ **Where is this person?**

■ **Why do you think he is reading?**

■ **Where do you like to read?**

The reading process explains what steps to take before, during, and after reading. It helps you understand and remember what you read.

1 **Before Reading**
- Set a purpose
- Preview
- Plan

2 **During Reading**
- Read with a purpose
- Connect

3 **After Reading**
- Pause and reflect
- Reread
- Remember

Key Concepts

A **purpose** is the reason for doing something.
A **process** is a series of small steps or actions.
A **strategy** is a plan to help you get from one step
of the process to the next.

Process

Purpose

Strategy

Steps in the Reading Process

Before Reading

Set a Purpose   Preview

Borders

Pat Mora

Why am I reading this?

Plan

eat American food

buy American toys

"Immigrants"

have American names

want to fit in

During Reading

Read with a Purpose

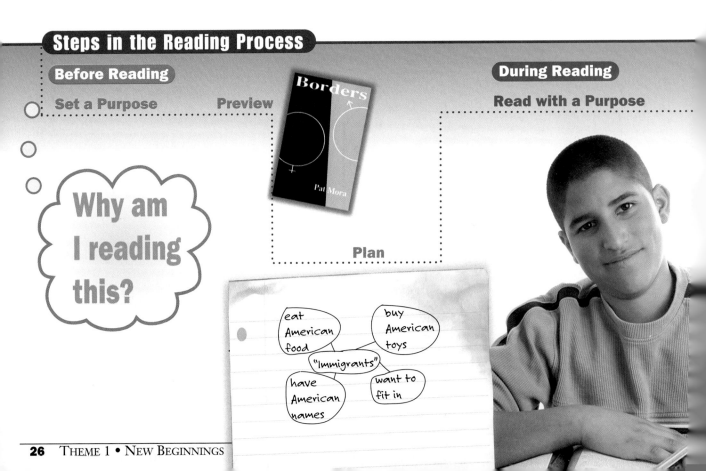

Taking Notes

When you take notes, you help yourself understand and remember what you read. Readers sometimes take notes to remember important facts. Other times they take notes to connect their own lives to the text. In a Double-entry Journal, you first write down interesting lines from your reading. Then try to explain what they mean in your own words.

Double-entry Journal

Quote	My Thoughts
"Will they like our boy, our girl, our fine american boy, our fine american girl?"	I remember wondering if the kids at school would like me when I first came to America.

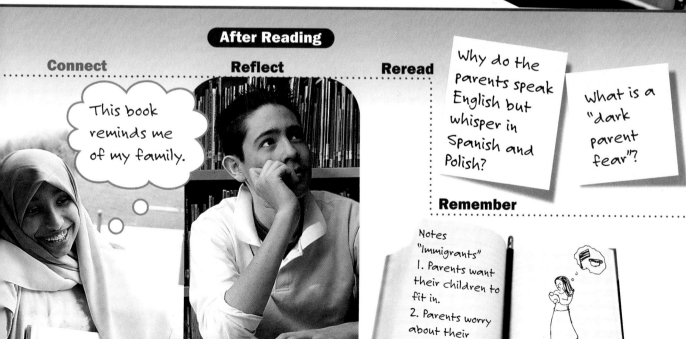

After Reading

Connect   **Reflect**   **Reread**

This book reminds me of my family.

Why do the parents speak English but whisper in Spanish and Polish?

What is a "dark parent fear"?

Remember

Notes
"Immigrants"
1. Parents want their children to fit in.
2. Parents worry about their children in a new country.

My parents try to help me fit in, too.

The Reading Process

When you use the reading process, you go step by step before, during, and after you read. To understand the reading process, first think about what reading really is.

What Is Reading?

Reading has a **purpose.** Reading is a thinking **process** and a **skill.**

READING HAS A PURPOSE

We read to understand, not just to say the words. Reading without meaning is not really reading. We read for different reasons: to **figure out** how to fix something, to learn about something new that interests us, or to enjoy an exciting story.

READING IS A THINKING PROCESS

When we read, we use what we already know to understand what the author is trying to tell us with printed words. Reading is thinking. It's thinking about the purpose, thinking about what we know, and thinking about what the author is saying.

READING IS A SKILL

Good readers have skills and **strategies** for understanding what they read. They look for the big ideas and think about how the ideas can be **organized.** When reading doesn't make sense, good readers figure out why. They may try to figure out the meanings of new words. They may try to take notes on the major points. Or, they may go back and reread some of the difficult parts.

TALK AND SHARE With a partner, talk about the process you use when you read. What 3 words describe it for you?

Language Notes

Homophones
These words sound alike, but they have different spellings and meanings.

- **new:** made a short time ago; not old or used
- **knew:** understood

- **know:** understand
- **no:** opposite of yes

VOCABULARY

purpose—a reason for doing something
process—a series of steps or actions
skill—something you get better at doing the more you practice it
figure out—solve or discover

strategies—plans that help you get from one step of a process to the next
organized—put together or arranged in an orderly way

Before Reading

The reading process begins before you even open up a book. Here are 3 steps to follow before you read.

SET A PURPOSE

People read for all kinds of reasons. Sometimes they read for fun, and sometimes they read to learn something. Whatever the reason, it is important to set a purpose before you read.

PREVIEW

Before you start to read, take time to get an idea about the **selection.** Start with a **preview.** Look at the book cover, the table of contents, and the selection itself. You can even read the first few sentences. What is it about?

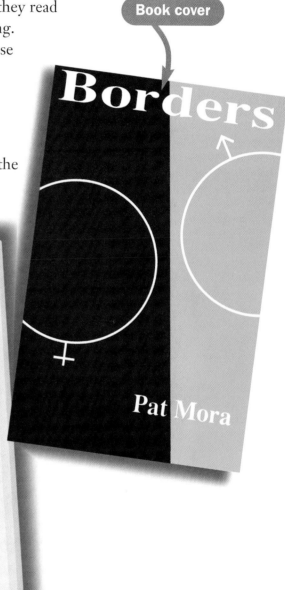

Book cover

Borders

Pat Mora

Table of contents

Borders

I

Title

Tomás Rivera	13
Immigrants	15
Border Town: 1938	16
Unnatural Speech	17
University Avenue	19
Sonrisas	20
Bilingual Christmas	21
The Grateful Minority	22
Echoes	23
Diagnosis	25
Withdrawal Symptoms	26
Tarahumara Mañanitas	27

VOCABULARY

selection—a story, article, poem, or chapter
preview—a look at something ahead of time

PLAN

A strategy is a plan for reading. It tells you how to do something. Different types of **texts** need different strategies. For example, you might **summarize** a chapter from a textbook. For a poem, you might read line by line and write notes in your Double-entry Journal.

Double-entry Journal

Quote	My Thoughts
"wrap their babies in the American flag, feed them mashed hot dogs and apple pie, name them Bill and Daisy,"	She's saying they're trying to make them American.

▲ How are these young women "wrapped in the American flag"?

TALK AND SHARE With a partner, talk about what you should do before you start to read. List 3 things.

VOCABULARY

texts—written materials. Poems, novels, and articles are texts.
summarize—tell the main points of something

During Reading

While you read, follow these two steps. They'll help you get the most out of your reading.

READ WITH A PURPOSE

As you read, look for information about your reading purpose. Your reading strategy helps you get the information you need. Taking notes, for example, helps you remember **details.** Writing your thoughts about lines in a poem can help you decide what the poem means. Use small **sticky notes** or write in your **reading journal.** Here is an example.

from "Immigrants"
by Pat Mora

buy them blonde dolls that blink blue eyes or a football and tiny cleats before the baby can even walk,

She's saying that the parents are giving the baby things that are American.

CONNECT

As you read, think about how the reading **connects** to, or is a part of, your life. Make personal connections between what you are reading and your own life. That keeps you interested in what you're reading. Plus, it is one of the best ways to understand a selection. You can do it by asking yourself these 3 questions.

| **1.** What does this remind me of? | **2.** How is this important to me? | **3.** What can I learn from this? |

from "Immigrants"
by Pat Mora

when the babies sleep, whisper
in a dark parent bed, that dark
parent fear, "Will they like
our boy, our girl, our fine american
boy, our fine american girl?"

My parents worry about me, too.

TALK AND SHARE Talk with a partner about how using a reading strategy can help you become a better reader.

VOCABULARY
connects—links, joins, or is a part of. Your hand *connects* to your arm.

After Reading

The reading process does not end after you read the last word in the text. To get the most out of your reading, take time to **pause and reflect, reread,** and **remember.**

PAUSE AND REFLECT

To pause and reflect means to stop and think carefully. After reading, look at what you learned and think about any questions you still have.

REREAD

You may still have some questions after reading. Rereading can help you answer those questions.

REMEMBER

No matter what you are reading, you will want to remember important parts of it. In a novel, it might be how a character changes. In a history textbook, it might be important dates. Write down your ideas after reading. It will help you remember. Keep a reading journal to help you keep track of your thoughts and remember what you read.

(**TALK AND SHARE**) **In a small group, talk about what to do after you read and how it can help you.**

Summary

The reading process explains what happens before, during, and after reading. Following these steps can help you understand and remember what you read.

Reading Tip

Use a Reading Journal

A journal is a notebook for writing down your thoughts and experiences. Start keeping a reading journal. A reading journal can help you understand and remember what you read. Here are some tips for keeping one. Write down important details from your reading and ideas you want to remember. Connect what you read to your own life. Tell how you feel about what you are reading or draw a picture.

VOCABULARY

pause and reflect—stop and think about carefully
reread—read a second or third time
remember—recall or be able to call up in your thoughts again

Explaining

Explaining the Steps in a Process

To *explain* means to make plain or clear. Explaining the steps in a process helps you remember the order. A Sequence Chart can help you organize notes on the important ideas. It shows how to go step by step. For example, this Sequence Chart lists the steps of the Before Reading part of the reading process.

Sequence Chart

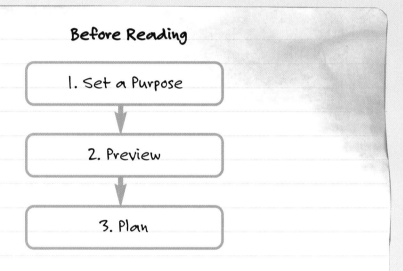

Before Reading

1. Set a Purpose

2. Preview

3. Plan

Practice Explaining

1. Tell   To a partner, explain the After Reading steps. Make a Sequence Chart like the one above. Fill in the 3 After Reading steps. Then tell your partner about each step in your chart.

2. Write   Explain all of the steps to follow in the reading process. First, list the steps in a Sequence Chart. Then, use your organizer to take notes. Write sentences that explain the steps. Use the Word Bank to help you.

Word Bank
first
second
third
next
last

Grammar Spotlight

The Verb *be* English uses the verb *be* all the time. It has many different forms. You'll need to memorize them.

Verb *be*	Singular	Example
am	I am	*I am a student.*
are	you are	*You are a reader.*
is	he is	*He is a teacher.*
	she is	*She is my aunt.*
	it is	*It is a reading strategy.*
	Plural	
are	we are	*We are readers.*
	you are	*You are good readers.*
	they are	*They are the best readers.*

Write your own sentences using *am*, *are*, and *is*.

Hands On

Make a Reading Poster In small groups, make a poster of the reading process. Use cardboard or a large sheet of paper. Divide it into 3 parts. Label them *Before Reading*, *During Reading*, and *After Reading*. Then cut out pictures from magazines or draw them to show the steps of the reading process. Share your poster with the class and explain how it shows the steps.

Oral Language

Teacher, Teacher With a partner, role-play a teacher explaining the reading process to a student. Begin this way:

STUDENT: *What is the reading process?*
TEACHER: *It is a series of steps to help you read.*
STUDENT: *What do I do before reading?*
TEACHER: *You think about why you are reading. Then you preview and make a plan for how to read.*

Keep going through the reading process. At the end, change roles and start over.

The Writing Process

Here you'll learn about the steps for becoming a better writer. You'll also learn how to write for an audience and practice summarizing steps of a process.

Building Background

▲ I like to write on my front porch when it's quiet outside.

- **What is this woman doing?**
- **What in the picture reminds you of something in your own life?**
- **What would you like to ask the woman in the picture?**

Use the steps of the writing process to become a better writer. First, you need to prewrite and draft your paper. Next, you revise, edit, and proofread. Then, you publish or present your paper.

1 Prewrite

Write a Draft 2

3 Revise

4 Edit and Proofread

5 Publish or Present

The first time I came to the United States, I was seven years old. I was very scared because many things were new, and so different. There were very tall buildings, and people running everywhere. Wherever I looked. I am from a very small town in Ecuador, and I am not used to the sounds of a large city. At night, I would sit by my open window and listen eries their deliveries. I

Key Concepts

A good writer will **organize** information in a way that is clear and easy to understand. When you **revise** your paper, you make changes to words and sentences to make your paper as clear as possible. This will help your **audience,** or people who read your writing, understand your paper.

Organize

My First Day in a New Country

By the end of the first day, the hardest part was over. As I met new people and tried new things, I started to feel more comfortable. It was a big challenge, but it was fun, too!

It was hard to move to a new country. The first day was the hardest of all.

At first it seemed like everyone was different. They spoke a different language and wore different clothes. I wondered if I would ever fit in.

Revise

My First Day in a New Country

It was hard to move to a new country. The first day was the hardest of all.

At first it seemed like everyone was different. They spoke a different language and wore different clothes. I wondered if I would ever fit in.

By the end of the first day, the hardest part was over. As I met new people and tried new things, I started to feel more comfortable. It was a big challenge, but it was fun, too!

Audience

The Writing Process

1. How to Prewrite

Brainstorm.

Narrow the topic.

Immigrants

first day

2. How to Draft

Use a computer.

Or, write with a pen.

My First Day in a New Country

It was hard to move to a new country. The first day was the hardest of all.

At first it seemed like everyone was different. They spoke a different language and wore different clothes. I wondered if I would ever fit in.

By the end of the first day, the hardest part was over. As I met new people and tried new things, to feel more comfortable. It was a big challenge, but it was fun, too!

3. How to Revise

My First Day in a New Country

It was hard to move to a new country. The first day was the hardest of all.

I thought I would never fit in because they were different and they wore different clothes and they had a different language.

By the end of the first day, the hardest part was over. As I met new people and tried new things, I started to feel more comfortable. It was a big challenge, but it was fun, too!

At first it seemed like everyone was different. They spoke a different language and wore different clothes. I wondered if I would ever fit in.

Change parts to make the meaning clearer.

Writing for an Audience

Your purpose is the reason you are writing. Your audience is the people who will read or hear what you write. Before you start writing, think about who your audience is.

Ask yourself these questions.

1. What does my audience already know about the subject?

2. Why will they read my work?

3. What do I think they want to learn from my writing?

This chart lists purposes and audiences for some different kinds of writing.

Purpose	Audience	Kind of Writing
To express your opinion	Students	Editorial in the school newspaper
To complain about a product	Company	Letter of complaint
To inform people about an event	The public	Poster

4. How to Edit and Proofread

Look up spelling.

Exchange papers and edit with a partner.

5. How to Publish or Present

Create a clean final draft.

> **My First Day in a New Country**
>
> It was hard to move to a new country. The first day was the hardest of all.
>
> At first it seemed like everyone was different. They spoke a different language and wore different clothes. I wondered if I would ever fit in.
>
> By the end of the first day, the hardest part was over. As I met new people and tried new things, I started to feel more comfortable. It was a big challenge, but it was fun, too!

Give a reading.

The Writing Process

The writing process has 5 steps: 1) prewriting, 2) drafting, 3) revising, 4) editing and proofreading, and 5) publishing or presenting.

Prewrite

Prewriting is the first step in the writing process. At this step, you choose a subject, gather information, and organize the details.

CHOOSE A SUBJECT

In school, sometimes you will be asked to write about a specific subject. Other times you can pick any subject you want. First, **brainstorm** ideas by thinking about all of the **possibilities.**

• Write about something you know. What are your experiences or interests? Write about what you know best.

• Think about your audience.

• Try not to choose a subject that is too **broad. Narrow** down your subject.

Example: <u>Immigrants</u> *is a very broad topic.*

Example: <u>The First Day in a New Country</u> *is a narrow topic.*

Web

the law

becoming citizens

Immigrants

starting over

first day in a new country

fitting in

VOCABULARY

prewriting—the first step in writing. It includes choosing a subject, gathering information, and organizing details.
brainstorm—think of many possible ideas
possibilities—options or choices that may work
broad—large in size
narrow—make smaller and easier to work on. You *narrow* down your subject so it is not too big.

GATHER INFORMATION

How do you find what to write about? Look in books, in magazines, or on the **Internet** for ideas. **Collect** information about your subject. Remember that the details you collect depend, in part, on what your audience already knows about the subject. Talk to friends and other people to get their ideas on your subject. Take notes on what you learn.

ORGANIZE THE DETAILS

Next, plan how you will **organize** the information. Put the information in an order that makes sense. You can make a list of your ideas or organize the details in a Web.

(**TALK AND SHARE**) **With your partner, talk about what happens during the prewriting step.**

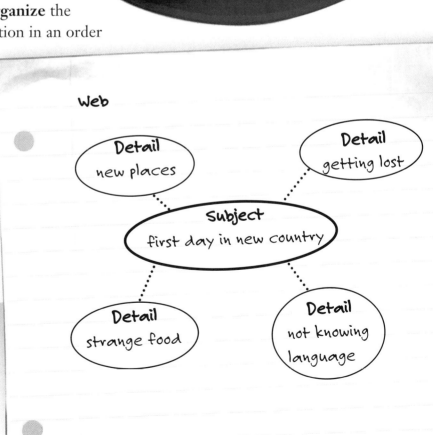

Web

Detail
new places

Detail
getting lost

Subject
first day in new country

Detail
strange food

Detail
not knowing language

Write a Draft

Writing a **draft** is the second step in the writing process. Here you try to get all of your ideas down on paper. Write freely. Organize what you want to say, but don't worry about all the details.

WRITE FREELY

In a draft, you simply write. Your goal is to get your ideas down on paper. Don't worry about making everything correct. You can cross out words that don't work or sound right. If you get stuck, move on and return to that part later.

ORGANIZE YOUR IDEAS

In your draft, organize your ideas. Try to create a strong beginning, middle, and ending.

Beginning	Middle	Ending
• Grab the reader's attention with an interesting fact. • Ask a question.	• Develop your subject. • Provide support with facts and definitions. • Add descriptive details.	• Summarize your main points. • Draw a conclusion.

Beginning of Draft

Grab attention →

On the first day I didn't know what. An immigrant is lost. On the first day, you can't find anything you remember. Everything is different. You are lost, like someone without anyplace to go. The language is different. The people look different. Even the food is different! Can you guess how that feels?

Ask a question

(TALK AND SHARE) **Talk with your partner about why you should write freely on a first draft.**

VOCABULARY
draft—the first, quick try at writing a paper

Revise the Draft

Later, after you have written your draft, read it again and **revise** it. To revise means to change the order of words or sentences. You can add words or cross them out. Look for the changes that will make your ideas clearer to the reader. Ask yourself the questions in the Revising Checklist.

~~On the first day I didn't know what.~~ An immigrant is lost. On the first day, you can't find anything you remember. Everything is different. You are lost, like someone without ~~anyplace to go.~~ a home The language is different. The people look different. Even the food is different! Can you guess how that feels?

TALK AND SHARE **Talk with your partner about how a checklist can help you revise your writing.**

Writing Tip

Revising Checklist

Good writers use a Revising Checklist to check their writing.

- ❐ Is my writing about one clear subject?
- ❐ Do I have a strong beginning, middle, and ending?
- ❐ Do I need to add more details or information to help my audience understand?
- ❐ Are some details not needed?
- ❐ Should the order of any sentences be changed?

VOCABULARY

revise—rethink and redo writing, changing sentences and ideas to make the writing clearer

Edit and Proofread

Editing means making sure you chose the right words. It is also the time you check to see that your sentences are complete and read smoothly. Ask yourself questions.

- Did I use the right word?

- Are all of the words spelled correctly?

- Are all of my sentences complete sentences?

- Do all of them end with the right punctuation?

Proofreading means checking your final draft for errors in **grammar, punctuation, capitalization,** and **spelling.** You might try reading your work out loud or exchanging papers with a friend. Below are a few useful proofreader's marks.

Proofreader's Marks

How to Mark	Meaning	Example
≡	Capitalize a letter.	Pat Mora wrote "immigrants."
/	Make a capital letter lowercase.	It's a good Poem.
⊙	Add a period.	Come to America⊙We'll welcome you⊙
sp.	Correct the spelling.	We went to (there) country.
ℓ	Take out or delete.	We should need to go.

(**TALK AND SHARE**) **Talk with your partner about how to use the proofreader's marks to add a period or to correct the capitalization.**

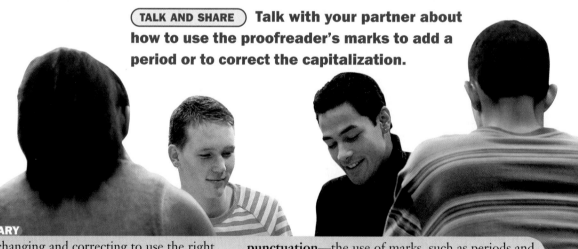

VOCABULARY

editing—changing and correcting to use the right words and complete, smooth sentences
proofreading—reading and marking corrections in grammar, punctuation, capitalization, and spelling
grammar—the rules for using words and sentences in language

punctuation—the use of marks, such as periods and commas, that make written work clearer
capitalization—the use of capital letters
spelling—the use of the correct letters to form a word

Publish or Present

When you **publish** or **present** your writing, you share it.

• Read your work out loud to a friend or partner.

• Put your work on the class bulletin board.

• Send your writing to the school newspaper.

 **With your partner, list two ways you can publish your writing.**

Summary

The writing process has 5 steps: prewriting, drafting, revising, editing and proofreading, and publishing or presenting. Follow these steps to make your writing better and easier to do.

Language Notes

Multiple Meanings
These words have more than one meaning.

▪ **draft**
1. a version or attempt at a paper
2. a light, cold breeze
3. an order to join the military

▪ **present**
1. show or display something
2. a gift

VOCABULARY

publish—make public or put on display for others to read; also to print something, such as a newspaper, magazine, or book

present—share or put in front of others for them to see and hear; display

Summarizing

Summarizing Steps of a Process

When you *summarize*, you tell only the most important information. You do not include all the details. You include only the important ones. A Summary Organizer can help you plan a summary.

Summary Organizer

Subject: What is prewriting?

Important Information:

1. Choose a subject.
2. Gather information.
3. Organize details.

Practice Summarizing

1. Draw Talk with a partner about what happens during the writing process. Together, draw pictures for a Summary Organizer. Show all of the steps in the writing process.

2. Write Tell about one step in the writing process: prewriting, drafting, revising, editing and proofreading, or publishing or presenting. First, complete a Summary Organizer. Tell the main point and what you do during that step in the process. Then, use your organizer to write a 3- or 4-sentence paragraph that summarizes that step. Be sure to check your writing using the checklist.

Check Your Writing

Make sure you

- ☐ Use complete sentences.
- ☐ Use a period at the end of each sentence.
- ☐ Spell all the words correctly.

Activities

Grammar Spotlight

Using Complete Sentences A sentence expresses a complete thought. A sentence may be a statement, a question, or an exclamation.

Type of Sentence	Example
Statement	*On the first day, you can't find anything you remember.*
Question	*Can you guess how that feels?*
Exclamation	*Even the food is different!*

A complete sentence begins with a capital letter. It ends with some kind of punctuation.

> *The language is different. The people look different. Even the food is different!*

Now write a complete sentence about your first day at school this year.

Hands On

Make a Poster With a partner, write the words *teacher* and *student* on separate index cards. Mix up the cards. Then choose one card. That's your audience. Make a poster for your audience about 3 ways that you can make a new student feel welcome at your school. Share your poster with your class. How are the posters alike? How are they different?

Oral Language

Chant Make a chant like the one below to help you remember the writing process. Then practice reading the chant aloud to your partner.

> *First, choose what to say.*
> *Don't let that take all day.*
> *Next, draft or write.*
> *It doesn't have to be all right.*
> *Later, revise or change.*
> *That's not so strange.*
> *Then, edit and proof to make it the best.*
> *You know the rest.*
> *Present it to other eyes.*
> *Then claim the prize.*

Active
Reading

Here you'll learn about how to become an active reader. You'll also learn how to do close reading and practice responding to what you read.

Building Background

▲ I like to write about what I read. It helps me remember it better.

- **What is the boy doing?**
- **What words best describe this picture?**
- **What would you tell someone about how and where you read?**

Be active when you read. You need to have different ways of taking notes so you can respond and connect, make judgments, draw conclusions, and compare and contrast.

"Immigrants"
by Pat Mora

Compare and Contrast

Why are they blonde dolls and not dolls with black hair?

Take Notes

Is this about how to be an American?

wrap their babies in the American flag,
feed them mashed hot dogs and apple pie,
name them Bill and Daisy,
buy them blonde dolls that blink blue
eyes or a football and tiny cleats
before the baby can even walk,
speak to them in thick English,
    hallo, babee, hallo,
whisper in Spanish or Polish
when the babies sleep, whisper
in a dark parent bed, that dark
parent fear, "Will they like
our boy, our girl, our fine american
boy, our fine american girl?"

Draw Conclusions

I think these things are on shoes.

Respond and Connect

My parents worry a lot, too.

Make Judgments

I think they will like them.

Key Concepts

Active reading means thinking about what you are reading. Active readers **mark, question, react, predict, visualize,** and **clarify** as they read.

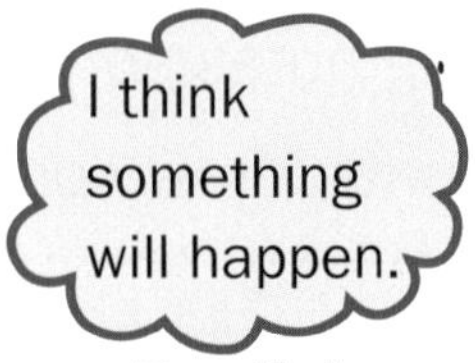

React

I think something will happen.

Predict

Question

Visualize

wisecrack = joke

Clarify

Mark

Reading Actively

React

Use a Double-entry Journal to respond to what you read.

Draw Conclusions

Use an Inference Chart to draw conclusions about a text.

Double-entry Journal

Quote	My Thoughts
"in a dark parent bed, that dark parent fear, 'Will they like our boy, our girl, our fine american boy, our fine american girl?'"	My parents worry a lot about me, too. They want me to fit in with everyone. I tell them that people like me just the way I am.

Inference Chart

Text	What I Conclude
"Not neither-nor, not maybe, but both, and not only The homes I've had, the ways I am"	I think she wants people to accept her for who she is—someone from two cultures.

Close Reading

Close reading is a good reading strategy for poems. It means reading slowly and carefully, word by word, line by line. By reading slowly and thinking about each word, you will understand the poem better.

Strategy Close Reading	
What It Is reading slowly and carefully, word by word and line by line	
Example "Beyond the red brick of Ellis Island where the two Slovak children who became my grandparents"	He is saying his grandparents were at Ellis Island as kids.

Compare and Contrast

A Venn Diagram can help you compare and contrast things you read.

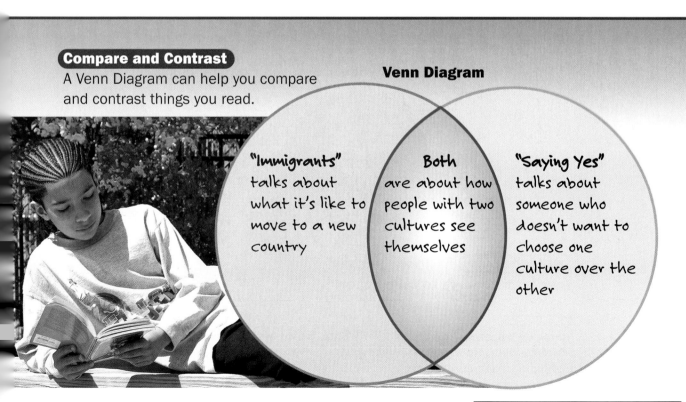

Venn Diagram

"Immigrants" talks about what it's like to move to a new country

Both are about how people with two cultures see themselves

"Saying Yes" talks about someone who doesn't want to choose one culture over the other

Active Reading

Active reading means thinking as you read. Active readers take notes, respond and connect, make judgments, draw conclusions, and compare and contrast as they read.

Reading and Thinking

Active readers are thinking all the time. They are not just sitting down and reading. Their **brains** are going fast because they are thinking and **reacting** to what they are reading.

As you read, you can be an active reader by taking notes. You can take notes in 3 different ways.

How to Take Notes

1. Mark or **highlight** the reading itself. Remember that, most of the time, you cannot mark in your school books.

a Circle Line ship slips easily
on its way to the island
of the tall woman, green
as dreams of forests and meadows

"tall woman, green"	must be the Statue of Liberty

2. Write and respond in your notebook.

3. Write sticky notes and put them on the page.

"tall woman, green" = Statue of Liberty

(**TALK AND SHARE**) **Tell your partner your favorite ways to take notes.**

VOCABULARY
brains—the brain is the part of your head that is used for thinking
reacting—acting in response to something
highlight—mark or call attention to something

Kinds of Notes

What do active readers do? They think as they read. Active readers usually take one or more of these 6 kinds of notes.

Kind of Notes	What It Is	Example
1. Mark or highlight	blonde dolls	buy them blonde dolls that blink blue
2. Ask questions	? ? ? ? ?	Why are they blonde?
3. React and connect	! ! ! ! !	That's crazy!
4. Predict	**I think _____ will happen.**	I think I'll like them.
5. Visualize		feed them mashed hot dogs and apple pie
6. Clarify	**Is this _____?**	Is this about how to be an American?

(**TALK AND SHARE**) **Ask your partner to tell you about 3 kinds of notes. Then tell him or her about 3 other kinds of notes.**

Responding and Connecting

When you read actively, you are constantly thinking about what you are reading. Your eyes are not just moving over the words. You are responding and **connecting** your life to those words. For example, when you read a line in a poem, stop and think about what each word means. Write your thoughts in a journal. Here are some ways you can start your sentences.

| I wonder why . . . | I think . . . | I can relate to this because . . . | This reminds me of . . . |

I wonder why these lands were invaded.

I think native lands are the same as American-Indian lands.

I can relate to this because my parents are from Peru and the Indian lands there were also invaded.

This reminds me of a story my grandfather told me about Incas in Peru.

from "Ellis Island"
by Joseph Bruchac

Another voice speaks
of **native** lands
within this nation.
Lands invaded
when the earth became owned.

TALK AND SHARE With a partner, talk about how reacting to a selection can help you get more out of your reading.

VOCABULARY
connecting—thinking about how you feel and how you have something in common with the reading
native—belonging to a place by birth

◄ Ellis Island symbolizes a new beginning for many immigrants. Angel Island is a similar place for immigrants on the West Coast.

Making Judgments

Any time you decide how you feel about something, you make a **judgment**. In a judgment, you decide what value something has for you. You make judgments every day. You decide what music you like, who your friends are, and what is important to you. When you do that, you are making judgments.

For example, which poem on pages 18–21 do you think is best?

☐ "Immigrants" by Pat Mora

☑ "Saying Yes" by Diana Chang

☐ "Ellis Island" by Joseph Bruchac

I liked "Saying Yes."
1. I felt the same way once.
2. It was short but strong.

When you make a judgment, you decide or form an **opinion.** You have **reasons** for the way you feel. Think about what they are. Try always to give two or more reasons to **support** your judgments.

(**TALK AND SHARE**) **With your partner, list 3 judgments you made today. Think about what you ate, what clothes you decided to wear, and what things you have said. Give reasons for each of your judgments.**

VOCABULARY
judgment—an opinion about what is good, bad, truthful, important, and so on
opinion—a belief that is based on what someone thinks or feels
reasons—causes or things that make you think, feel, or act in a certain way
support—explain; give evidence

Drawing Conclusions

A **conclusion** is a final, or last, **decision.** A conclusion is not just made up. It is a decision made after looking at many bits of information. What conclusion would you draw from these lines?

from "Ellis Island"
by Joseph Bruchac

Another voice speaks

of native lands

within this nation.

Lands invaded

when the earth became owned.

Lands of those who followed

the changing Moon,

knowledge of the seasons

in their **veins.**

My Conclusion
"Another voice" must be his Native-American grandparents.
1. The voice talks about being born in the United States.
2. He writes that their land was invaded.
3. He writes that seasons were important to their way of life.

(**TALK AND SHARE**) **With your partner, draw a conclusion about one of the other poems in this unit. Give one or two reasons why you came to that conclusion.**

VOCABULARY
conclusion—a final judgment or decision made after careful thought
decision—the act of making up one's mind
veins—tubes in the body that carry blood

◄ Native Americans watch the sun rise.

Comparing and Contrasting

When you **compare,** you show how two things are alike. When you **contrast,** you show how two things are different. Poets make comparisons to help you see things in new ways. As an active reader, you make pictures in your mind. That helps you **visualize** what the writer is saying. Use what you already know to **clarify** what the writer is saying.

Here one reader made a sketch and wrote notes to understand the comparison in a poem.

"Fame Is a Bee"
by Emily Dickinson

Fame is a bee.
   It has a song—
It has a sting—
   Ah, too, it has a wing.

The writer is comparing fame to a bee. Both have a sting.

Reading Tip

Metaphor
   Emily Dickinson compares fame to a bee. This kind of figurative language is called a *metaphor.* By comparing fame to an everyday thing, she helps you understand it in a new way. Comparing fame to a bee helps you see the "buzz" of fame and its "sting." This metaphor shows you that fame might not always be as great as it seems at first.

TALK AND SHARE With your partner, compare happiness to something. Use a metaphor if you can.

Summary

   Active readers always think and take notes as they read. They respond and connect to what they're reading. Active readers also make judgments, draw conclusions, and compare and contrast.

VOCABULARY

compare—show how things are alike
contrast—show how things are different
visualize—make pictures in your mind so that you can "see" what you are reading

clarify—make clear
fame—public popularity or respect

Responding

Responding to a Text

Responding to a text means reacting to what you read in writing or by talking. One way to respond is with a Double-entry Journal. It can help you look at one part of a reading. For example, this Double-entry Journal shows a response to lines in Joseph Bruchac's poem "Ellis Island."

Double-entry Journal

Quote	My Thoughts
"Yet only one part of my blood loves that memory. Another voice speaks of native lands within this nation."	He is thinking about his Native-American ancestors. I think he is "hearing" them talk about their land.

Practice Responding

1. Draw   With a partner, choose one of the poems on pages 18–21. Talk together about your reactions to it. Think of two ways to connect the poem to your lives. Make a drawing to show how it relates to you.

2. Write   From one of the poems on pages 18–21, choose some lines that you like. Use a Double-entry Journal to organize your thoughts about them. Write in your journal how you connect your life to the lines in the poem. The words in the Word Bank may help you. Start your response with one of these prompts.

I wonder why . . .
What I liked was . . .
I felt that . . .

Word Bank
whisper
fear

neither
nor
both
only

dreams
waiting

Activities

Grammar Spotlight

Plurals of Nouns That End in y To form the plurals of nouns that end in *y*, follow these two rules.

Nouns That End in:	Rule	Example	
vowel + *y*	add s	boy	*Will they like our boys?*
consonant + *y*	change *y* to *i*, and add es	baby	*"wrap their babies in the American flag"*

Write two sentences using the plural form of *day* and *country*.

Oral Language

Read Aloud Look back at the lines from Emily Dickinson's poem "Fame Is a Bee" on page 57. Practice reading it closely. Then practice reading it aloud to a partner. Change roles and have your partner read the poem aloud to you. Then talk about your reactions to each line with your partner.

Hands On

Stick It On Get a pad of sticky notes. Pick the poem on pages 18–21 that you liked the best. Read the poem again. Then use the sticky notes to make 3 different kinds of notes for the poem. See the examples below. Stick the notes on the poem in your book.

1. Predict
I think this will be sad.

2. Clarify
This means she's not sure what she is.

3. Respond and connect
I feel like a stranger sometimes, too.

Understanding
Sentences

Here you'll learn about sentences. You'll also learn how to combine sentences and practice synthesizing ideas.

▲ This looks like a place near my aunt's house. It's really far away.

■ **What do you see here?**

■ **What does the picture remind you of?**

■ **What sentence would you use to describe it to a friend?**

A sentence is a group of words that shows a complete thought. There are different parts to sentences and different kinds of sentences. All sentences begin with a capital letter and end with punctuation.

Read the paragraph below and pay attention to each sentence. Note that each one begins with a capital letter and ends with punctuation.

Begins with a capital letter

from *Lasting Echoes*
by Joseph Bruchac

Ends with a period

When I was growing up, my formal education was filled with the traditional courses in American history. I was taught about the "founding fathers" of this country, the major battles of the Civil War, and the like. But another part of me longed to know another history, the history of my American Indian ancestors.

each sentence = a new thought

George Washington was one of the founding fathers of America. ▶

Two Crows was a Native-American chief from the Crow tribe. ▶

Key Concepts

A sentence has many parts. The **subject** and **predicate** are the main parts. The subject tells *who does the action.* The predicate tells *what the action is.* A **phrase** and **clause** are parts that may be added on to explain more.

sentence

Subject	Predicate	Phrase	Clause
the part of the sentence that tells who or what does the action of the sentence	the part of the sentence that names the action	a group of words that adds information and *does not* have a subject or a predicate	a group of words that adds information and *does* have a subject and a predicate

Sentence Parts . . . and Problems

Sentence Parts

A sentence has two main parts: the subject and the predicate.

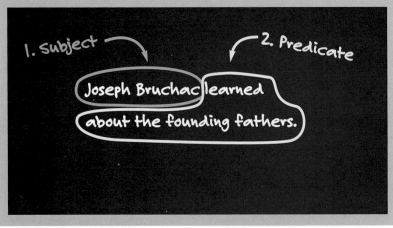

1. Subject   2. Predicate

Joseph Bruchac learned about the founding fathers.

Combining Sentences

When you combine sentences, you turn two short sentences into one more interesting sentence. You can combine two sentences in a number of ways.

- Move a group of words into another sentence.

  Native Americans lived in America. **They were many different groups of people.**

  Many different groups of *Native Americans lived in America.*

- Put two sentences together by using a connecting word, such as *or*, *and*, or *but*.

  Native Americans hunted buffalo. **They moved from place to place.**

  Native Americans hunted buffalo **and moved from place to place.**

▲ The Sioux were one group of Native Americans that moved from place to place.

A Sentence Fragment
It is a part of a sentence that is missing a subject or predicate.

A Run-on Sentence
It is two or more sentences put together without connecting words or punctuation.

Fragment

Learned about the founding fathers.

Run-on Sentence

I learned about them, I read more about their lives and I came to learn they looked at life differently.

What's wrong?
It's not a complete thought and has no subject.

What's wrong?
It has too many thoughts that run together.

Understanding Sentences

A sentence expresses a complete thought. It begins with a capital letter and ends with a period, question mark, or exclamation mark. Sentences can be simple, compound, or complex.

Sentence Basics

To become a good writer, you need to be able to write a good **sentence.** Your writing is built word by word and sentence by sentence. Here are some sentence basics.

PARTS OF A SENTENCE

Sentences have two basic parts: the **subject** and the **predicate.**

Sentence Part	What It Does	Example
SUBJECT	Does something or is talked about	*Native-American people hunted on the plains.*
PREDICATE	Says something about the subject	*Native-American people hunted on the plains.*

▲ This girl is Native American and from the Crow tribe.

The *simple subject* in the example is *people.* The *complete subject* (*Native-American people*) includes the simple subject and all of the words that **modify** it.

The *simple predicate* in the example is the verb *hunted.* The *complete predicate* includes the simple predicate and all of the words that modify it (*hunted on the plains*).

VOCABULARY
sentence—one or more words that express a complete thought
subject—who or what the sentence is about
predicate—what the subject does or what happens
modify—limit or change the sense of

▲ Native Americans hunt buffalo on the plains.

PHRASES AND CLAUSES

A **phrase** is a group of words that does not have a subject or a predicate.

> *on the plains*

A **clause** is a group of words that has a subject and a predicate.

> _{SUBJECT PREDICATE}
> *When they hunted buffalo,* *the Native Americans roamed the plains.*

There are two types of clauses. A ***dependent*** *clause* does not express a complete thought. It is not a sentence by itself.

> *When they hunted buffalo*

An ***independent*** *clause* expresses a complete thought. It can stand by itself.

> *The Native Americans roamed the plains.*

(**TALK AND SHARE**) **With a partner, make a chart. Show an example of each part of a sentence: subject, predicate, phrase, and clause.**

VOCABULARY

phrase—a short group of words that is meaningful
clause—a group of words within a sentence that has a subject and a predicate
dependent—must rely on someone or something else
independent—not controlled by anything or anyone else; free

Language Notes

Homophones
These words sound alike, but they have different spellings and meanings.

- **piece:** part or bit
- **peace:** not fighting; not at war

- **plains:** large areas of flat land
- **planes:** airplanes; vehicles with wings that fly in the air

Sentence Problems

Two of the most common problems with sentences are **fragments** and **run-ons**.

SENTENCE FRAGMENTS

A sentence is a complete thought. It expresses a whole idea. If it does not express a complete thought, it is called a *sentence fragment*, or piece of a sentence. A fragment may be missing a subject or a predicate.

Incorrect

*hunted on the **plains**.*   (missing the subject)
My ancestors of long ago   (missing a predicate)

You can often find a sentence fragment by reading a sentence out loud. You can correct the fragment by adding what is missing.

Correct

*My ancestors of long ago hunted on the **plains**.*

Native Americans hunted buffalo in late winter. ▼

VOCABULARY
fragments—parts or pieces
run-ons—two or more sentences that are put together without correct punctuation

RUN-ON SENTENCES

Another mistake is running two or more sentences (and ideas) together. That happens when a writer doesn't use the correct **punctuation** or a connecting word. This is called a *run-on sentence*.

> **Incorrect**
> *I admired my grandfather he told me stories of the Native Americans of long ago he taught me songs.*

Correct the run-on sentence by adding punctuation or a connecting word, such as *and*, *but*, or *or*.

> **Correct**
> *I admired my grandfather. He told me stories of the Native Americans of long ago, and he taught me songs.*

(**TALK AND SHARE**) **Tell your partner which sentence problem is hardest for you. Then ask your partner which one he or she thinks is the most difficult.**

A mother and child from the Sioux tribe live on the plains. ▼

◀ A grandfather and grandson from the Crow tribe talk in the Montana countryside.

VOCABULARY

punctuation—the use of periods, commas, and other marks to make the meaning of written material clear

Kinds of Sentences

Good writers use different kinds of sentences. The punctuation you use depends on the kind of sentence.

Statements

A **statement** tells something about a person, a place, a thing, or an idea. It ends with a period.

The Native Americans hunted on the plains.

Commands

In a command, the subject *you* is not stated.

Be quiet! (This sentence means "You be quiet!")

A command is called an **imperative.** It can end with an exclamation mark or a period. (*Listen to me.*)

Exclamations

An **exclamation** shows strong emotion or surprise.

I can't believe it!

Read these two sentences out loud:

I love it.   *I love it!*

Notice how the emotion of the sentence changes when you replace a period with an exclamation mark.

Questions

An **interrogative sentence** asks a question. Interrogative sentences end with question marks.

Did Native Americans hunt on the plains?

Use different kinds of sentences in your writing. They give writing variety and make it more interesting to read.

(TALK AND SHARE) **Explain to your partner which punctuation marks are used to end sentences. Tell what marks you use with each of the 4 kinds of sentences.**

VOCABULARY

statement—something expressed in words
imperative—a sentence expressing a command or request
exclamation—a sudden, strong outcry
interrogative sentence—a sentence that is a question

Simple, Compound, and Complex Sentences

Sentences can be long or short. Ideas can be simple or **complicated.** Writers use different kinds of sentences to hold different kinds of ideas.

1. A *simple sentence* expresses a complete thought. It has only one independent clause.

   > *Native Americans lived off the land.*

2. A *compound sentence* is two or more independent clauses joined together. It uses a connecting word (*and, but,* or *or*). Each clause needs punctuation.

   > *Some Native Americans lived on the plains, and they hunted buffalo for food.*

   A semicolon can also be used to join the sentences instead of *and* or *or.*

   > *Some Native Americans lived on the plains; they hunted buffalo for food.*

3. A *complex sentence* has one independent and one or more dependent clauses. Note the main clause is in blue and the dependent clause is in yellow.

   > *When the Native Americans roamed the plains, they hunted buffalo for food.*

(TALK AND SHARE) Write examples of a simple sentence, a compound sentence, and a complex sentence. Share them with your partner.

▲ Buffalo provided food, shelter, and tools for Native Americans.

Summary

A sentence expresses a complete thought. A sentence has parts, and there are many kinds of sentences. Sentences begin with a capital letter and end with a punctuation mark.

VOCABULARY
complicated—very hard and difficult

Synthesizing

Synthesizing Ideas

When you *synthesize*, you look at many parts of a text and pull all of the ideas together. Then you make a general statement from the details.

Use a Details and Statement Organizer to help you synthesize information.

Details and Statement Organizer

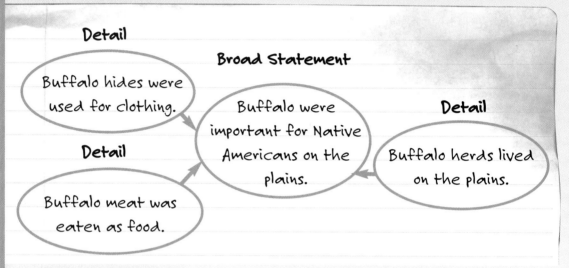

Detail

Buffalo hides were used for clothing.

Broad Statement

Buffalo were important for Native Americans on the plains.

Detail

Buffalo herds lived on the plains.

Detail

Buffalo meat was eaten as food.

Practice Synthesizing

1. Tell   Copy the 3 short sentences below as details in a Details and Statement Organizer. Add a main idea. Then give your paper to your partner. Ask your partner to synthesize the ideas together into one longer sentence and read it aloud.

> *Joseph Bruchac is a poet. He is a writer.*
> *He writes about his ancestors.*

2. Write   Write 4 different kinds of sentences about "new beginnings." Write one statement, one question, one command, and one exclamation. Synthesize your ideas into a paragraph. Use the Check Your Writing checklist to improve your paragraph.

Check Your Writing

Make sure you

- ☐ Use complete sentences.
- ☐ Use a period at the end of each sentence.
- ☐ Spell all the words correctly.

Using *and, or,* and *but* The words *and, or,* and *but* are sentence connectors. They help you combine ideas to make more interesting sentences.

Word	What It Does	Example
and	connects two ideas that are alike	*The student wrote a story, and she read a book.*
or	gives a choice	*The students can read a story, or they can read a book.*
but	shows contrast	*The students wrote a story, but they did not read a book.*

When you connect two complete sentences into a compound sentence, be sure to add a comma before the connector.

They hunted buffalo, and they roamed the plains.

Write one sentence each with *and, or,* and *but*. Share your sentences with your partner.

Changing Sentences In a small group or with a partner, read the 4 statements below. Then try to change each sentence into at least one other type of sentence: a command, an exclamation, or a question.

I love apples.   *Let's go to the store.*
Felipe likes you.   *Benjy says, "Hello."*

Matching Parts With a partner, make cards for the words *subject, predicate, phrase,* and *clause*. Then make 4 cards for the sentence parts shown at the bottom of the page. Work with your partner to match the sentence part to the part of the sentence that goes with it.

Subject   **Predicate**   **Phrase**   **Clause**
Native Americans hunted buffalo on the plains because they needed food and clothing.

Theme 2
People Like Us

People everywhere want to fit in. They want to feel like they belong and have friends. When they meet new people, they want to be accepted and to be treated well.

- **What is happening in the photographs?**
- **How would you describe the people in these photos?**
- **Which photo reminds you most of your family? Why?**

Understanding Tone and Mood

Tone is the feeling, or attitude, the writer has toward the subject. The writer may be serious or silly, cheerful or sad, about the subject.

When you read, the words often make you feel a certain way. That's the mood of the writing. **Mood** is the feeling you get when you read. It might be sad or scary, happy or silly.

Before Reading Activities

Oral Language

Discussing Tone and Mood   With a partner, tell what you think about one of these topics: your neighbors, your home, or your family. Tell what *tone* you would take when you talk about that topic. Then tell what *mood* your description of the topic would give a listener or reader.

Partner Practice

People Like You   With a partner, share information about your family. Have a conversation by asking and answering these questions.

Where were you born?
I was born in ____.

Where were your parents and
grandparents born?
My parents were born in ____.
My grandparents were born in ___.

What does your family like
to do?
My family likes to ____.

The House on MANGO STREET

by Sandra Cisneros

This story is about a young girl named Esperanza. Esperanza and her family are always moving from place to place. In each new neighborhood, Esperanza meets new people and learns a lot along the way.

As you read the story, think about what Esperanza says and how she feels. What parts remind you of something in your own life? How would you describe Esperanza to a friend?

My Name

In English my name means hope. In Spanish it means too many letters. It means sadness, it means waiting. It is like the number nine. A muddy color. It is the Mexican records my father plays on Sunday mornings when he is shaving, songs like **sobbing.**

It was my great-grandmother's name and now it is mine. She was a horse woman too, born like me in the Chinese year of the horse—which is supposed to be bad luck if you're born female—but I think this is a Chinese lie because the Chinese, like the Mexicans, don't like their women strong.

VOCABULARY

sobbing—crying with short, quick breaths. The songs sounded like someone crying.

My great-grandmother. I would've liked to have known her, a wild horse of a woman, so wild she wouldn't marry. Until my great-grandfather threw a sack over her head and carried her off. Just like that, as if she were a fancy **chandelier.** That's the way he did it.

And the story goes she never forgave him. She looked out the window her whole life, the way so many women sit their sadness on an elbow. I wonder if she made the best with what she got or was she sorry because she couldn't be all the things she wanted to be. Esperanza. I have **inherited** her name, but I don't want to inherit her place by the window.

At school they say my name funny as if the **syllables** were made out of tin and hurt the roof of your mouth. But in Spanish my name is made out of a softer something, like silver, not quite as thick as sister's name—Magdalena—which is uglier than mine. Magdalena who at least can come home and become Nenny. But I am always Esperanza.

I would like to **baptize** myself under a new name, a name more like the real me, the one nobody sees. Esperanza as Lisandra or Maritza or Zeze the X. Yes. Something like Zeze the X will do.

(TALK AND SHARE) **How does Esperanza feel about her name? Talk to a partner about it.**

VOCABULARY

chandelier—a light that hangs from the ceiling
inherited—received from a person who has died
syllables—parts of a word that you hear separately. You
  hear 4 syllables when you say her name: *Es per an za.*

baptize—give a new beginning or rebirth to.
  Esperanza wants to *baptize* herself and start
  over with a new name.

Cathy Queen of Cats

She says, I am the great great grand cousin of the queen of **France.** She lives upstairs, over there, next door to Joe the baby-grabber. Keep away from him, she says. He is full of danger. Benny and Blanca own the corner store. They're okay except don't lean on the candy counter. Two girls **raggedy as rats** live across the street. You don't want to know them. Edna is the lady who owns the building next to you. She used to own a building big as a whale, but her brother sold it. Their mother said no, no, don't ever sell it. I won't. And then she closed her eyes and he sold it. Alicia is stuck-up ever since she went to **college.** She used to like me but now she doesn't.

VOCABULARY

France—a large country in Europe
raggedy as rats—poor, worn out, dirty
college—a school of higher learning after high school

Cathy who is queen of cats has cats and cats and cats. Baby cats, big cats, skinny cats, sick cats. Cats asleep like little donuts. Cats on top of the **refrigerator.** Cats taking a walk on the dinner table. Her house is like cat heaven.

You want a friend, she says. Okay, I'll be your friend. But only till next Tuesday. That's when we move away. Got to. Then as if she forgot I just moved in, she says the neighborhood is getting bad.

Cathy's father will have to fly to France one day and find her great great **distant** grand cousin on her father's side and inherit the family house. How do I know this is so? She told me so. In the meantime they'll just have to move a little farther north from Mango Street, a little farther away every time people like us keep moving in.

(**TALK AND SHARE**) **Why is Cathy moving away? With a partner, discuss what she says.**

VOCABULARY

refrigerator—an appliance, often in the kitchen, used to keep food cold
distant—far away. A great, great, grand cousin is a very *distant* family member.

Responding to Literature

Explore the Reading

Talk with a partner about each question below.

1. What do you think of Esperanza?

2. What parts of the story remind you of something that has happened to you?

3. How does Esperanza tell you about her name?

4. What is the mood in the story? What is the tone?

5. How would you describe Cathy?

6. How do you think Esperanza feels when Cathy says "the neighborhood is getting bad"?

Learn About Literature

Style

Style is the way someone writes. The words a writer chooses, the tone he or she takes, the length of sentences—all of these make up the writer's *style*.

Read this example. The reader looked at part of the reading and drew conclusions about the author's style.

Text	My Thoughts
Okay, I'll be your friend. But only till next Tuesday. That's when we move away. Got to. Then as if she forgot I just moved in, she says the neighborhood is getting bad.	• sounds like talking (Okay, I'll be your friend.) • short sentences or parts (Got to.) • not correct or formal (no marks around a speaker's words)

Now read this sentence from *The House on Mango Street*. With a partner, choose 3 or 4 words you would use to describe the style.

> In the meantime they'll just have to move a little farther north from Mango Street, a little farther away every time people like us keep moving in.

Activities

Hands On

Who's Your Neighbor?   Tell a partner about one of your neighbors. Then draw a picture of your neighbor. Add details (like pets, what the person wears, what he or she says and does). Title your picture "People Like Us." Talk about how you and your neighbor are alike and different. Tell about what feelings and dreams you have in common.

Oral Language

Your Name   Ask your family what your name means or how you got the name you have. Many dictionaries give meanings for names. If you can, look in one of them. Then, in a small group, share what you learned about your name.

Partner Practice

Talk About Tone   In one part of *The House on Mango Street*, Esperanza says her name is "A muddy color. It is the Mexican records my father plays on Sunday mornings when he is shaving, songs like sobbing." Talk with a partner about the tone. Does the tone change when Esperanza talks about taking a new name, such as Zeze the X? How?

Know the Author

Sandra Cisneros

Sandra Cisneros was born in Chicago in 1954, 1 of 7 children. Like her character Esperanza, Cisneros moved around a lot as a child. She attended college at Loyola University in Chicago and became well known as a writer after graduating from the Writer's Workshop at the University of Iowa. After school, she worked as a teacher of high school dropouts and as a poet-in-the-schools. Besides *The House on Mango Street*, Cisneros is known for *Woman Hollering Creek and Other Stories* (1991) and *Caramelo* (2003). Her story about Esperanza, a young girl who grew up in Chicago, comes from her own experiences.

Reading
Paragraphs

Here you'll learn about paragraphs. You'll also learn how to draw conclusions and practice evaluating details.

Building Background

▲ The streets near my house are always filled with families walking around.

- **What are these people doing?**
- **What are the streets like around your neighborhood?**
- **How would you describe these people to a friend?**

To find the main idea of a paragraph, first look for the topic, or subject. Then look for what the writer says about that topic. Sometimes the main idea will be stated. Most of the time you'll need to infer the main idea.

from *The House on Mango Street*
by Sandra Cisneros

Everybody in our family has different hair. My Papa's hair is like a broom, all up in the air. And me, my hair is lazy. It never obeys barrettes or bands. Carlos' hair is thick and straight. He doesn't need to comb it. Nenny's hair is slippery—slides out of your hand. And Kiki, who is the youngest, has hair like fur.

Topic Details Main Idea

Hair

What the author says about the topic

1 Papa's hair is like a broom.

2 The speaker's hair never obeys.

3 Carlos' hair is thick and straight.

4 Nenny's hair is slippery.

5 Kiki's hair is like fur.

Everybody in our family has different hair.

Key Concepts

paragraph   topic   subject   main idea

A **paragraph** is a group of sentences about one idea. The **topic,** or **subject,** is who or what the paragraph is about. What the author is saying about the topic is the **main idea.**

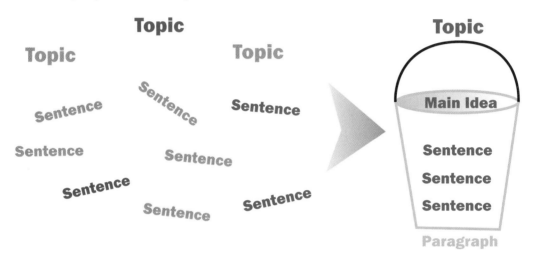

Parts of a Paragraph

1. Topic and topic sentence

Topic = hair

Topic sentence = Everybody in our family has different hair.

2. Details about the topic

Papa's hair is like a broom.

The speaker's (Esperanza's) hair never obeys.

Drawing Conclusions

You draw conclusions every day. As you read a paragraph, collect facts and bits of information. Put them together with information you already know. Draw conclusions to help you figure out the main idea.

For example, think about these 3 things.

- The sky is dark and gray.
- You see lots of clouds in the sky.
- You hear thunder.

What conclusion do you draw? You put these facts together to conclude that it's going to rain.

Fact + Fact + Fact = Conclusion

Carlos' hair is thick and straight.

Nenny's hair is slippery.

Kiki's hair is like fur.

Reading Paragraphs

How do you read a paragraph? First, look for the subject, or what the paragraph is about. Then, find out what the author says about the subject. Sometimes the main idea is easy to find. Other times you have to make an inference.

Finding the Subject

When you read a paragraph, you need to break it down to really understand it.

- First, find the **subject,** or **topic.**
- Then, find out what the writer says about the subject.

Here is the way you can find the subject of a paragraph.

1. LOOK AT THE TITLE

Begin by looking at the title or heading.

Here the title of the story tells you that the subject will be the character's name. If you are reading a textbook, look at the chapter title and the headings inside the chapter.

Remember that the subject of a paragraph is not always given in the title or heading.

This story is about a young girl named Esperanza. Esperanza and her family are always moving from place to place. In each ne̶ neighborhood, Esperanza meets new people and learns a lot along the way.

As you read the story, think about what Esperanza says and ho̶ she feels. What parts remind you of something in your own life? How would you describe Esperanza to a friend?

Title

My Name

In English my name means hope. In Spanish it means too many letters. It means sadness, it means waiting. It is like the number nine. A muddy color. It is the Mexican records my father plays on Sunday mornings when he is shaving, songs like **sobbing.**

It was my great-grandmother's name and now it is mine. She was a horse woman too, born like me in the Chinese year of the horse—which is supposed to be bad luck if you're born female—but I think this is a Chinese lie because the Chinese, like the Mexicans, don't like their women strong.

2. LOOK AT THE FIRST SENTENCE

You should also look at the first sentence to find the subject of a paragraph.

from *The House on Mango Street*
by Sandra Cisneros

We didn't always live on Mango Street. Before that we lived on Loomis on the third floor, and before that we lived on Keeler. Before Keeler it was Paulina, and before that I can't remember. But what I remember most is moving a lot. Each time it seemed there'd be one more of us. By the time we got to Mango Street we were six—Mama, Papa, Carlos, Kiki, my sister Nenny and me.

In this paragraph, the first sentence tells you that the family in the story hasn't always lived in the house on Mango Street.

3. LOOK FOR REPEATED WORDS

If an author uses a word or phrase more than once, it's probably important. The words *lived on* are repeated two times in the paragraph above. This tells you that they are **key words.** The words *Mango Street* and names of other streets are included (Loomis, Keeler, Paulina). They tell you that *living in different places* is probably the subject, or topic.

Remember that the subject is what the paragraph is about. To find the main idea, you need to know what the writer is saying *about* the subject.

▲ City streets in Chicago, Illinois

(TALK AND SHARE) **With a partner, talk about where you look for the subject of a paragraph.**

VOCABULARY
key words—very important words. *Key* means "important."

Finding Stated Main Ideas

Some paragraphs state the main idea in the very first sentence. That makes your job as a reader easy.

> **from *The House on Mango Street***
> **by Sandra Cisneros**
>
> Cathy who is queen of cats has cats and cats and cats. Baby cats, big cats, skinny cats, sick cats. Cats asleep like little donuts. Cats on top of the refrigerator. Cats taking a walk on the dinner table.

In the example above, the writer states the main idea in the first sentence (Cathy has lots of cats). That is the **topic sentence.** The other sentences give **examples** and **facts.** These **supporting details** help the reader understand the main idea.

Other times the paragraph starts with examples and ends with the main idea. The paragraph begins first with one detail, then another, and then another. Finally, in the last sentence, the paragraph states the main idea.

TALK AND SHARE Explain to a partner why supporting details are important in a paragraph, and name two types of supporting details.

Main idea in the last sentence

VOCABULARY

topic sentence—the sentence that states the main idea of a paragraph
examples—details an author uses to prove a point or make something clear
facts—things that can be shown to be true. *The cats walk on the dinner table* is a fact.
supporting details—facts and examples that add to or explain the main idea.

Finding an Implied Main Idea

In most paragraphs you read, the main idea will not be stated. When the main idea is not directly stated, it is **implied.** This means that you have to decide what the main idea is on your own, using what you learn as you read.

1. NOTE THE DETAILS

Read the paragraph below. As you do, ask yourself, "What is the author saying about the topic? What do the 4 details show?"

▲ A house in France

from *The House on Mango Street*
by Sandra Cisneros

1 Cathy's father will have to fly to France one day and find her great great distant grand cousin on her father's side and 2 **inherit** the family house. How do I know this is so? She told me so. In the meantime they'll just 3 have to move a little farther north from Mango Street, a little farther away 4 every time people like us keep moving in.

VOCABULARY

implied—not said directly. An *implied* idea is suggested by the information given.
inherit—receive land, money, or other things from a person who has died

2. LOOK AT WHAT YOU LEARNED

After you look at the details in the paragraph, make a list of what you learned. Write the list in your notebook.

The example below shows the details one reader wrote after reading the same paragraph.

Characterization

What you learn about a character in a story is called *characterization*. It includes:

- How a character feels
- What a character does or believes
- What others think or say about the character

For example, in *The House on Mango Street*, you learn how Esperanza feels about her home, her name, and her neighbor Cathy.

Notes

1. Cathy's father will have to fly to France.

2. He will inherit the family house.

3. Cathy's family will have to move a little farther north from Mango Street.

4. They will move every time people like Esperanza's family keep moving in.

Now that you have a list of what you learned, you need to draw a conclusion about, or **infer,** the main idea.

VOCABULARY

infer—conclude; arrive at an idea by putting together clues or bits of information; figure it out

3. MAKE AN INFERENCE

As a reader, you need to make an **inference** about what you learned. To make an inference, put together what you know with what you learned.

What I learned + What I know = Inference

An Inference Chart can help you find the implied main idea in a paragraph. In the first column, write what you learned. Then put it together with what you know, and write your inference in the second column.

Think how you would feel if someone said they were moving away from people like you. Now you know what Esperanza is saying. She is upset that Cathy thinks she is better than "people like us." Cathy's feeling that she's better than everyone else is the implied main idea of the paragraph, but it is never stated.

(**TALK AND SHARE**) **Explain to your partner how you can find an implied main idea.**

Inference Chart

Notes from Text	My Inference
1. Cathy's father will go to France. 2. inherit a house 3. leave Mango Street 4. move away from people like Esperanza and her family	Cathy makes her family sound like they're important, rich, and don't like to be around people like Esperanza's family. Cathy thinks she's better than everyone else.

Summary

To read a paragraph, first look for the subject, or topic. Then look for what the writer says about the subject. In some paragraphs, the main idea will be stated. Most of the time you will have to infer the main idea from the information you learn in the paragraph.

VOCABULARY

inference—a conclusion you come to by putting together facts or ideas

Evaluating

Evaluating Details

Writers use a lot of interesting details. You need to know which details are important and which ones are not. To evaluate details means to look at them carefully to see how well they help you understand a character or a story.

Use a Main Idea Organizer to help you find important details. Write the details about the main idea on the left. Put the other details on the right.

Main Idea Organizer

Main Idea: Cathy thinks she's better than Esperanza and her family.

Important Details	Unimportant Details
• inherit the house	find her great great distant grand cousin
• have to move	
• leave when people like Esperanza's family move in	

Practice Evaluating

1. Tell Talk to your partner about the character Cathy, Queen of Cats. Then list things you learned about her. Include lots of details in your list. Then talk with your partner about which details are important and which ones don't help you understand who she is.

2. Write Now draw a picture of a neighbor you've met. Include as many details as you can remember. Then write a paragraph about your neighbor. Use a Main Idea Organizer before you begin writing. Read your paragraph to a partner. Then give your paper to your partner and check each other's writing.

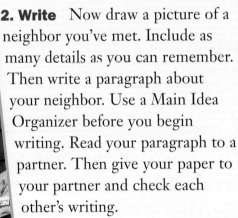

Check Your Writing

Make sure you

- Use complete sentences.

- Use a period at the end of each sentence.

- Spell all the words correctly.

Activities

Grammar Spotlight

Using *a* and *an* Use *a* or *an* when you talk or write about one person, place, or thing.

Rule	Example
Use *a* before words that start with consonant sounds.	*a family, a house, a broom*
Use *an* before words that start with vowel sounds.	*an uncle, an apartment, an eye*

Work with a partner. One person names an object. The other says a sentence about the object using *a* or *an* correctly.

Oral Language

Do a Choral Reading Work in small groups. Choose a paragraph and take turns doing a choral reading. For example, try doing a choral reading with this paragraph.

1st group *Cathy who is queen of cats has cats and cats and cats.*
2nd group *Baby cats, big cats, skinny cats, sick cats.*
3rd group *Cats asleep like little donuts.*
1st group *Cats on top of the refrigerator.*
2nd group *Cats taking a walk on the dinner table.*
3rd group *Her house is like cat heaven.*

Partner Practice

Make a Details Wall With a partner, list as many details as you can about the people in your neighborhood. Write each detail on a file card or piece of paper. Display the details on a bulletin board. Evaluate which details are important to understanding how you feel about the people in your neighborhood. Compare the details you used with the ones your partner used. Talk about how your lists are alike and how they are different. Then draw some conclusions about your neighborhood.

Ways of Organizing

Paragraphs

Here you'll learn about how ideas and details in a paragraph can be organized. You'll also learn how to visualize and practice identifying likenesses and differences.

Building Background

▲ My brother runs every morning. I like to exercise, but not that early!

- **What do you see here?**
- **Where and when do you run?**
- **What would you like to say to this person?**

Paragraphs can be organized in different ways. If you learn how the ideas and details are organized, it will help you understand the paragraph. Here are 5 common ways of organizing paragraphs.

1 Compare and Contrast Order

Details can show how things are *alike* and *different*.

2 Order of Importance

The *most important* idea can be first or last.

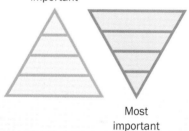

Most important

Most important

3 Time Order

Details can show *when* something happens.

4 Location Order

Details can explain what happens *where*.

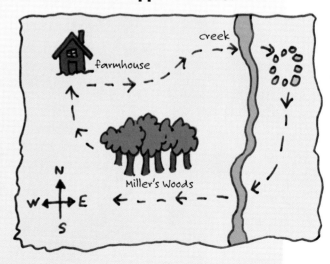

5 Cause and Effect Order

Details can show *why* something happens.

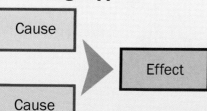

Cause

Cause

Effect

Key Concepts

To **organize** means to put something together in a way that makes sense. When you organize ideas in writing, you **arrange** them in **order** and show how they are related or connected.

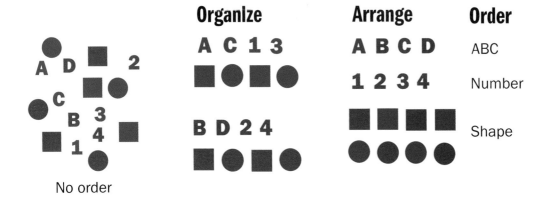

Organize

A C 1 3
■ ● ■ ●

B D 2 4
■ ● ■ ●

Arrange

A B C D

1 2 3 4

■ ■ ■ ■

● ● ● ●

Order

ABC

Number

Shape

No order

Kinds of Order

Compare and Contrast Order

Order of Importance

Time Order

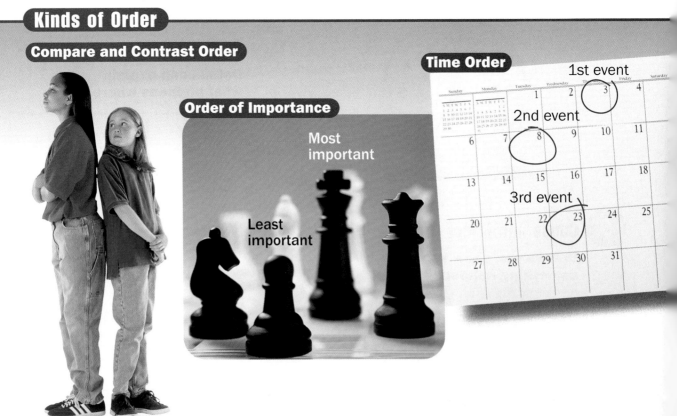

Most important

Least important

1st event

2nd event

3rd event

Visualizing

To understand paragraphs, try to picture, or visualize, what you are reading. Make a picture in your mind. Sometimes it helps to draw, or sketch, what you see.

As you read, make sure you:

1. Organize the ideas.

2. Try to draw what you see in your mind.

3. Use graphic organizers whenever you can.

Now read this passage. Try to visualize it in a timeline.

Timeline
- grew up in New York City
- got in trouble as a young man
- went to prison
- began writing in prison
- worked with young people

> Piri Thomas grew up in Spanish Harlem in New York City. As a young man, he often got into trouble. As a result, he spent time in prison. There he began writing. After prison, he decided to work with young people to help them turn away from crime.

Location Order

Left

Middle

Right

Cause and Effect Order

What happens first

What happens as a result

Ways of Organizing Paragraphs

Writers organize the ideas in paragraphs in 5 different ways. As a reader, look for the way the ideas are arranged. It will help you understand more of what you read.

Compare and Contrast Order

Sometimes a writer will develop a paragraph by showing how things are alike and different. The writer **compares** and **contrasts** one set of details with another. Note how Piri Thomas compares and contrasts Antonio and Felix here.

---

from **"Amigo Brothers"**
by Piri Thomas

Each had fought many **bouts** representing their community and had won two gold-plated medals plus a silver and bronze **medallion.** The difference was in their style. Antonio's lean form and long reach made him the better boxer, while Felix's short and muscular frame made him the better slugger. Whenever they had met in the ring for **sparring** sessions, it had always been hot and heavy.

▲ Two boys spar at a gym in Los Angeles, California.

VOCABULARY

compares—shows how things are alike
contrasts—shows how things are different
bouts—fights or contests. Each fight or match is a bout.
medallion—a large medal. The winner gets a medallion.
sparring—boxing for practice or training

Venn Diagram

To help you **visualize** a paragraph with compare and contrast order, use a Venn Diagram. It helps you **organize** details.

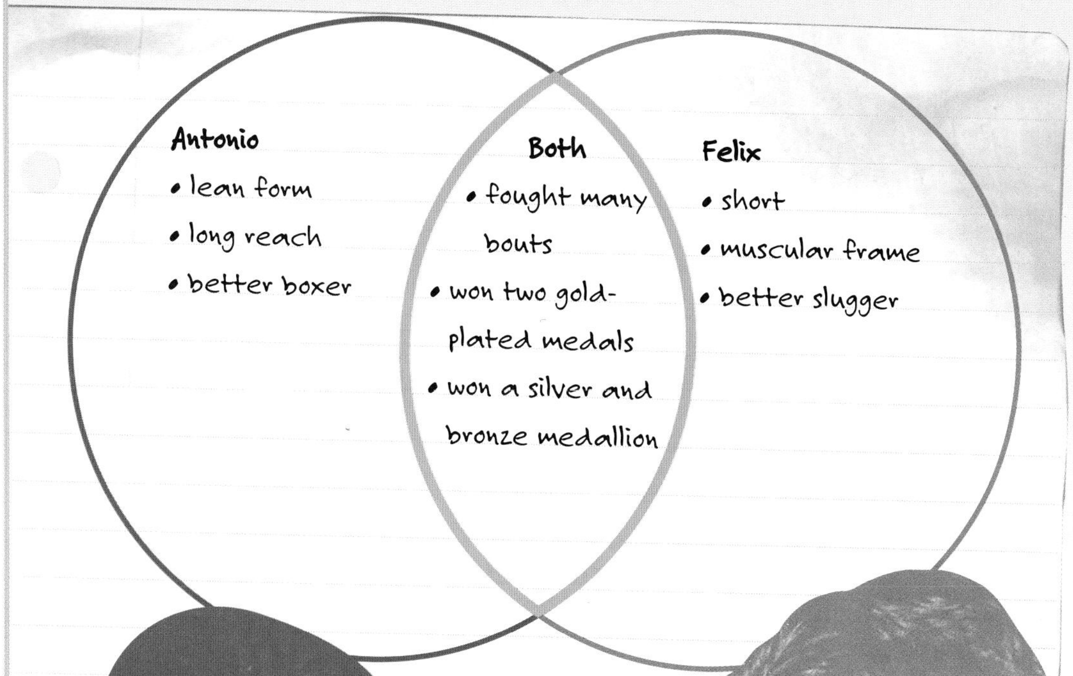

Antonio
- lean form
- long reach
- better boxer

Both
- fought many bouts
- won two gold-plated medals
- won a silver and bronze medallion

Felix
- short
- muscular frame
- better slugger

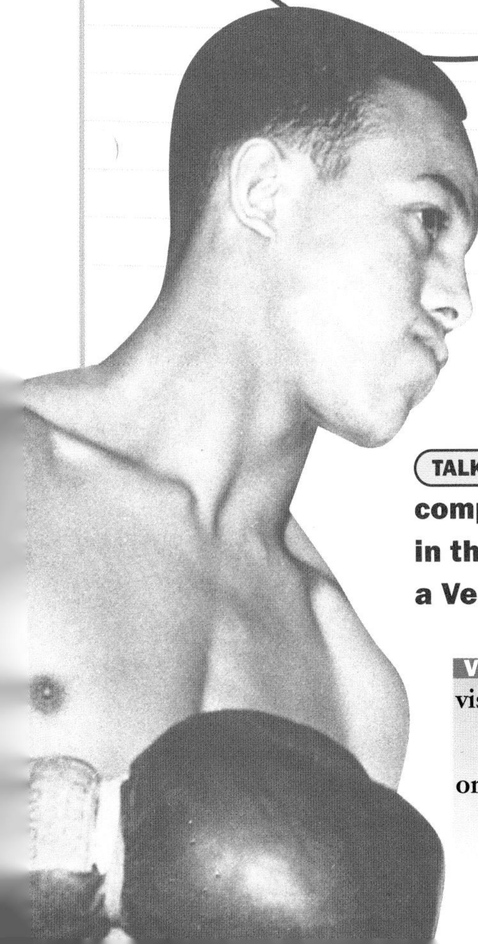

(**TALK AND SHARE**) **With a partner, compare and contrast two things in the classroom. Together, make a Venn Diagram.**

VOCABULARY

visualize—see or picture in your mind. Once you *visualize* something, you can draw or sketch it.

organize—put together in a way that makes sense

A winner gets a champion belt. ▼

▲ Two boxers work out in New York City.

Order of Importance

In some paragraphs, the most important idea is stated first. Less important details follow after that. This is one way of organizing ideas *by importance*. Other times writers start with details. Then they end with the most important idea.

How is the paragraph below organized?

> **Events in order of importance**
>
> from **"Amigo Brothers"**
> by Piri Thomas
>
> **Main idea**
>
> Each youngster had a dream of someday becoming **lightweight champion** of the world. Every chance they had the boys **worked out,** ① sometimes at the Boy's Club on 10th Street and Avenue A and sometimes at the pro's gym on 14th Street. Early morning sunrises would find them ② running along the East River Drive, wrapped in ③ sweat shirts, short towels around their necks, and ④ handkerchiefs Apache style around their foreheads.
>
> **Details**

Here the most important idea comes first. Then smaller, less important details come later and **support** that main idea.

TALK AND SHARE) **With a partner, talk about two ways to organize paragraphs by order of importance.**

VOCABULARY

lightweight—a boxer who weighs between 127 and 135 pounds
champion—a winner ahead of or above all others

worked out—ran, lifted weights, and exercised
support—add to or help make stronger. The details help make the main point clearer and stronger.

Time Order

In a paragraph organized by *time order*, the writer tells a series of events in the order they happen. The writer tells what happened first, next, after that, and in the end. Writers sometimes help you keep track of what's going on by giving times and dates. Other times writers will use **signal words**, such as *first, next, after, then, later,* and *finally.*

Note how the author gives the details in this paragraph.

▲ This apartment building is in New York City.

---

from "Amigo Brothers"
by Piri Thomas

Felix had returned to his apartment early in the morning of August 7th and stayed there, hoping to avoid seeing Antonio. He turned the radio on to **salsa music** sounds and then tried to read while waiting for word from his manager.

Events in time order

> early in the morning of August 7th
>
> ↓
>
> turned the radio on
>
> ↓
>
> then tried to read

(**TALK AND SHARE**) **With your partner, tell how a writer can show time order.**

Reading Tip

Point of View

How an author tells a story is called *point of view*. In the *third-person point of view*, the person telling the story, called the narrator, is not a character in the story. The narrator uses pronouns such as *he, they,* and *them*. "Amigo Brothers" is told from the third-person point of view.

In the *first-person point of view*, the story is told by one of the characters in the story. The character uses pronouns such as *I* or *me*. A first-person narrator takes part in the action. The reader knows only as much as the character telling the story knows, thinks, and feels. *The House on Mango Street* is told from the first-person point of view.

VOCABULARY

signal words—words that point out or show something
salsa **music**—a popular kind of Latin-American music

Location Order

A paragraph organized by **location** order shows what is happening where. Writers often move slowly and very clearly from one place to another. They want to make it easier for you, the reader, to "see" where the action takes place.

What details about location can you find here?

from "Amigo Brothers"
by Piri Thomas

The local junior high school across from Tompkins Square Park served as the dressing room for all the fighters. Each was given a separate classroom with desk tops, covered with mats, serving as resting tables. Antonio thought he caught a glimpse of Felix waving to him from a room at the far end of the **corridor.** He waved back just in case it had been him.

Different locations

You can often draw what you read. Try to visualize the details of a paragraph as you read.

TALK AND SHARE **Talk with a partner about the things in your classroom. Tell where each thing is, starting at the door and going to the right.**

VOCABULARY
location—a place where something is found
corridor—a long hallway with rooms opening off of it. The hallway in your school is a corridor.

Cause and Effect Order

A paragraph with **cause** and **effect** order tells *why* something happened. The cause is the event that happens first. The event or events that happen as a result are the effects. Look for a word that signals cause-effect relationships as you read, such as *because* or *reason.* In cause-effect paragraphs, you might read about the cause or the effects first. What is important is which event occurs first, not the order in which you read about them.

Language Notes

Signal Words:
Cause-Effect
These words are clues to discovering why something happened.

- why
- because
- as a result
- reason

---

from ***The House on Mango Street***
by Sandra Cisneros

Cause — I like Alicia because once she gave me a little leather purse with the word **GUADALAJARA** stitched on it, which is home for Alicia, and one day she will go back there. But today she is **Effect** listening to my sadness because I don't have a house.

Cause-Effect Organizer

CAUSE	EFFECT
Alicia gave the narrator a leather purse.	→ The narrator likes Alicia.
The narrator doesn't have a house.	→ The narrator is sad.

(TALK AND SHARE) **With a partner, talk about how you can tell when a paragraph is organized by cause and effect.**

Summary

Details in paragraphs can be organized in at least 5 different ways. Knowing how paragraphs are organized helps you understand them.

VOCABULARY
cause—someone or something that makes something else happen
effect—something brought about by a cause
Guadalajara—a city in western Mexico

Identifying

Identifying Likenesses and Differences

Identifying means telling what something is. For example, you can identify "Amigo Brothers" as fiction because it is an imaginary story. Antonio and Felix may seem like real people, but they are characters created in the mind of the author.

On a test you may be asked to identify how two stories are alike and different. In the Venn Diagram below, "Amigo Brothers" is compared to *The House on Mango Street*.

Venn Diagram

"Amigo Brothers"
- main characters are Antonio and Felix
- told by someone outside the story (third-person point of view)

Both
- fiction
- realistic

The House on Mango Street
- main character is Esperanza
- told by someone in the story (first-person point of view)

Practice Identifying

1. Create Identify two ways you are like your partner and two ways you are different. Create a Venn Diagram to show how you are alike and how you are different.

2. Write Write a paragraph about you and someone else in your family. First, make a Venn Diagram. Write how you are alike and different. Identify the kind of organization you are using in your paragraph. Use words from the Word Bank if you can.

Word Bank
fair
strong
kind
funny
tall
short

want
dream

Identifying When to Use *am*, *is*, and *are* In the present tense, the verb *be* has 3 forms: *am*, *is*, and *are*.

Form of *be*	Rule	Example
am	used with *I*	*I am*
is	used with *he,* *she,* or *it*	*he is, she is, it is*
are	used with *you,* *we,* or *they*	*you are, we are, they are*

Remember to watch for compound subjects. A compound subject has two or more simple subjects. You need to use *are* with compound subjects. For example:

SUBJECT SUBJECT VERB
Antonio and Felix are boxers. (two people)

SUBJECT SUBJECT VERB
The boys and girls are jogging. (many people)

Now write a sentence using a compound subject and the word *are*.

Hands On

Visualize! Describe the places in your neighborhood to your partner. Give your partner plenty of details so he or she can visualize your neighborhood. Then draw a map of it. Look at the drawing to see if it matches your neighborhood. Then switch roles.

Oral Language

Read Aloud Choose one of the paragraphs in the lesson. Read it aloud to your partner. Ask your partner to identify the kind of order used in the paragraph. Read the paragraph a second time sentence by sentence. Ask your partner to picture, or visualize, details from each sentence and tell you about them.

Partner Practice

Because, Because Make up a sentence using *so*, *because*, or *as a result*. For example, you might say: *It is raining today, so I wore my raincoat.* Ask your partner to identify the cause and the effect. Then have your partner make up a sentence and ask you to identify the cause and effect.

Descriptive
Paragraphs

Here you'll learn about descriptive paragraphs. You'll also learn how to choose words carefully and practice describing a person.

Building Background

▲ I wonder where he's going. He looks like he's running fast.

■ **What words would you use to describe this picture?**

■ **How do you feel when you see it?**

■ **What questions would you ask the boy?**

A descriptive paragraph describes someone or something. It has a main idea, details, and adjectives. A descriptive paragraph also creates images that help readers see, hear, feel, smell, or taste something.

from ***Maniac Magee***
by Jerry Spinelli

If you listen to everybody who claims to have seen Jeffrey-Maniac Magee that first day, there must have been ten thousand people and a parade of fire trucks waiting for him at the town limits. Don't believe it. A couple of people truly remember, and here's what they saw: a scraggly little kid jogging toward them, the soles of both sneakers hanging by their hinges and flopping open like dog tongues each time they came up from the pavement.

1 **Details** ten thousand people and a parade of fire trucks

2 **Adjectives** scraggly little

3 **Image** the soles of both sneakers hanging by their hinges and flopping open like dog tongues

Key Concepts

Details are words and examples that help create images. **Sensory images** are pictures created by words that help the reader see, hear, feel, smell, or taste things. **Adjectives** are words that describe nouns.

A **descriptive paragraph** has colorful words and creates vivid pictures in a reader's mind.

Details

Sensory Images

Adjectives

We walked along the banks of the muddy river. Outside of town we bought some slimy, slippery worms. The day was warm, and the air felt wet and heavy.

Descriptive Paragraph

Tips for Writing a Descriptive Paragraph

1. Choose an interesting subject.
2. Decide what you want to say about the subject.
3. Use words that help your readers *see, hear, feel, smell,* and *taste* what you are describing.

See **Sees a sky full of cotton clouds**

Hear **Hears a soft song**

Choosing Words Carefully

Good writing contains vivid, well-chosen words. When you write, choose your words carefully.

1. Use concrete nouns. They name things that can be touched or seen.

2. Use action verbs. They tell what someone or something is doing.

3. Use strong adjectives. They describe nouns, and they should be clear, colorful words.

When you revise your writing, try to use even better words. Look for just the right word. Replace overused, tired words such as *nice* and *good* with better words.

Vivid Words

Concrete Nouns	
fire truck	suitcase
explosion	

Action Verbs	
jog	leap
scream	

Strong Adjectives	
scraggly	frosty
vicious	

Overused	**Better**
It is a nice day.	*It is a bright, sunny day.*
The band is good.	*The band is awesome.*

Feel Feels rough like an elephant's trunk

Smell Smells sweet like a field of flowers

Taste Tastes sour like a lemon

Descriptive Paragraphs

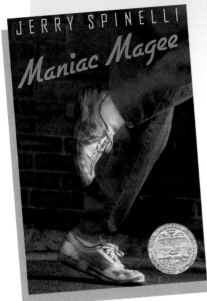

Most paragraphs have a subject and a main idea. What makes a descriptive paragraph? It's the details, images, and adjectives that form a picture in the reader's mind.

Subject, Main Idea, and Details

How can you make your writing lively? Follow these steps.

1. CHOOSE A SUBJECT.

2. DECIDE ON THE MAIN IDEA.

3. ADD DETAILS AND IMAGES.

SUBJECT

First, choose a **subject** you know well. A subject can be almost anything, including a person, place, thing, or idea.

Example: *Maniac Magee*

MAIN IDEA

Second, decide what to say about the subject. What you say about the subject is the **main idea** of your paragraph.

Example: *Maniac Magee started running.*

VOCABULARY

subject—who or what the paragraph is about
main idea—what the writer is saying about the subject

DETAILS AND IMAGES

Third, choose just the right words and details to describe your subject. Details can include facts and small points that help build a **scene.** They help create images in the reader's mind. Notice the details in the scene as Maniac runs away.

SEE pastel dresses

2 HEAR screaming

from ***Maniac Magee***
by Jerry Spinelli

And that's when the running started. Three **springy** steps down from the **risers**—girls in **1 pastel** dresses **2** screaming, the music director **lunging**—a leap from the stage, out the side door and into the starry, **3** sweet, onion-grass-smelling night.

3 SMELL AND TASTE sweet, onion-grass-smelling

(**TALK AND SHARE**) **With a partner, take turns explaining 3 steps to take when you write a descriptive paragraph.**

Add Details

A good descriptive paragraph has carefully chosen words. These words should give details about what is being described. Details help readers see something in their minds, or **visualize** it.

As you read the paragraph below, look for words that give specific details about Amanda.

① around eight in the morning, and Amanda was heading for grade school

② she was carrying a suitcase

> ## from *Maniac Magee*
> ### by Jerry Spinelli
>
> It was **①** around eight in the morning, and Amanda was heading for grade school, like hundreds of other kids all over town. What made Amanda different was that **②** she was carrying a suitcase, and that's what caught Maniac's eye. He figured she was like him, running away, so he stopped and said, "Hi."

TALK AND SHARE   Talk with your partner about the details in this picture. What words would you use to describe the picture?

Writing Tip

Use a Personal Voice

In *Maniac Magee*, Jerry Spinelli writes, "He figured she was like him, running away, so he stopped and said, 'Hi.'" This sentence has a personal voice. It sounds the way a person talks. When you read *Maniac Magee*, you feel as if the author is talking right to you. Jerry Spinelli won the Newbery Award in 1991 for *Maniac Magee*. Its personal voice helped make him a winner! When you write, try to give your own writing a personal voice. Choose words that make your writing sound just like you and the way you talk.

VOCABULARY
visualize—picture something in your mind

Use Clear Adjectives

Adjectives are words that describe nouns. An adjective can tell how a person, place, or thing looks, sounds, feels, smells, and tastes. Sometimes an adjective tells which one. Use strong, clear adjectives when you write a descriptive paragraph.

> ### from *Maniac Magee*
> ### by Jerry Spinelli
>
> To the ordinary person, Cobble's Knot was about as friendly as a nest of **yellowjackets.** Besides the tangle itself, there was the **weathering** of that first year, when the Knot hung outside and became hard as a rock. You could barely make out the individual strands. It was **grimy, moldy,** crusted over. Here and there a loop stuck out, maybe big enough to stick your **pinky** finger through, pitiful **testimony** to the challengers who had tried and failed.

Look for the nouns described by the adjectives. Ask yourself, "What does this word tell me about?" (*First* tells you something about which year. *Hard* tells you how the knot felt. *Grimy, moldy* tells how it looked. *Pinky* tells you which finger.) Sometimes an adjective is not right next to the noun. In this paragraph, *hard* describes the knot.

(**TALK AND SHARE**) **Give your partner an example of 5 clear adjectives. Then listen to his or her adjectives.**

VOCABULARY

yellowjackets—wasps; yellow winged insects, like bees, that sting

weathering—a change or hardening of something caused by the weather

grimy—covered with dirt

moldy—covered with a fuzzy, often greenish, growth

pinky—the little finger

testimony—a statement used as proof

Create Sensory Images

A descriptive paragraph presents a clear picture, or image, of something. A sensory image helps readers experience something through any of the 5 senses. It uses words that describe how things look, sound, feel, smell, and taste.

Read the paragraph below about the character Maniac Magee. What images do the words in yellow create in your mind?

from *Maniac Magee*
by Jerry Spinelli

But the ball never quite reached Hands. Just as he was about to cradle it in his big brown loving mitts, it **vanished.** By the time he recovered from the shock, a little kid was weaving upfield through the **varsity** football players. Nobody laid a paw on him. When the kid got down to the soccer field, he turned and **punted** the ball. It sailed back over the up-looking gym-classers, **spiraling** more perfectly than anything Brian Denehy had ever thrown, and landed in the outstretched hands of still **stunned** Hands Down. Then the kid ran off.

Remember, choose your words carefully and create sensory images when you write a descriptive paragraph.

VOCABULARY

vanished—disappeared suddenly
varsity—the team that represents a school in a sports competition
punted—kicked the ball after dropping it and before it touched the ground

spiraling—moving in a circling way; moving in the shape of a screw or coil
stunned—amazed, confused, or shocked

Writing a Descriptive Paragraph

When you write a descriptive paragraph, include:

Details

> banks of the muddy
> We walked along the ‸river.

Clear adjectives

> Outside of town, we bought
> slimy, slippery
> some ‸worms.

Sensory images

> warm, and   wet and heavy
> The day was ‸nice the air felt ‸good.

When you edit and revise your descriptive paragraph, add more details, clear adjectives, and sensory images.

TALK AND SHARE With your partner, give examples of a sensory detail, a clear adjective, and a specific detail.

Summary

A descriptive paragraph has a main idea and details. It uses clear adjectives and sensory images to create a picture in the reader's mind.

Describing

Describing a Person

When you describe a person, help your listeners or readers visualize by including descriptive details. A Paragraph Organizer can help you organize and plan your descriptive paragraph. Before you write, brainstorm some details, adjectives, and images to include.

Paragraph Organizer

Main Idea: Maniac Magee didn't look unusual, but he was.

Details	Adjectives	Images
• a leap from the stage • out the side door	• scraggly • little	• soles of sneakers flopping open • the music director lunging • girls in pastel dresses

Practice Describing

1. Draw   Think of an unusual person that you can describe. Draw a picture of the person to show what you want to describe. Then talk with your partner about what specific details, clear adjectives, and sensory images you can add to your description. Remember to choose your words carefully.

2. Write   Write a paragraph to describe a person. First, work with a partner to create a Paragraph Organizer like the one above. Use the details, adjectives, and images you created with your partner to write a paragraph. Use words and details from the Word Bank if you can.

Word Bank

happy
funny
friendly

tall
short

interesting
wild
different

Activities

Grammar Spotlight

Placing Adjectives You can place an adjective before a noun or after a linking verb like *is, was, are,* or *were*. Be careful not to place the adjective after the noun.

> **Example:** Say *"tall trees"* (not *"trees tall"*).

Adjectives Before Nouns	Adjectives After Linking Verbs
scraggly little kid	*He <u>is</u> scraggly and little.*
pastel dresses	*The dresses <u>are</u> pastel.*
starry night	*The night <u>was</u> starry.*
weird parents	*The parents <u>were</u> weird.*

Now write two sentences using the adjective *bright*. Put it before a noun in one sentence and after a linking verb in another sentence.

Hands On

Word Wall Work with a small group. On a bulletin board or on chart paper on the wall, write the heading "Add to Descriptive Paragraphs." Then, on file cards, write examples of specific details, clear adjectives, and sensory images. Put them in rows under the headings "Details," "Adjectives," and "Images." Make sure to choose your words carefully. Use concrete nouns, action verbs, and strong adjectives.

Oral Language

Choral Reading Form 3 groups. Practice reading the sentences below from *Maniac Magee* with your group. Then read all 3 sentences together in a choral reading for the rest of the class.

1st group *It was around eight in the morning, and Amanda was heading for grade school, like hundreds of other kids all over town.*

2nd group *What made Amanda different was that she was carrying a suitcase, and that's what caught Maniac's eye.*

3rd group *He figured she was like him, running away, so he stopped and said, "Hi."*

Understanding
Nouns

Here you'll learn about naming words. You'll also learn how to use proofreader's marks and practice analyzing a character.

▲ At first I was afraid to ride buses, but now I ride one every day.

- **What is happening here?**
- **What do you know about Rosa Parks?**
- **How do these photographs make you feel about her?**

A noun is a naming word. Nouns name people, places, things, and ideas. They can show how many or who owns something.

Note the underlined nouns in this paragraph.

from ***Rosa Parks: My Story***
by Rosa Parks with Jim Haskins

One <u>evening</u> in early <u>December 1955</u> I was sitting in the front <u>seat</u> of the colored <u>section</u> of a <u>bus</u> in <u>Montgomery, Alabama</u>. The white <u>people</u> were sitting in the white <u>section</u>. More white <u>people</u> got on, and they filled up all the <u>seats</u> in the white <u>section</u>. When that happened, we black <u>people</u> were supposed to give up our <u>seats</u> to the <u>whites</u>. But I didn't move. The white <u>driver</u> said, "Let me have those front <u>seats</u>." I didn't get up. I was tired of giving in to white <u>people</u>.

1 Person
Rosa Parks

2 Thing bus

3 Place
Montgomery, Alabama

Montgomery is the capital of the state of Alabama. ▶

▲ The bus Rosa Parks was arrested on is now in the Henry Ford Museum in Dearborn, Michigan.

Key Concepts

A **noun** is any word that names a person, place, thing, or idea. A **proper noun** names a specific person, place, thing, or idea. It starts with a capital letter. All other nouns are **common nouns**. A **singular noun** names one person, place, thing, or idea. A **plural noun** names more than one.

Proper Noun:
Rosa

Common Noun:
woman

Singular Noun:
girl

Plural Noun: girls

Capitalizing Proper Nouns

Capitalize the names of proper nouns.

1. Specific people, places, and things
Jorge, Washington Middle School, *The Montgomery Advertiser*

2. Historical events
World War II, Civil Rights Act of 1964

3. Days, months, and holidays
Tuesday, July, Martin Luther King, Jr., Day

▲ Protesters made headlines by refusing to ride on segregated buses.

▲ Civil Rights march

Skill Building

Using Proofreader's Marks

After you write, you need to edit and proofread your work. Use proofreader's marks to help you fix mistakes in your writing.

Use a capital letter with all proper nouns. Show that a word should be capitalized this way:

The work of leaders such as ̲rosa p̲arks and
̲dr. k̲ing led to the Civil Rights ̲act of 1964.

Make a letter lowercase this way:

I like reading about famous people in /History.

	Proofreader's Marks
≡	Make a capital letter.
/	Make a letter lowercase.
ℓ	Delete.
⊙	Insert a period.
∧	Insert here.
SP.	Correct the spelling error.

---

4. Languages, races, and religions
Spanish, Arab, Hinduism

5. Titles of books, magazines, and songs
To Be a Slave, *The New York Times Magazine*, "Go Down, Moses"

6. Titles and abbreviations
Senator Edward Kennedy, FBI

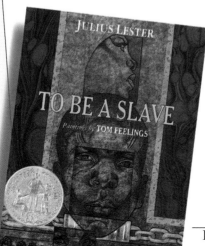

Understanding Nouns

mother
and child

Two kinds of nouns are common nouns and proper nouns. Some nouns tell how many, and others name things that you cannot count. Possessive nouns tell who owns something.

Common and Proper Nouns

A *common noun* is any word that does not name a particular person, place, thing, or idea. A *proper noun* names a **specific** person, place, thing, or idea.

Common Nouns	Proper Nouns
mother	Leona Edwards
school	Payne University
city	Montgomery
state	Alabama
book	*The Struggle for Civil Rights*
language	Italian
month	December
holiday	Martin Luther King, Jr., Day

Martin Luther
King, Jr.

What 3 common nouns can you see right now? What proper nouns can you see?

(TALK AND SHARE) **Explain to your partner the difference between common and proper nouns.**

VOCABULARY

specific—definite, precise, or particular. Rosa Parks is a *specific* person.

Count Nouns

Look around you. You can see a floor, ceiling, road, or window. There can be one of these or many of them. Count nouns name things that can be counted. They can show one or can be changed to show more than one: *road* or *roads*.

SINGULAR NOUNS

Nouns that name one person or thing are called **singular** nouns. These words are all singular nouns.

desk   fox   dress   baby

PLURAL NOUNS

A **plural** noun names two or more people or things. In most cases, you can make a noun plural just by adding *s*. However, if the noun ends in *sh*, *ch*, *x*, *s*, or *z*, you need to add *es* to make it plural. If a noun ends in a consonant plus *y*, the *y* changes to *i* before *es* is added.

desks   foxes
dresses   babies

Singular and Plural Nouns

Singular	Plural
law	laws
dish	dishes
church	churches
box	boxes
kiss	kisses
story	stories

If you are not sure how to spell the plural form of a word, look it up in a dictionary.

fox (fŏks) *n.*, *pl.* fox • es A small mammal, with a long bushy tail, that is related to the dog and the wolf.

baby

babies

MORE ABOUT PLURAL NOUNS

With some nouns, you have to change the spelling to form the plural. These are called **irregular** nouns. With irregular nouns, you have to **memorize** the plural form.

> *Children had to attend segregated schools.*

Under **segregation**, African-American children didn't receive fair treatment. ▶

The word *children* is irregular because it is plural but does not end in *s*. Irregular plurals don't follow any rules. Luckily, there are only a few irregular plurals. Here are some of the more common irregular plurals.

Irregular Plural Forms

Singular	Plural
child	children
man	men
foot	feet
tooth	teeth
goose	geese
mouse	mice

(**TALK AND SHARE**) **Explain to your partner what an irregular plural noun is. Give two examples. Then have your partner explain what a regular plural noun is.**

VOCABULARY
irregular—something that does not follow the rule; strange or unusual; not normal
memorize—learn well enough that you can remember
segregation—the system that kept African Americans apart from white Americans

Noncount Nouns

You can count "1 pencil," "2 pencils," but you can't count "1 homework," "2 homeworks." Nouns for things we don't count are called **noncount nouns.** You will find many noncount nouns in English. See the list below.

Noncount Nouns

air	corn	ice	shopping
baggage	dust	meat	soccer
beef	electricity	oil	sugar
biology	fog	oxygen	sunshine
blood	garbage	poetry	syrup
clothing	gold	rice	toast

You don't make noncount nouns plural.

> *The ice is in the glasses.*
>
> *Sunshine is better than clouds.*

Some nouns can be count or noncount, depending on how they are used.

> *The beauty of the photo was amazing.*
>
> *The jewels were real beauties.*

(TALK AND SHARE) **Make a list with your partner of 5 noncount nouns you can think of. Then take turns using them in sentences.**

▼ Photo of a sunset in Alabama

VOCABULARY

noncount nouns—words that name things you cannot count. These words do not have plural forms.

Words That Show Ownership

Words that show **ownership** are called **possessive nouns.** In most cases, you can turn a singular noun into a possessive noun by adding an **apostrophe** (') and *s*.

Forming Possessive Nouns

▲ A restaurant sign

Singular Possessive

Rosa ignored the <u>driver's</u> demand.
The <u>boss's</u> voice was loud.

To turn a singular noun ending in s into a possessive, add just an apostrophe and an s.

Plural Possessive (ending in s)

Three <u>drivers'</u> caps are on the table.

To turn a plural noun ending in s into a possessive, add just an apostrophe.

Plural Possessive (not ending in s)

The <u>children's</u> lesson is now.

To turn a plural noun that does not end in s into a possessive, add an apostrophe and an s.

Grammar Tip

Apostrophes

An apostrophe is a common mark of punctuation in English. It has 3 main uses.

1. To form possessives
   Jose's book, the ladies' umbrellas, Chris's brother

2. To form contractions
   isn't, I'll, don't

3. To show letters or numbers are missing
   '03 (for 2003)   'em (for them)

Learn these 3 ways apostrophes are used and what they signal. It can improve your understanding of what you read.

VOCABULARY

ownership—owning something; having something that is yours
possessive nouns—words that show who or what owns something. *Anna's* milk, the *cat's* paw, and the *girls'* game are examples of possessive nouns.
apostrophe—a mark of punctuation (') used with possessive nouns and with contractions, such as *isn't*

1. SINGULAR POSSESSIVE NOUNS

You use a singular possessive noun to show ownership. A singular possessive shows that something belongs to one person.

> The _marcher's_ sign was held high.

This sentence means there is one marcher, and she held her sign high.

2. PLURAL POSSESSIVE NOUNS

You use a plural possessive noun to show ownership by a group or more than one person.

> The _marchers'_ signs were held high.

This sentence means there were many marchers, and they held their signs high.

3. OTHER PLURAL POSSESSIVE NOUNS

When a possessive noun _does not_ end in _s_, add an apostrophe and _s_ to show ownership.

> The _children's_ parents were marching.

This sentence means there was more than one child, and their parents were the ones marching.

(TALK AND SHARE) **Talk with your partner about how to form the possessive of the words _boy, girls,_ and _women_.**

◀ The marcher's sign was held high.

Summary

Nouns are naming words. They name people, places, things, and ideas. Nouns also show how many or who owns something.

Analyzing

Analyzing a Character

When you analyze something, you look at it closely. To *analyze* means to divide into parts to see what something is or how it works. In school, you may be asked to analyze a character in a story. First, pull together what you know in a Web. Then look closely at the things you put in your Web. What do the things in this Web tell you about Rosa Parks?

Web

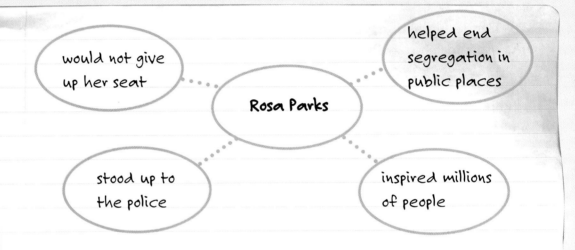

would not give up her seat

helped end segregation in public places

Rosa Parks

stood up to the police

inspired millions of people

Practice Analyzing

1. Create   With a partner, decide on a person or character to analyze. Discuss your topic for 3 or 4 minutes. Then create a Web based on what you decided. Use the Web on Rosa Parks above as a model.

2. Write   Make a Web about a person or character. Then write a paragraph of 3 or 4 sentences about that person or character. When you finish, circle the nouns. Then share your work with a partner. Ask him or her to underline any plural nouns in the paragraph. Then exchange papers and check each other's writing. Use proofreader's marks to show your partner how to fix mistakes.

Check Your Writing

Make sure you

- Use complete sentences.
- Use a period at the end of each sentence.
- Spell all the words correctly.

Grammar Spotlight

Choosing *a*/*an* or *the* Use *a* or *an* with singular count nouns. Use *the* with all nouns. Use *a* or *an* when you're talking about something in general. Use *the* when you mean something in particular.

a or *an*	*the*
It was an evening in December.	It was the evening when we began to march.
Luis lived near a park.	Luis lived near the large park.
Maria lived in an apartment.	Maria lived in the apartment over the store.

Remember to use *a* with words that begin with a consonant sound. Use *an* with words that begin with a vowel sound, such as *evening* and *apartment*.

Now write a sentence about *a law*. Write another sentence about *the law*.

Hands On

Portraits of People Like You Use photographs or pictures that you find or draw to make an album. Show people who have made a difference in your own life. Title your album "People Like Me." The people in your album may be family members, friends, or public people. Label the people in your album. Then tell your partner about the people and how they made a difference for you.

Oral Language

Interviewing Rosa Parks Rosa Parks has been interviewed many times by reporters. With a partner, prepare some questions you would want to ask her. Then answer the questions as you think Rosa would. Take turns being the interviewer and Rosa Parks. Here is an example.

Question: *Why didn't you give up your seat on the bus?*

Answer: *I was tired of giving up my seat.*

Question: *How could you have been so brave?*

Answer: *I was angry and tired of being mistreated.*

Theme 3
Becoming Who We Are

The people we meet, the places we go, and the experiences we have all shape who we are.

■ **What are these people doing?**

■ **How do they remind you of your own life?**

Understanding Point of View

Do you know why no two people ever tell the same story in the same way? That happens because people have different **points of view.** This means that people see and understand things in different ways. In an **autobiography,** the author writes about his or her **experiences** from his or her own point of view.

Points of View
opinions; the
ways people see
something

Autobiography
a true story
about a person's
life written by
that person

Experiences
things that
happen in
someone's life

Before Reading Activities

Hands On

Make a Web Explore your own point of view. Think about the special people, places, and experiences in your life. How did they help you become who you are? Make a Web like the one shown here. Explain it to a partner.

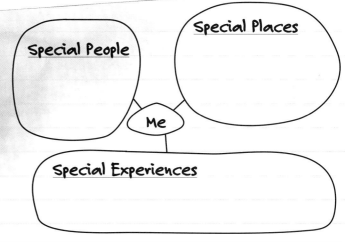

Special People

Special Places

Me

Special Experiences

Oral Language

Preview with a Partner With a partner, preview the selection on pages 130–133. Read the title and first line. Look at all the pictures in the selection. Talk to your partner about them. Then answer these questions.

• What do you think the reading will be about?

• Where do you think it takes place?

The Invisible Thread

by Yoshiko Uchida

▲ A family worships together at a Japanese temple.

Yoshiko Uchida wrote about growing up as a Japanese American during the 1930s and 1940s in her autobiography The Invisible Thread. *In it, she shares how she felt about visiting Japan and meeting new people. Yoshiko also tells how her experiences helped shape who she became.*

As you read the selection, look carefully at the events Yoshiko talks about. Ask yourself questions such as: How did she feel about visiting Japan? How did her experiences change the way she saw herself? Have you ever felt the way Yoshiko did? Write your thoughts in your reading journal.

One of the happiest times for my parents and Grandma Uchida was our stay in Kyoto, with its temples and hills and their beloved Doshisha University. The first friends Obah San wanted to visit were Dr. and Mrs. Learned, for whom she had worked so long ago.

They seemed so old and frail to me, like pale white **shadows** in a sea of Japanese faces. They **showered us with** love and affection, and gave Keiko and me the American names we had long wanted to have. Keiko was named Grace, and I was given the name Ruth. But somehow it didn't make me as happy as I thought it

VOCABULARY

shadows—dark images made when light is blocked
showered us with—gave us a lot of

would. I just didn't feel like a Ruth, and I never used the name.

Keiko and I **tolerated innumerable** long dinners and lunches with our parents' many friends, but when things got too boring, we would count the number of times people bowed to each other. In Japan no one hugged or shook hands. They just bowed. And bowed. And bowed some more. My mother set the record, with thirteen bows exchanged in one **encounter.**

What I liked best was going to temples and **shrines** on festival days, when the celebration, with costumed dancers and booming drums, was like a holiday parade and carnival rolled into one.

But I liked the celebration of Obon (All Souls' Day), too. That was when the spirits of the dead were believed to return home, and some families lit tiny **bonfires** at their front gate to welcome them at dusk. Inside, there were tables **laden** with all sorts of delicious dishes, prepared especially for the returning spirits.

In Japan the dead seemed to blend in with the living, as though there were no great black separation by death. And I found that a comforting thought.

▲ Kyoto, Japan, has many temples and shrines.

(**TALK AND SHARE**) **What did Yoshiko like about Japan? What did she not like? Talk to a partner about it.**

VOCABULARY
tolerated—allowed or put up with
innumerable—too many to count
encounter—a meeting
shrines—places of worship
bonfires—fires built outside for a celebration
laden—completely covered; loaded with

from *The Invisible Thread*

Sometimes we climbed wooded hills that rose behind ancient temples to visit graveyards filled with moss-covered **tombstones.** And one day we went to pay our respects to our **samurai** grandfathers whom we had never known. Using small wooden scoops, we poured cold water on their tombstones to refresh their spirits, and left them handfuls of summer lilies.

I wondered what they thought of us—their grandchildren from far-off America, dressed in strange clothing and **babbling** in a foreign **tongue.** I hoped they liked us.

Once we stayed with an uncle and some cousins at a rural inn, where at the end of the day, we all went to the **communal** tub to have a pleasant soak together.

Then, wearing cool cotton kimonos provided by the inn, we gathered around the low table, where the maids brought us miso soup, broiled eel, and slivered cucumber on individual black lacquer trays.

After dinner we sat on the **veranda** and had sweet bean paste cakes and tea, watching a full moon rise over the mountains. The talk was gentle, and

VOCABULARY

tombstones—stones that mark graves
samurai—a kind of Japanese soldier
babbling—talking that can't be understood
tongue—a language
communal—used by everyone in a community
veranda—a porch or balcony that usually has a roof

from *The Invisible Thread*

whenever it stopped, we could hear the swarms of **cicadas** in the pine trees buzzing **in unison** like some **demented** chorus.

As I sat watching the fireflies **darting** about in the darkness, I thought maybe I could get quite used to living in Japan. Here, at least, I looked like everyone else. Here, I blended in and wasn't always the one who was different.

And yet, I knew I was really a foreigner in Japan. I had felt like a complete idiot when an old woman asked me to read a bus sign for her, and I had to admit I couldn't read Japanese.

Deep down inside, where I really **dwelled,** I was thoroughly American. I missed my own language and the **casual banter** with friends. I longed for hot dogs and chocolate sodas and bathrooms with plumbing.

But the sad truth was, in America, too, I was **perceived** as a foreigner.

So what was I anyway, I wondered. I wasn't really totally American, and I wasn't totally Japanese. I was a **mixture** of the two, and I could never be anything else.

(**TALK AND SHARE**) **Talk to a partner about what Yoshiko thinks of herself.**

▲ This painting is *Geisha Visiting a Shrine* by Suzuki Harunobu. A *geisha* is a Japanese girl trained to sing and dance. A *shrine* is a religious or sacred place.

▲ Yoshiko (second from left) and her sister, Keiko (far right), are shown with their friends in California.

VOCABULARY
cicadas—insects; the males make a high-pitched sound
in unison—all together
demented—insane; crazy
darting—moving quickly and suddenly
dwelled—lived
casual banter—light, playful talk or conversation
perceived—looked at; seen as
mixture—a little of each; a combination

Responding to Literature

Explore the Reading

In a small group or with a partner, talk about each question below.

1. What did you think of the narrator Yoshiko?

2. What do you think Yoshiko meant when she said, "Here, at least, I looked like everyone else. Here, I blended in and wasn't always the one who was different"?

3. At the end of the story, how did Yoshiko feel about who she is? Why did she feel that way?

4. What in your own life did this story remind you of?

5. How would you describe the author's point of view?

6. Who would you say Yoshiko was? Who was she becoming?

Learn About Literature

Genre

Literature has many *genres*, or kinds of writing. The chart below can help you understand some of the most common genres.

Genre	Description
Autobiography	A true story about a person's life written by that person
Biography	A true story about a person's life written by someone else
Drama	A written story that can be performed on stage by actors
Essay	A short piece of writing that gives information or the writer's opinion about something
Novel	A long made-up story that comes from the writer's imagination
Poetry	A short piece of writing that usually has rhyme, imagery, or rhythm
Short Story	A short made-up story

With a partner, choose 3 books from the library from 3 different genres. Bring the books to class and tell how you know the genre of each book.

Activities

Hands On

Draw the Author Make a drawing of the author Yoshiko and some of the things that are special to her. Write 3 sentences about her at the bottom of your drawing. Then share it with a partner.

Oral Language

Oral Story String In a small group, make an oral Story String about *The Invisible Thread*. The first person in the group tells the first event in the story. Then the next person says the second event. Take turns until you finish telling the whole story. You might start like this.

> **Student 1:** *First, Yoshiko and her family went to Japan.*
> **Student 2:** *Then, she met Dr. and Mrs. Learned.*

Partner Practice

Write a Poem Write a poem that starts with "I am" in each line. Then read it to a partner. Here is an example.

> I am Stefan.
>
> I am a fun and caring brother.
>
> I am Polish American.
>
> I am happy when I spend time with my friends and family.
>
> I am proud of who I am.

Know the Author

Yoshiko Uchida

Yoshiko Uchida was born in California in 1922 to Japanese-American parents. Uchida began writing when she was 10 years old and she made tiny books out of brown wrapping paper. Uchida grew up to write more than 20 books for young people. Her books explore what it means to be both Japanese and American. Some of her best-known books include *The Dancing Kettle and Other Japanese Folk Tales*, *Jar of Dreams*, and *Journey to Topaz*.

Reading an
Autobiography

Here you'll learn about autobiographies. You'll also learn how to look for cause and effect and practice synthesizing key ideas.

Building Background

▲ Once I visited another country and learned to get around by myself.

- **What is happening here?**
- **Where do you think these people are going?**
- **What might their lives be like?**

An autobiography is a true story about a person's life written by that person.

When you read an autobiography, focus on 3 things.

1 Key events in the author's life
2 How the author's life changed
3 How you feel about the author

▲ Yoshiko (left) and her sister, Keiko (right)

from ***The Invisible Thread***
by Yoshiko Uchida

They seemed so old and frail to me, like pale white shadows in a sea of Japanese faces. They showered us with love and affection, and gave Keiko and me the American names we had long wanted to have. Keiko was named Grace, and I was given the name Ruth. But somehow it didn't make me as happy as I thought it would. I just didn't feel like a Ruth, and I never used the name.

1 **Key events**

2 **How the author's life changed**

I agree with her. I wouldn't want someone to change my name either.

3 **How I feel about the author**

Key Concepts

In an autobiography, the author shares **key events** from his or her life. Key events are important things that happen in a person's life. Authors also show a **point of view** by giving an opinion or saying how they feel about something. Think about what you learned and form an **impression,** or feeling, about the author.

Key Events

Birth School Moved to U.S.

Point of View

Impression

Types of Nonfiction

Nonfiction is about real people and real events. Here are 5 types of nonfiction.

Autobiography

The story of the author's life written by the author

Biography

The story of a person's life written by someone else

Looking for Cause and Effect

When you read an autobiography, look for causes and their effects to learn how the author became who she or he is.

1. The *causes* are the key events in the author's life.

2. The *effects* are what happened as a result of those events.

For example, look at the organizer below. What happened when Yoshiko was given an American name?

CAUSE

Yoshiko was given the name Ruth.

EFFECT

Yoshiko didn't feel like a Ruth. She never used her American name.

Newspaper
Short news articles

Magazine
Articles about people and events

Essay
Thoughts and ideas of a writer

Sacred Places

There is a place, a round, trampled patch of the red earth, near Carnegie, Oklahoma, where the Kiowa Gourd Dances were held in the early years of the century. When my father was six or eight years old, my grandfather, who was a member of the *Tian-paye*, or Gourd Dance Society, took him there. In one of the intervals of the dance there was a "giveaway," an ancient Plains tradition of giving gifts as a public expression of honor and esteem. My grandfather's name was called, and he let go of my father's hand and strode out upon the dance ground. Then a boy

Reading an Autobiography

An autobiography is about people and important events that shaped the author's life. After you read an autobiography, decide how you feel about the author.

Read for Key Events

Key **events** are important things that happened to the **author.** Pay close attention to the information in these events. They usually tell you two things.

1. Clues about important parts of the author's life

2. What the author learned

Read the example below. What key event does Yoshiko describe? What does she tell you about her family?

from *The Invisible Thread*
by Yoshiko Uchida

Key event

Sometimes we climbed wooded hills that rose behind ancient temples to visit graveyards filled with moss-covered **tombstones.** And one day we went to pay our respects to our **samurai** grandfathers whom we had never known. Using small wooden scoops, we poured cold water on their tombstones to refresh their spirits, and left them handfuls of summer lilies.

I wondered what they thought of us—their grandchildren from far-off America, dressed in strange clothing and **babbling** in a foreign tongue.

Yoshiko thinks this is how her grandfathers might see her. Maybe they don't!

VOCABULARY

events—things that happen
author—a person who writes a book or other type of text

tombstones—stones that mark graves
samurai—a kind of Japanese soldier
babbling—talking that can't be understood

Cause-Effect Organizer

CAUSE		EFFECT
Visited samurai grandfathers	→	Wonders what they would think of her

Key events tell you about important parts of the author's life, such as **character traits** and **major achievements.** Autobiographies usually touch on these common subjects.

- Growing up
- Character traits
- Major achievements
- Family
- School or work
- Major problems

Once you find a key event, use Key Topic Notes to help you keep track of the important details. In the first column, write the topic. Then write important details about the topic in the second column. Look at the example below.

▲ A samurai with a sword was photographed in 1860.

Key Topic Notes

Key Topic	Notes from Reading
family	Yoshiko and her family visited her grandfathers' graves. The visit was very respectful. Yoshiko wondered what her grandfathers might think of her and her American ways.

(TALK AND SHARE) **With a partner, talk about why it's important to look for key events in an autobiography.**

VOCABULARY
character traits—qualities a person has; parts of a person's personality
major—main; most important
achievements—great things you gain by working hard; accomplishments; successes

Look at How Events Shaped the Author's Life

Verb Phrases
These phrases have special meanings.

- **keep track of:** maintain a record of

- **touch on:** tell about or mention

Read about key events carefully. Decide how they changed the author's life. Ask yourself questions.

- What did the author learn from these events?

- How did the author change his or her **view** on life?

- How did the author change?

Read the excerpt below. How did Yoshiko's visit to Japan shape her **identity?**

from *The Invisible Thread*
by Yoshiko Uchida

And yet, I knew I was really a **foreigner** in Japan. I had felt like a complete idiot when an old woman asked me to read a bus sign for her, and I had to admit I couldn't read Japanese.

Deep down inside, where I really dwelled, I was thoroughly American. I missed my own language and the casual banter with friends. I longed for hot dogs and chocolate sodas and bathrooms with plumbing.

But the sad truth was, in America, too, I was **perceived** as a foreigner.

So what was I anyway, I wondered. I wasn't really totally American, and I wasn't totally Japanese. I was a **mixture** of the two, and I could never be anything else.

How the event changed the author's life

VOCABULARY

view—a belief; an opinion; a position about something
identity—who a person is; how one knows oneself and is known by others

foreigner—a person from another country or place
perceived—looked at; seen as
mixture—a little of each; a combination

Key event → **Key event** → **Key event** = **Life is changed.**

An autobiography usually describes a **series** of events in an author's life. Look for them and decide how they changed the author's life. Keep track of those events with a Timeline or with Sequence Notes. Look at the example below.

Sequence Notes

1st Event
went to Japan and liked traditions →

2nd Event
couldn't read Japanese bus sign →

3rd Event
liked Japan, but missed America

Reading Tip

Using a Double-entry Journal

Autobiographies usually have a lot of information. How can you keep track of important details? A Double-entry Journal can help. A Double-entry Journal has two columns. In the first column, write notes or quotes from the text. In the second column, write what you think or how you feel about the quotes.

Example

Quote	My Thoughts
"I was a mixture of the two, and I could never be anything else."	Yoshiko can't be only American or only Japanese. She'll always be both. That's how I feel, too.

TALK AND SHARE With a partner, make a list of two things you can do to figure out how events shaped an author's life.

VOCABULARY
series—a number of similar things in a row or following one another; a sequence

Yoshiko stands next to her mother on the left. ▼

Decide How You Feel About the Author

When you have a good idea of what the author is really like, decide how you feel about him or her. Do you like or **admire** this person? Why or why not?

As you read, write down your thoughts on sticky notes.

from ***The Invisible Thread***
by Yoshiko Uchida

As I sat watching the fireflies darting about in the darkness, I thought maybe I could get quite used to living in Japan. Here, at least, I looked like everyone else. Here, I blended in and wasn't always the one who was different.

I don't agree with her. Sometimes it's okay to be different.

VOCABULARY

admire—have a high opinion of someone or something

Record Your Thoughts

> 1. Look at what the author says, does, and feels.

> 2. Draw a conclusion about how you feel about him or her.

Create an Inference Chart to help you form your own **impressions.** In the first column, write notes about what the author said or did. In the second column, write the inferences you made to form your impressions.

Sometimes you may not immediately have a clear impression. When this happens, go back and reread for key details. Then ask yourself, "What do these details tell me about the author?"

(TALK AND SHARE) **How can you decide how you feel about an author? Use sticky notes or your reading journal to record your thoughts about Yoshiko. Talk to your partner about it.**

Inference Chart

What the Author Said, Did or Felt	My Inferences
Yoshiko doesn't like to always be different.	• She thinks a lot about who she is and where she fits in the world. • Yoshiko deeply wants to feel like she belongs somewhere. I think everyone feels that way.

Summary

Autobiographies are true stories about a person's own life. Read them carefully to see how key events shaped the author's life. After you read an autobiography, decide how you feel about the author.

Synthesizing

Synthesizing Key Ideas

Synthesizing means looking at many small parts and deciding what they mean as a whole. It is like gathering the pieces of a puzzle and figuring out how they fit together.

You need to synthesize information when you read an autobiography. Use a Character Trait Web like the one below. With it, you can find the details that are proof of the character traits you see in the author.

Character Trait Web

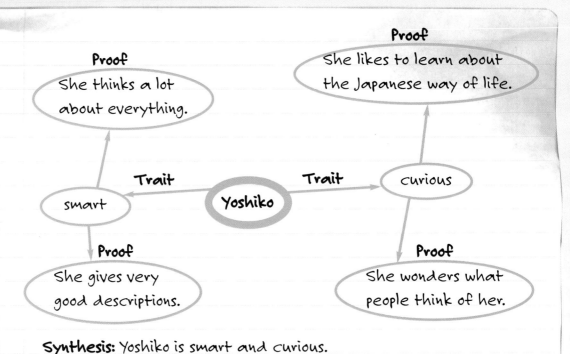

Synthesis: Yoshiko is smart and curious.

Practice Synthesizing

1. Draw   With a partner, talk about your backgrounds and lives. Then draw what you learned about your partner in a Character Trait Web.

2. Write   Make a Character Trait Web about yourself. Then write an autobiographical paragraph. Trade paragraphs with a partner, and check each other's work.

Check Your Writing

Make sure you

- ☐ Use complete sentences.
- ☐ Use a period at the end of each sentence.
- ☐ Spell all the words correctly.

Activities

Grammar Spotlight

Subject-Verb Agreement with Two or More Subjects   When two subjects are connected by *and*, use a plural verb. When two subjects are connected by *or*, the verb should agree with the subject closest to the verb.

Rule	Example
Use a singular subject with a singular verb.	*Yoshiko visits Japan.*
When two or more subjects are connected by *and,* use a plural verb.	*Yoshiko <u>and</u> her sister visit Japan.*
When two or more subjects are connected by *or,* use a plural verb <u>if the subject closest to the verb is plural.</u>	*Either my dad <u>or</u> my aunts are going to Japan.*
When two or more subjects are connected by *or,* use a singular verb <u>if the subject closest to the verb is singular.</u>	*Either my aunts <u>or</u> my dad is going to Japan.*

Write a sentence using *and*. Use the subjects *my parents* and *my sister* in your sentence. Then rewrite the sentence using *or*.

Hands On

My Story   Bring 3 things from home that are important to you. Tell a partner why each thing is important. Then ask your partner to form an impression based on what he or she has learned.

Oral Language

Read Together   Think about the Japanese ways of life you read about in *The Invisible Thread*. Are any of those ways of life like ones you have? Read the passage on page 140 again. Then take turns reading the sentences aloud with a partner.

Partner Practice

Sharing Who We Are   Think about key events in your life that helped you become who you are. What were the events? How did they change you? Describe them in a Sequence Notes Organizer like the one on page 143. Then explain your organizer to a partner.

Reading

Graphics and Websites

Here you'll learn about reading graphics and websites. You'll also learn how to paraphrase and practice interpreting graphics.

▲ I know lots of things about the people in my city.

■ **Who do you think these people are?**

■ **How are they like or different than the people where you live?**

■ **What words would you use to describe this picture?**

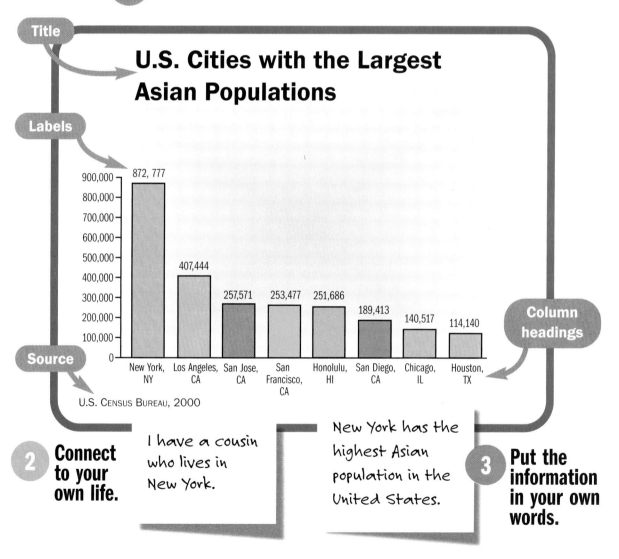

When you read graphics or websites:

1 Read all of the labels and text on the graphic.

2 Connect the graphic to your own life.

3 Put what the graphic says in your own words.

1 **Read labels and text.**

Title

U.S. Cities with the Largest Asian Populations

Labels

872, 777

900,000
800,000
700,000
600,000
500,000
400,000
300,000
200,000
100,000
0

| New York, NY | Los Angeles, CA | San Jose, CA | San Francisco, CA | Honolulu, HI | San Diego, CA | Chicago, IL | Houston, TX |

407,444
257,571
253,477
251,686
189,413
140,517
114,140

Column headings

Source

U.S. CENSUS BUREAU, 2000

2 **Connect to your own life.**

I have a cousin who lives in New York.

New York has the highest Asian population in the United States.

3 **Put the information in your own words.**

Key Concepts

Some common types of **graphics** are graphs, maps, photos, and timelines.

The **Internet** is a system of computers from around the world that shares information. It has billions of **websites**.

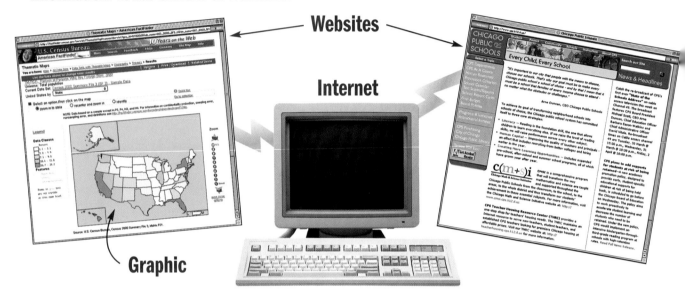

Websites

Internet

Graphic

Types of Graphics

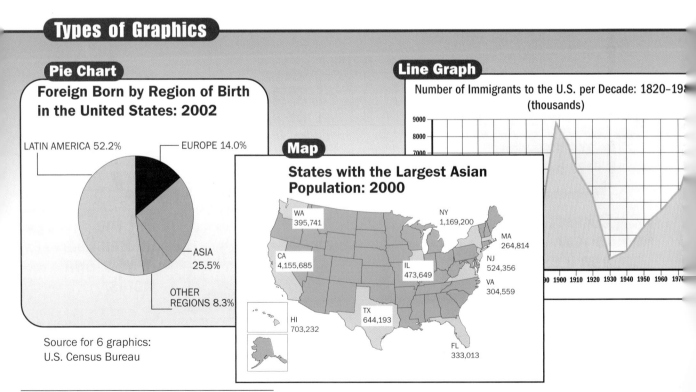

Pie Chart

Foreign Born by Region of Birth in the United States: 2002

LATIN AMERICA 52.2%

EUROPE 14.0%

ASIA 25.5%

OTHER REGIONS 8.3%

Source for 6 graphics:
U.S. Census Bureau

Line Graph

Number of Immigrants to the U.S. per Decade: 1820–198
(thousands)

9000
8000
7000

90 1900 1910 1920 1930 1940 1950 1960 1970

Map

States with the Largest Asian Population: 2000

WA 395,741

NY 1,169,200

MA 264,814

CA 4,155,685

NJ 524,356

IL 473,649

VA 304,559

HI 703,232

TX 644,193

FL 333,013

Paraphrasing

When you *paraphrase*, you use your own words to explain something you've read. Paraphrasing can help you understand and remember the most important details in a graphic. To paraphrase, create a Paraphrase Chart and ask yourself these questions.

1. What is the graphic about?

2. What are the important details?

3. What do I think about the information?

Paraphrase Chart

Subject	Cities with the largest number of Asians
My Paraphrase	New York has the highest Asian population out of all 8 cities. Houston has the lowest Asian population.
My Thoughts	Wow! I didn't know that New York had such a high Asian population.

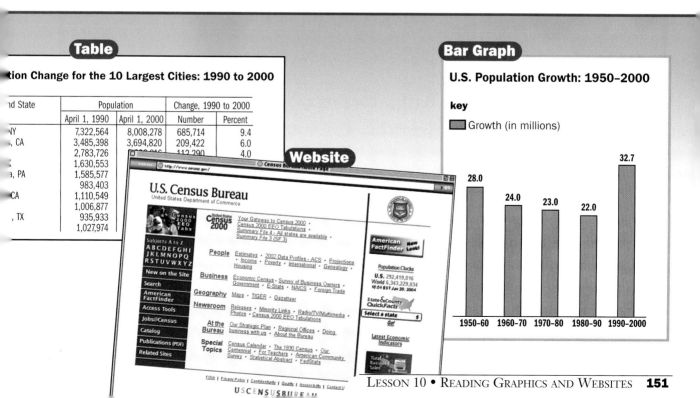

Table

tion Change for the 10 Largest Cities: 1990 to 2000

nd State	Population		Change, 1990 to 2000	
	April 1, 1990	April 1, 2000	Number	Percent
NY	7,322,564	8,008,278	685,714	9.4
, CA	3,485,398	3,694,820	209,422	6.0
	2,783,726		112,290	4.0
	1,630,553			
, PA	1,585,577			
	983,403			
CA	1,110,549			
	1,006,877			
, TX	935,933			
	1,027,974			

Bar Graph

U.S. Population Growth: 1950–2000

key

☐ Growth (in millions)

				32.7
28.0				
	24.0	23.0	22.0	
1950–60	1960–70	1970–80	1980–90	1990–2000

Website

U.S. Census Bureau
United States Department of Commerce

LESSON 10 • READING GRAPHICS AND WEBSITES **151**

Reading Graphics and Websites

Graphics organize information in a visual way. Websites use text and graphics. Read all the labels. Connect graphics and websites to your own life. Then put what you learn in your own words.

Looking at a Graphic

Before you read a graphic, follow two important steps.

1. **Preview** the graphic.

2. Look at how the graphic is organized.

PREVIEW

Think about your purpose for reading a graphic. What is the graphic about? To find out, preview the title, labels, **source,** and headings.

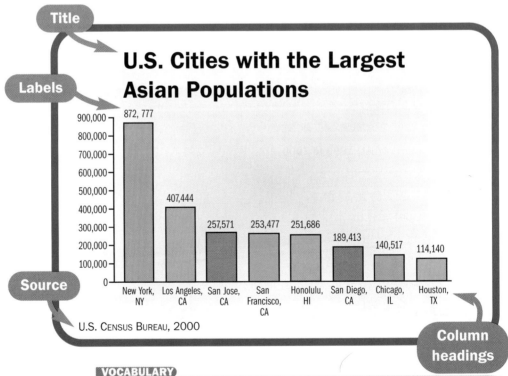

Title

Labels

Source

Column headings

U.S. Cities with the Largest Asian Populations

- New York, NY — 872, 777
- Los Angeles, CA — 407,444
- San Jose, CA — 257,571
- San Francisco, CA — 253,477
- Honolulu, HI — 251,686
- San Diego, CA — 189,413
- Chicago, IL — 140,517
- Houston, TX — 114,140

U.S. Census Bureau, 2000

VOCABULARY

preview—look at something quickly before reading it carefully
source—something or someone that gives information; where information came from or started

LOOK AT HOW THE GRAPHIC IS ORGANIZED

One common type of graphic is a bar graph. Bar graphs have the shape of an "L." The vertical line is called the *y* **axis.** The *y* axis gives amounts. The horizontal line, or *x* axis, labels places or things. When you read a bar graph, read "up and over" or "over and up." See the yellow arrow in the bar graph below.

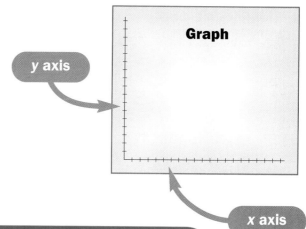

y axis

x axis

y axis: Population

x axis: Cities

U.S. Cities with the Largest Asian Populations

U.S. CENSUS BUREAU, 2000

This bar graph compares the Asian **population** in different cities. The yellow arrow shows how you read over to the city you want to find and up to the population.

(TALK AND SHARE) **With a partner, find a graphic in a textbook and preview it. Then point to all of the parts.**

VOCABULARY

axis—a straight line in a chart that contains measurements or presents information

population—all the people in a place

Reading a Graphic

When you read a graphic, think about what you want to learn and what the graphic tells you.

READ CAREFULLY

First, read all of the words in and around the graphic. Pay close attention to details, such as amounts, numbers, or dates. If you are looking at a line or bar graph, make sure you know what the *x* and *y* axes are showing. Then, find out what the **symbols** mean in the **key** or **legend**. Finally, make sure the **source** of the information is current and **reliable.**

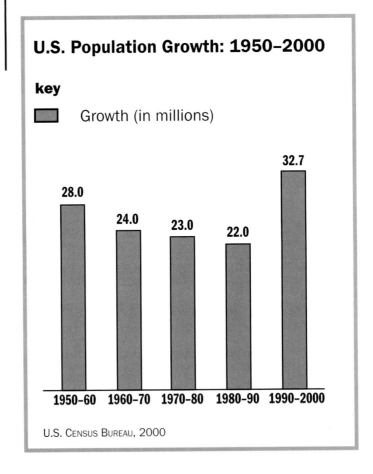

U.S. Population Growth: 1950–2000

key

☐ Growth (in millions)

- 1950–60: 28.0
- 1960–70: 24.0
- 1970–80: 23.0
- 1980–90: 22.0
- 1990–2000: 32.7

U.S. CENSUS BUREAU, 2000

VOCABULARY

symbols—things that stand for or represent something else. For example, the pink bars in the graph above stand for millions of people.

key, legend—a caption on a map or chart that explains symbols used in it

source—where something comes from. The U.S. Census Bureau is a good source for information about population. Its job is to count the number of people.

reliable—worthy of trust; dependable

PARAPHRASE

When you read graphics, you need to be able to understand
a   ense of the information. First, figure out the subject
           phic is showing you. Then, put the information
           o your own words, or paraphrase it. That will help
           and and remember the information you learned.

se Chart

	U.S. population growth from 1950 to 2000
..ase	Between 1950 and 1990, U.S. population growth decreased. It was lowest between 1980 and 1990. Population growth was the highest between 1990 and 2000.
My Thoughts	Even though the growth had been decreasing, the U.S. population grew the most between 1990 and 2000. That surprised me a lot!

(TALK AND SHARE) **Find a graphic in a magazine or newspaper. Then paraphrase it for your partner.**

Reading Websites

The Internet is like a huge library on a computer. You can find out just about anything you need to know—from the latest news stories to recipes to biographies of your favorite authors. The Internet is a **valuable** research source if you use it correctly. When you read websites, follow these two steps.

1. Know your **purpose.**

2. **Evaluate** the source.

KNOW YOUR PURPOSE

When you are searching the Internet to find information, decide what your purpose is before you begin. Ask yourself these questions.

1. What do I need to find out?

2. What questions do I have?

3. What information do I need?

You may need to **expand** or widen your search as you go. Have a clear purpose in mind. It will keep you focused.

Reading Tip

Using a Search Engine

A *search engine* can make research on the Internet easy to do. Search engines are tools that keep huge collections of information. Ask your teacher or school librarian for a list of good search engines. When you're ready to begin searching, type in specific key words that describe what you are looking for. *U.S. population* would help you with the information in this lesson. Then look at the websites the search engine lists. Remember that not all sites are reliable. Be sure to double-check the information you find.

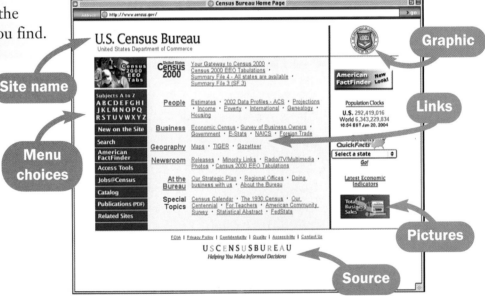

VOCABULARY

valuable—having great importance; worthy
purpose—a reason for doing something; a goal

evaluate—decide the value or importance of something
expand—increase in number or size; make larger

EVALUATE THE SOURCE

Anyone can make a website and fill it with anything, even if the information is not true! For this reason, it's important that you check the source of the websites you use. Make sure your information is from a good source. To find out if a source is good, ask yourself questions.

1. Does the site name its source?

2. Is the source well known?

3. Is the site's goal to sell a product or to **promote a cause?** Or does it give fair information?

4. Is the information up-to-date?

5. Is the site free of errors in spelling, grammar, and facts?

A Website Profiler like the one below can help you keep track of the websites you use and the information on them.

Website Profiler

Name and Website Address	
Source	Date
Point of View	Information ☐ weak ☐ average ☐ very good
My Thoughts	

(TALK AND SHARE) With a partner, find a website. Look at it. Then talk about how to evaluate it with a Website Profiler.

Summary

Read all the words in a graphic or website. Then connect the graphic or website to your own life. Finally, put what you learn in your own words.

VOCABULARY

promote a cause—speak, write, or act in support of an idea or belief

Interpreting

Interpreting Graphics

When you interpret a graphic, you decide what its information means. To interpret a graphic, follow these steps.

1. Read the information carefully. Pay close attention to labels and changes in amounts or numbers.

2. Figure out the most important piece of information in the graphic.

3. Ask yourself, "What is the big idea in this graphic?"

4. Use Summary Notes to help you interpret it.

Summary Notes

Title or Topic: Cities with highest Asian populations

Main Point: New York ranks far above the rest.

1. New York has about 873, 000 Asians.
2. The city with the next highest population has only about 407,000 Asians. That's less than half of what New York has.
3. Most of the top 8 cities have between 100,000 and 260,000 Asians.

Practice Interpreting

1. Tell With a partner, find a population graph on www.census.gov. Then fill out Summary Notes and talk about it.

2. Write Research a population graph on www.census.gov with a partner. Fill out Summary Notes, and write an interpretation of 3 to 4 sentences. The Word Bank may help you.

Word Bank

highest
lowest
biggest
smallest

population
group
graphic

Grammar Spotlight

Phrases A phrase is a group of related words that does not have a subject or a predicate. A phrase is never a complete sentence, but it can be part of one.

Phrase	Phrase Used in a Complete Sentence
during the year 2000	*During the year 2000, the Asian population in the United States kept growing.*
before the end of the year	*The census was completed before the end of the year.*

Now write two complete sentences that have phrases. Then underline the phrase in each of your sentences.

Hands On

Make a Poster Make a poster on how to preview a graphic or how to read a website on the Internet. Paraphrase what you learned in this lesson. Give 3 to 4 steps for how to read a graphic. Then explain your poster to the class.

Oral Language

Show and Tell Find a graphic in a newspaper or magazine. Do not show it to your partner, but describe the information it presents. Have your partner draw the graphic you explained. Then compare your partner's graphic to the one you found.

Partner Practice

Draw a Graph Draw a line or bar graph about your class. Talk with your partner to decide what to show. For example, you might show how many boys and girls are in the class or how many children are in students' families. Then give your graph a title, add labels to the x and y axes, and share it with the class.

Writing an
Expository Paragraph

Here you'll learn about expository paragraphs. You'll also learn how to use time order and practice identifying reasons.

▲ I wonder where these people are. I've never seen a place like this.

- **What do you think is happening here?**
- **Where do you think the people are?**
- **Why might they be there?**

Expository paragraphs give information or explain subjects using facts and details. Expository paragraphs often use cause-effect order or time order.

The expository paragraph below tells when and why Japanese internment camps were started during World War II.

Explains *When*   **Explains *Why***

Japanese Internment Camps

On December 7, 1941, the Japanese military attacked the U.S. fleet at Pearl Harbor. This made many Caucasian Americans angry at Japan and at Japanese Americans. Before this day, Japanese Americans were seen as friends and as Americans. Now they were seen as the enemy. Japanese Americans were strongly against the Pearl Harbor attack. But the United States government ordered them to move to internment camps. The military took 112,000 people to live in camps that looked like prisons. Most of the people they took were American citizens.

Japanese planes bombed American ships at Pearl Harbor on December 7, 1941. ▼

Key Concepts

Expository paragraphs give information or explanations. People write expository paragraphs to **inform** or to **explain** a subject.

To inform means to tell about a subject. To explain a subject means to make it clear or easy to understand.

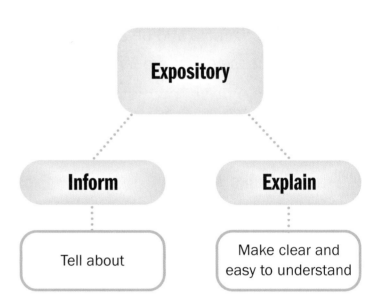

Expository

Inform

Tell about

Explain

Make clear and easy to understand

Developing an Expository Paragraph

Add facts and details.

On December 7, 1941, Japanese war planes attacked the U.S. fleet at Pearl Harbor.

Give examples.

Topaz is an example of a Japanese internment camp.

Using Time Order

Writers often use time order in expository paragraphs. Time order is the order in which events happened. These steps can help you use time order.

1. Give dates and times when you can.

2. Use words that signal time order, such as *first*, *next*, *before*, *while*, and *after*.

   Look at the paragraph here. The highlighted words signal time order.

> ### Japanese Internment Camps
>
> Life soon changed for many Japanese Americans. In late April of 1942, the United States government ordered Japanese and Japanese Americans to move to internment camps. While preparing for the move, many had to sell their homes and everything they owned. They had to leave friends, jobs, and their lives behind. After they moved to the camps, they were forced to stay there for a long period of time.

Create definitions.

Internment means being held and kept in prison.

Tell about personal experiences.

My life changed after the attack. I was sent to the internment camp two weeks before I would have graduated from college.

Writing an Expository Paragraph

Expository paragraphs explain a subject in a clear and detailed way. You can use time order or cause-effect order for an expository paragraph.

Steps for Writing an Expository Paragraph

All writers need time to plan their ideas. First, they think about what they want to write and how they will do it. Then, they decide which **details** they want to include. Here are 3 steps to follow when writing an **expository** paragraph.

1. Choose a subject.
2. Decide on a main idea.
3. Make a plan.

1. CHOOSE A SUBJECT

Write about what you know. The better you know a **subject,** the easier it is to write about it. It's important to do some **research,** too. Try to find at least two **sources** about the subject you choose.

Example: *Yoshiko Uchida*

▲ Yoshiko (right) plays with her family in happy times.

VOCABULARY

details—single items or facts about something
expository—a type of writing that gives information (such as an explanation, directions, or how to do something)
subject—a topic; what a paragraph is about

research—the work done to learn about a subject. Usually research is done by studying books about the subject at the library or by searching the Internet for information.
sources—books, magazines, websites, or encyclopedias that give information

2. DECIDE ON A MAIN IDEA

Next, decide what you want to say about your subject. This will be the main idea of your paragraph.

> **Example:** *Yoshiko Uchida overcame many challenges to become a writer.*

3. MAKE A PLAN

After you choose your main idea, use an organizer to plan your paragraph. A Main Idea Organizer can help you support your main idea and stay on track when writing your paragraph.

Main Idea Organizer

Main Idea: Yoshiko Uchida overcame many challenges to become a writer.

Detail 1:	Detail 2:	Detail 3:
Yoshiko and her family were forced to live at a Japanese internment camp during World War II.	Yoshiko had to leave college to go to the camp.	Yoshiko finally graduated from college and became a famous writer.

A letter from the U.S. government dismissed Yoshiko from college before she graduated. *Dismissed* means to be sent away. ▼

▲ Yoshiko needed a new identification card during internment.

TALK AND SHARE What would you write about in an expository paragraph? Talk to a partner about your ideas.

Cause-Effect Order

▼ Yoshiko and her family were photographed on the day they left the Topaz internment camp.

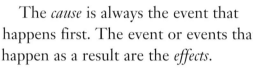

If the purpose of your paragraph is to explain *why* something happened, use cause-effect order. You can give the cause first and then the effects. Or you can give the effects and then the cause. Either way works as long as you clearly state which event happened first.

The *cause* is always the event that happens first. The event or events that happen as a result are the *effects*.

Cause-Effect Organizer

Effect

Yoshiko and her family were forced to live at the camp.

Cause

During World War II, President Roosevelt ordered Japanese Americans to be sent to internment camps.

Effect

During her senior year, Yoshiko had to leave college to go to the camp.

Effect

Yoshiko later wrote about her experiences at the camp and became a famous author.

▲ Yoshiko Uchida

Writing an Expository Paragraph

> 1. Make a Cause-Effect Organizer.
>
> 2. Use cause-effect signal words.

Use your Cause-Effect Organizer to write your paragraph. Remember to use words that signal cause-effect relationships, such as *because, so, since, why, cause, as a result,* and *reason.*

Yoshiko Uchida's Life During WWII

During World War II, President Roosevelt ordered that Japanese Americans be sent to internment camps. As a result, Yoshiko Uchida and her family had to leave their home and move to a camp. The order caused Yoshiko to leave college during her last year. Yoshiko wrote about her **experiences** at the camp and became a famous writer.

▲ Japanese-American children move to an internment camp.

(TALK AND SHARE) **Make a Cause-Effect Organizer about some change that happened to you. Explain it to a partner.**

Writing Tip

Add Details

Details help make your writing interesting. In an expository paragraph, the details can help readers "see" the steps you're writing about. Good details can turn a dull explanation into a lively and interesting one. Where can you find the details you need? First, start with *you*. Consider what you've seen, heard, tasted, touched, and smelled. Also, your own personal experiences—things that have happened to you—make good details. Other sources can be books, magazines, newspapers, the Internet, or experts—people who know the subject really well.

VOCABULARY

experiences—things that happen to a person

A 1942 poster asks Americans to remember the attack on Pearl Harbor. ▼

...we here highly resolve that these dead shall not have died in vain...

REMEMBER DEC. 7th!

Time Order

If you want to write an expository paragraph to tell about several events, use time order. When you use time order, you tell a **series** of events in the order they happened. You write what happened first, second, third, and so on. Sequence Notes can help you plan the order of events. The Sequence Notes below show the series of events that led to the start of Japanese internment camps.

Sequence Notes

Japan attacked Pearl Harbor.

↓

The United States declared war on Japan.

↓

Prejudice against Japanese Americans grew.

↓

President Roosevelt ordered that the **military** could tell people where they could and could not go.

↓

Japanese Americans were sent to live in internment camps.

▲ President Franklin D. Roosevelt signs the declaration of war on Japan.

▲ A truck takes Japanese Americans to an internment camp.

VOCABULARY

series—a number of similar things in a row or following one another; a sequence

prejudice—a strong feeling or opinion formed before knowing all the facts

military—the army, navy, and air force

Planning an Expository Paragraph

1. List events in Sequence Notes.

2. Connect events using signal words.

After you finish making Sequence Notes, you can start writing your paragraph. When possible, use dates in your paragraph and connect the events using signal words.

Look at the example below.

Language Notes

Signal Words:
Time Order
These words are clues to the order in which things happened.

- at first
- soon
- first
- later
- second
- after
- then
- last
- next
- finally

Japanese Internment Camps

First, Japan attacked Pearl Harbor during World War II. Then, the United States declared war on Japan. Prejudice against Japanese Americans grew greatly. Soon, the government was involved. President Roosevelt ordered that the military could tell people where they could and could not go. At first, Japanese Americans couldn't live, work, or travel on the West Coast of the United States. Later, Japanese Americans were sent to live in internment camps.

TALK AND SHARE Make Sequence Notes for 3 key events in your life. Then talk about the events with a partner. Use signal words.

Summary

Expository paragraphs give information about a subject. Use time order or cause-effect order as a way to organize expository paragraphs.

Identifying

Identifying Reasons

When you identify reasons, you tell what caused something to happen. For example, what if your teacher asked you, "What is the reason that you're late to school?" You would say what caused you to be late. (*I'm late because I missed the bus*, *I woke up late*, and so on.)

A Cause-Effect Organizer can help you list the reasons you identify. The Cause-Effect Organizer below lists the reasons that Yoshiko Uchida may have become a writer.

Cause-Effect Organizer

Cause

She had many stories to tell.

Cause

She liked to write.

Effect

Yoshiko Uchida became a writer.

Cause

She wanted to share her experiences at the internment camp.

Practice Identifying

1. Draw Draw a Cause-Effect Organizer to identify the reasons that Japanese internment camps were started. Then share your Cause-Effect Organizer with a partner.

2. Write Use a Cause-Effect Organizer to explain an event that happened in your own life. Then use those reasons to write an expository paragraph of 3 to 4 sentences. Use the checklist to help you revise your paragraph.

Check Your Writing

Make sure you

- ☐ Use complete sentences.
- ☐ Use a period at the end of each sentence.
- ☐ Spell all the words correctly.

Activities

Grammar Spotlight

Using the Simple Present Tense   Use the simple present tense when you talk about facts (things that are true) or things that happen over and over again.

Use the Simple Present Tense . . .	Example
To talk about a fact	*The Japanese celebrate Obon (All Souls' Day).*
To talk about something that happens over and over	*We study at school every day.*

Now write two sentences about your own life using the simple present tense.

Hands On

How to Develop a Paragraph   With a partner, make a poster about how to develop an expository paragraph. Look at the description on pages 162–163. Then, together with your partner, choose a subject and give an example of a fact, a definition, and a personal experience.

Oral Language

Make a Rap   With a partner or small group, think about something you want to explain or demonstrate to the class. Write an expository rap about it. Here is an example.

> *First, pick a subject that's important to you.*
> *It can be something special or a how-to.*
> *Then, figure out what you want to say.*
> *Make a good plan, and you're on your way.*

Partner Practice

Time Order Picture   Think about something important that happened to you. Make a picture about it. Write 4 or 5 sentences about the event. Remember to use time order and words such as *first, next, before, after, last,* and *finally.* Then explain your picture to a partner.

Understanding
Verbs

Here you'll learn about verbs. You'll also learn how to revise your writing and practice identifying tenses.

▲ My brother and I take karate lessons. Kicks are my favorite moves to practice.

- **What does this remind you of?**
- **How does the picture make you feel? Why?**
- **What words would you use to describe what's happening?**

Big Idea

Verbs show action or a state of being. Verbs match, or agree with, the subject. Verb tenses are forms of verbs that show time or when something happened.

Some verbs show action.

Some verbs show state of being.

from *Two or Three Things I Know for Sure*
by Dorothy Allison

At twenty-four I joined a karate class and learned for the first time how to run without fear pushing me. It was not what I had intended. I never expected to join the class at all. I showed up because I had been told there were no women allowed and my newfound feminist convictions insisted someone had to do something about that. Along with my friend Flo, I dressed in loose clothes and hitched a ride out to the university gardens very early one Monday morning.

hitched a ride

dressed

Key Concepts

A **subject** is the part of the sentence that is doing something or is what the sentence is about. A **verb** shows what the subject is, does, feels, or thinks. The **predicate** is the part of the sentence that names the action. It includes one or more verbs.

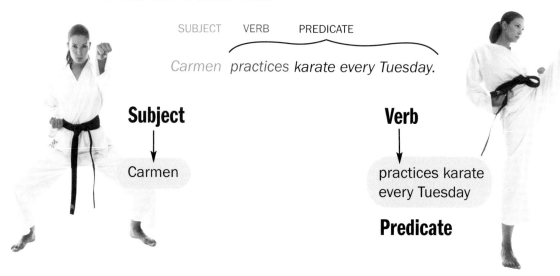

SUBJECT   VERB   PREDICATE

Carmen practices karate every Tuesday.

Subject
Carmen

Verb
practices karate every Tuesday
Predicate

Verb Types

Verbs

Show action . . .
Dorothy practices her moves.

or a state of being.
Dorothy is in class today.

Revising Your Writing

Good writers use strong verbs and the active voice in their writing. The *voice* of a verb tells whether the subject is acting or being acted upon.

- *Active voice* means that the subject is acting, or doing something.

- *Passive voice* means that the subject is being acted upon.

	Subject	Verb
Active	Dorothy	took
	Dorothy took a karate class.	
	Action	Received by
Passive	was taken	Dorothy
	A karate class was taken by Dorothy.	

Active voice makes writing more direct and lively. Use active verbs when you write. As you revise your writing, look for any places where you can use active voice.

Linking Verbs

Linking verbs join the subject to other words in the sentence.

Anne feels good about her high kick.

Helping Verbs

Helping verbs are added to another verb to make the meaning more clear.

Dorothy will return for class next week.

Understanding Verbs

Verbs are important. Verbs tell you what the subject of the sentence is doing, thinking, or feeling, and they match the subject. There are 3 main types of verbs and 3 main tenses.

Action verbs

Talk

Watch

Stand

Throw

Fall

Types of Verbs

What are the different types of **verbs?** Here you will learn about 3 basic types of verbs and how you can recognize them.

1. ACTION VERBS

Action verbs tell what the subject does. Here are examples of some action verbs.

> jump   run   read
> shout   laugh   write

In the example below, the action verb *kicks* tells what Dorothy does.

Example: *Dorothy kicks her leg high.*

2. LINKING VERBS

Linking verbs join the subject to other words in the sentence. In the sentence below, the verb *is* links the adjective *happy* to the subject *Dorothy*.

Example: <u>Dorothy</u> is <u>happy</u> with her
karate skills.

The most common linking verb is a form of *be*, such as *am, are, is, was,* and *were*. Other common linking verbs include *feel, become, grow, look, remain, seem, smell, sound, stay,* and *taste*.

VOCABULARY

verbs—words that show action or state of being
linking verbs—verbs that join the subject to a noun or an adjective in the predicate

3. HELPING VERBS

Helping verbs are added to another verb to make the meaning clear.

> **Example:** *Dorothy and her team can <u>compete</u> at the karate competition, too.*

Here are the most common helping verbs: *do, does, did, have, has, had, should, will, would, could, can, may, might,* and forms of the verb *be*.

Usually you will find one main verb and one or more helping verbs.

Examples

- *Dorothy's team may win the competition.*

- *They will have won three times in a row.*

- *Their coach has given them **some** words of wisdom.*

Language Notes

Homophones
These words sound alike, but they have different spellings and meanings.

- **to:** toward; or a part of a verb
- **too:** also
- **two:** the number 2

- **their:** belonging to them
- **there:** in that place
- **they're:** a contraction for *they are*

- **some:** a number of
- **sum:** the total when adding numbers

(**TALK AND SHARE**) **With a partner, talk about the 3 types of verbs. Give one example of each kind of verb to your partner.**

VOCABULARY
helping verbs—verbs added to other verbs to make the meaning clear

Matching Verbs and Subjects

A subject tells who or what the sentence is about. The verb tells what the subject is doing or feeling. For a sentence to be correct, the verb and subject must match, or **agree.**

SINGULAR SUBJECTS

A **singular** subject needs a singular verb.

> SINGULAR SUBJECT   SINGULAR VERB
> **Example:** *Dorothy <u>kicks</u> higher than anyone in her class.*

When singular subjects are joined by *or* or *nor*, they also require a singular verb.

> SINGULAR SUBJECT   SINGULAR VERB
> **Example:** *Neither Dorothy nor Flo <u>is</u> ever late.*

Watch out for subjects such as *everybody, everything, everyone, someone, anybody, somebody, nobody, each, either, neither, one,* and *another.* These subjects are singular, and they require a singular verb.

> SINGULAR SUBJECT   SINGULAR VERB
> **Example:** *Everyone <u>is</u> trying to get to class on time.*

> SINGULAR SUBJECT   SINGULAR VERB
> **Example:** *Either <u>fits</u> me.*

VOCABULARY

agree—be the same in number. When a verb and noun agree, they are both singular or both plural.
singular—naming one person, place, or thing

PLURAL SUBJECTS

Some sentences have a **plural** subject. That means more than one person, place, or thing is the subject. Plural subjects are sometimes connected with the word *and*. They **require** a plural verb to match, or agree.

PLURAL SUBJECT   PLURAL VERB
Example: *We <u>are</u> excited about the karate class.*

PLURAL SUBJECT   PLURAL VERB
Example: *She and I <u>are</u> taking another class next year.*

PLURAL SUBJECT   PLURAL VERB
Example: *Dorothy and Flo <u>run</u> two miles every day.*

▲ Students warm up at a karate tournament.

SPECIAL CASES

In sentences with compound subjects connected by *or* or *nor*, the verb must agree with the subject closer to the verb.

SINGULAR SUBJECT + PLURAL SUBJECT   PLURAL VERB
Example: *The uniform or the belts <u>are</u> on sale.*

PLURAL SUBJECT + SINGULAR SUBJECT   SINGULAR VERB
Example: *The belts or the uniform <u>is</u> on sale.*

(**TALK AND SHARE**) **With your partner, take turns giving examples of sentences that correctly match verbs to subjects.**

VOCABULARY
plural—naming more than one person, place, or thing
require—must have something; need

Verb Tenses

The **tense** of a verb tells *when* the action takes place.

Present Tense	The verb shows an action that is happening now or an action that happens all the time.	start	The competition starts now. The competitions start at 11 A.M. on Saturdays.
Past Tense	The verb shows an action that happened earlier.	started	The competition started an hour ago.
Future Tense	The verb shows an action that will happen in the future.	will start	The competition will start in an hour.

PRESENT TENSE

The present tense is used to:

• Show an action that is happening now

> **Example:** *The students practice now.*

• Show an action that happens all the time

> **Example:** *Tomás and Pati exercise at 7 each morning.*

Use the regular form of the verb to make the present tense.

First-person pronouns (*I, we*)	I practice. We practice.
Second-person pronoun (*you*)	You practice.
Third-person plural pronoun (*they*)	They practice.

To form the present tense with third-person singular nouns or pronouns (*he*, *she*, or *it*), you can usually just add an *s* to the end of the verb.

> *He practices.*

VOCABULARY

tense—the form of the verb that tells when the action takes place.

PAST TENSE

The past tense is used to tell about an action that happened at a particular time in the past. With most verbs, you can just add *ed* to the end of the present-tense verb to form the past tense.

Example: *Yesterday the students <u>walked</u> to the gym from school.*

FUTURE TENSE

The future tense tells about an action that will happen in the future. To form the future tense, add *will* in front of the verb.

Example: *I <u>will join</u> the karate class next year.*

(TALK AND SHARE) **What is a present-tense verb? What are past-tense and future-tense verbs? Talk to a partner about verb tenses. Give an example for each kind of tense.**

Grammar Tip

Helping Verbs and Verb Tenses

You've already learned that helping verbs are added to another verb to make the meaning clear. Helping verbs are also added to form some tenses. Often, the verb tense shows *when* something happens.

The helping verb *will* forms the future tense.
Example: *Laura <u>will walk</u> two miles tomorrow.*

The helping verb *has* forms the present perfect tense. This tense is used with an action that began in the past but continues or is completed in the present.
Example: *Laura <u>has walked</u> two miles every day for a year.*

Summary

Verbs are the words that show action or a state of being. Verb tenses show time or when the action happened. Verbs always match, or agree with, the subject.

Identifying

Identifying Tenses

Tenses tell you about the time of an action. Is something happening now? That's the present tense. Did it happen earlier? That's the past tense. Will it happen in the future? That's the future tense. Look at the endings of verbs to identify, or tell, the tense. Also, look for helping verbs, such as *will*. A Verb Chart can help you identify the tenses.

Verb Chart

Present Tense	Past Tense	Future Tense
enjoy	enjoyed	will enjoy
watch	watched	will watch
like	liked	will like

Practice Identifying

1. Create   Get together with a partner. Make a list of 4 action verbs. Talk about how to form their present, past, and future forms. Then create a Verb Chart showing each verb's present, past, and future tenses.

2. Write   With a partner, cut out 3 magazine pictures. Pick pictures that show action, or use the pictures below. Then write a story about the pictures. Use verbs in each of the tenses: present, past, and future. Choose the strongest verbs you can. Use the checklist to revise your story.

Check Your Writing

Make sure you

☐ Use complete sentences.

☐ Use a period at the end of each sentence.

☐ Spell all the words correctly.

Adding *ed* to Verbs You can form the past tense of most verbs by adding *ed*.

Verb	+ *ed*	Past Tense	Example
join	ed	joined	*We join<u>ed</u> the karate class.*
kick	ed	kicked	*We kick<u>ed</u> the soccer ball.*

With some verbs, you need to change the spelling to form the past tense.

If the verb ends in . . .	The spelling rule is . . .	Example	
A consonant + *y*	Change *y* to *i* and add *ed.*	*try*	*tried*
A consonant + vowel + consonant and has one syllable	Double the consonant and add *ed.*	*tip*	*tipped*
A vowel + *w, x,* or *y*	Do not double the consonant. Add only *ed.*	*stay* *fix*	*stayed* *fixed*

Now write two sentences of your own. Use two different verbs that are in the past tense and end in *ed*.

Make a Chart With a partner or small group, make a chart to show

- What a subject is and what a predicate is
- What the 3 kinds of verbs are
- What the present, past, and future forms for verbs are

Say a Chant Say this chant aloud to a partner.

> *The present tense shows what's happening now.*
> *Like, "I'm saying a chant right about now."*
> *It also shows what happens all the time.*
> *Like, "I learn every time I say a rhyme."*
> *The past tense shows what happened back then.*
> *Like, "Yesterday, I stayed up till 10."*
> *The future tense says what's yet to come.*
> *Like, "I will learn my tenses by the time I'm done."*

Theme 4
Life Journeys

Here you will learn how life is like a journey. You will read about the life journeys of different people and the ways people feel about being free.

- What are these people doing?
- What journey, or long trip, have you taken in life?
- How is life like a journey?

Understanding Fact and Opinion

In nonfiction, you read about real people and places. You read a lot of facts, but you also read a lot of opinions. Learn how facts and opinions are different.

fact—something that can be proved to be true

> **Example:** *Harriet Tubman led slaves to freedom.*

opinion—a belief. It may or may not be true.

> **Example:** *Harriet Tubman is America's greatest hero.*

Before Reading Activities

Hands On

Understanding Facts and Opinions   Choose a famous person. If you can, cut out a picture of him or her from a magazine and paste it on a large piece of paper. Then, tell two facts and two opinions about that person. Copy them onto your poster. List the facts on one side and opinions on the other.

Oral Language

Your Life Journey

With a partner, talk about your own life journey. Make a list of things that have happened to you since you were born. Think of two great times and think of two hard times. Create a graph of your life like the one shown here.

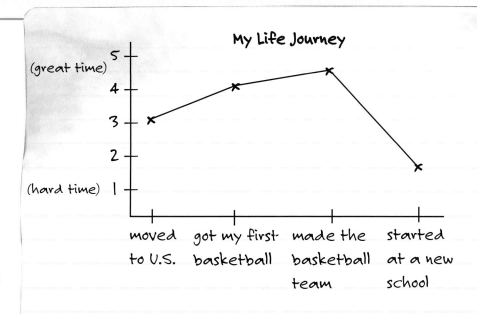

Harriet Tubman

CONDUCTOR ON THE UNDERGROUND RAILROAD

by Ann Petry

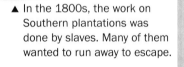

▲ In the 1800s, the work on Southern plantations was done by slaves. Many of them wanted to run away to escape.

In 1849, Harriet Tubman escaped slavery and began helping other slaves escape through the Underground Railroad. The Underground Railroad was a long, secret path of homes, tunnels, and roads set up to help slaves escape from the South. They fled to places where slavery was not legal. The journey was long and dangerous, but Harriet Tubman was not afraid. She traveled to the South 19 times and helped close to 300 slaves escape. She was never caught and never lost a slave. In this passage, Tubman is leading a group of slaves to freedom.

But there were so many of them this time. She knew moments of doubt when she was half-afraid, and kept looking back over her shoulder, imagining that she heard the sound of **pursuit.** They would certainly be pursued. Eleven of them. Eleven thousand dollars' worth of flesh and bone and muscle that belonged to **Maryland planters.** If they were caught, the eleven runaways would be whipped and sold South, but she—she would probably be hanged.

VOCABULARY

pursuit—the act of chasing after something
Maryland planters—owners of large farms called plantations, in the state of Maryland, where slaves worked. The planters owned the slaves.

from *Harriet Tubman*

They tried to sleep during the day but they never could **wholly** relax into sleep. She could tell by the positions they assumed, by their restless movements. And they walked at night. Their progress was slow. It took them three nights of walking to reach the first stop. She had told them about the place where they would stay, promising warmth and good food, holding these things out to them as an **incentive** to keep going.

(TALK AND SHARE) **Why did Tubman and her group have to travel by night? Why did she look back over her shoulder? Talk to a partner about it.**

The painting *Harriet Tubman's Underground Railroad* by Paul Collins shows Tubman leading a group of runaway slaves. ▼

VOCABULARY

wholly—totally; completely
incentive—what pushes a person to do something or to make a special effort

from *Harriet Tubman*

When she knocked on the door of a farmhouse, a place where she and her parties of runaways had always been welcome, always been given shelter and plenty to eat, there was no answer. She knocked again, softly. A voice from within said, "Who is it?" There was fear in the voice.

She knew instantly from the sound of the voice that there was something wrong. She said, "A friend with friends," the **password** on the Underground Railroad.

The door opened, slowly. The man who stood in the doorway looked at her coldly, looked with **unconcealed astonishment** and fear at the eleven **disheveled**

▼ Slaves escape the South.

runaways who were standing near her. Then he shouted, "Too many, too many. It's not safe. My place was searched last week. It's not safe!" and slammed the door in her face.

She turned away from the house, **frowning.** She had promised her **passengers** food and rest and warmth, and instead of that, there would be hunger and cold and more walking over the frozen ground. Somehow she would have to **instill** courage into these eleven people, most of them strangers, would have to feed them on hope and bright dreams of freedom instead of the fried pork and corn bread and milk she had promised them.

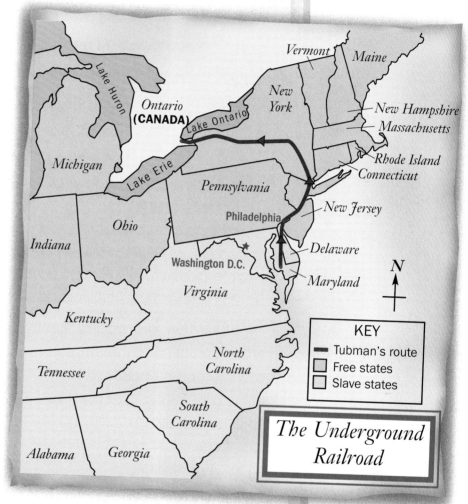

The Underground Railroad

▲ In Tubman's time, the United States was divided. In some states, it was legal to own slaves. In others it was not.

(**TALK AND SHARE**) **What was Tubman worried about? Make a list with a partner.**

VOCABULARY

frowning—looking unhappy or upset
passengers—people on a trip or journey
instill—fill with

Responding to Literature

Explore the Reading

Talk with a partner about each question below.

1. What happened to Tubman in 1849?

2. How would you describe the journey of the runaway slaves?

3. What did you learn about Harriet Tubman's life journey from this reading?

4. What facts did you learn about Harriet Tubman?

5. What is your opinion of her?

6. Who or what in your own life does Harriet Tubman remind you of?

Learn About Literature

Dialogue

Writers use *dialogue* to make people or characters come alive. Dialogue is what a character says. In *Harriet Tubman: Conductor on the Underground Railroad*, Ann Petry uses this example of dialogue:

> One of the runaways said, again, "Let me go back. Let me go back," and stood still, and then turned around and said, over his shoulder, "I am going back."
>
> She lifted the gun, aimed it at the despairing slave. She said, "Go on with us or die."

Two signals help to set off dialogue.

1. A comma before a quote: *She said, "Go on with us or die."*

2. Quotation marks around the words of the speaker: *"Go on with us or die."*

Note the end punctuation appears *inside* the closing quotation marks.

Now try writing some dialogue of your own. Write what the slave might say in reply to Harriet Tubman.

> She said, "Go on with us or die."
>
> In reply, the slave said . . .

Activities

Hands On

Map Harriet Tubman's Journey   In small groups, trace Harriet Tubman's journey with the runaway slaves. On the map on page 189, find Maryland, Delaware, Philadelphia, and Ontario, Canada. Then explain the route Tubman took in leading the slaves to freedom.

Oral Language

Create a Dialogue   With a partner, write a dialogue between two characters. For example, imagine a dialogue between two of the runaway slaves traveling with Tubman. What would they say to each other about Tubman? Then read your dialogue aloud to another group.

Partner Practice

Fact or Opinion?   With a partner, think of 3 statements about Harriet Tubman. Write them on a piece of paper, as shown here. Then work with your partner to decide whether each statement is a fact or an opinion.

1. Harriet Tubman was courageous.
   opinion
2. She led around 300 slaves to freedom.   fact
3. Tubman escaped slavery in 1849.   fact

Know the Author

Ann Petry

Ann Petry was born in 1908. She started writing stories in the 1940s. Her story "Like a Winding Sheet" was named the Best American Story in 1946. In addition to her well-known biography of Harriet Tubman, Petry wrote novels about the life journeys of other African Americans. Her novel *The Street* was one of the first novels written by an African American that sold more than one million copies.

Reading

Textbooks

Here you will learn about reading textbooks. You'll also learn how to preview a text and practice comparing and contrasting textbooks.

▲ Sometimes I like to go outside to read.

DO NOT LOCK BIKES TO RAILINGS
PLEASE USE BIKE RACKS

■ **How would you describe what these students are doing?**

■ **Where are they?**

■ **What does this remind you of?**

When you read your textbooks, use the reading process. You also need to take notes.

1 Use the reading process.

Before Reading

↓

During Reading

↓

After Reading

2 Take notes on your school reading.

The Underground Railroad

By 1860 there were more than 500,000 free African Americans living in the United States. Some had been born to parents who were free. Some had bought their freedom or had been freed by their owners. Others had escaped **slavery** by running away.

Over the years thousands of slaves tried to gain their freedom by running away. Some ran away alone. Others tried to escape with their families or friends.

Once away from their owners' land, runaway slaves had to find safe places to

The Underground Railroad

Key word	Notes
slavery	• 1860—more than 500,000 free African Americans • some bought their freedom

Key Concepts

The **table of contents** in a textbook tells what's in it. It lists the **chapters** and often the **headings** in each chapter. You can use these to help you with **note-taking**.

Table of Contents

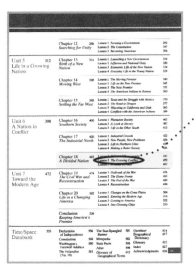

Chapters and Headings

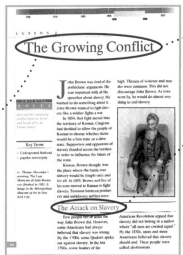

Note-taking

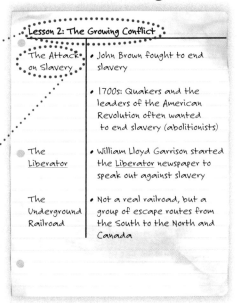

Parts of Textbooks

Table of Contents

This information in the front of a book tells you what is in the book.

Boldface Terms and Headings

These terms stand out because they are important.

Heading

· UNIT ·

1

The Land and Early People

The Underground Railroad

By 1860 there were more than 500,000 free African Americans living in the United States. Some had been born to parents who were free. Some had bought their freedom or had been freed by their owners. Others had escaped **slavery** by running away.

Boldface term

Previewing

When you preview, you take a look at the parts of a text before you begin reading. It can help you know what to expect. It will also help you think about what you already know about the subject.

Before you begin reading a chapter in your textbook, preview the items listed below.

Preview Checklist

☐ The title

☐ The first and last paragraphs

☐ The headings

☐ Names, dates, or words that are in boldface type or repeated

☐ Photos or graphics and their captions

Photos and Captions

Photos show more information about facts in the text. Captions explain the photos.

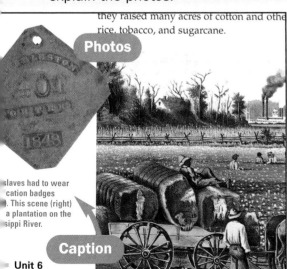

they raised many acres of cotton and othe rice, tobacco, and sugarcane.

Photos

slaves had to wear cation badges). This scene (right) a plantation on the sippi River.

Caption

Unit 6

Glossary

A glossary lists important vocabulary words and definitions. Usually the words are in alphabetical order.

segregation (se•gri•gā´shən) The practice of keeping people in separate groups based on their race or culture. p. 484
self-rule (self•rōōl´) Control of one's own government. p. 168
self-sufficient (self•sə•fi´shant) Able to provide for one's own needs without help. p. 147
sharecropping (sher´krāp•ing) A system of working the land in which the worker was paid with a "share" of the crop. p. 483
siege (sēj) A long-lasting attack. p. 393
slash and burn (slash and bûrn) A method of clearing land for farming that includes cutting and burning of trees. p. 87
slave state (slāv stāt) A state that allowed slavery before the Civil War. p. 437
slavery (slā´va•rē) The practice of holding people against their will and making them carry out orders. p. 66
society (sə•sī´ə•tē) A human group. p. 10
sod (sod) Earth cut into blocks or mats, held together by grass and its roots. p. 82
sound (sound) A long inlet often parallel to the coast. p. 28

Index

The index is at the back of a textbook. It lists important people and subjects, with page numbers to help you find them in the book.

Sequence, 105, 301
Sequoias, 37
Serbia, 576
Serpent Mound, 66
Serra, Junípero, 148, 148, 174, 175
Servant, indentured. *See* Indentured servant
Settlements
See also Colonies
British Colonies, m238
Carolina Colony, 235
Dutch, 210–213
English, 156–164, 166–170, 188–199
European, m101, 171
first Americans, 56–59
French, 150–155
Georgia Colony, 236–237
Indian, 64–67, 70–72, 82–85, 86–90
Maryland Colony, 240
patterns of, 46–47
of the South, 232–239
Spanish, 146–149

Slater, Samuel, 416
Slave, 203, 236, 437, 445
slavery
See also African Americans
abolition of, 477
from Africa, 145, 163, 250
during American Revolution, 310
definition of, 66
disagreements over, 437–441
division over, 437–438
and the economy, 444–445
and the Emancipation Proclamation, 461–463
field slaves, 243
freedom of, 461–462
house slaves, 244
identification badges, 444
Indians in, 144–145
and the law, 243–244, 438–440, 445
life of, 243
Lincoln on, 452
Lincoln's view, 450

See also
Charles
Fort Sur
and the 225
plantati
secessio
South Dak
South Kore
South Pole
South regio
South, sett
South Viet
Southern C
Southern C
Southern F
Southern r
Southern p
Southern S
443
Southwest,
Sovereign
Soviet Uni
Space shut
Spain, 108

Reading Textbooks

Reading textbooks is easier when you use the reading process. Take notes to help you remember what you have read.

Use the Reading Process

You can make your reading for school easier when you follow certain steps as you read. Those steps are called the *reading process*. The reading process can help you learn and remember more of what you read.

BEFORE READING

Reading begins when you hear the assignment: "Read chapter. . . ." First, **set your purpose.** This means figure out what you need to learn. Ask yourself questions, such as, "What do I need to learn or remember?"

Then, **preview** the chapter so that you know what to expect. Look at the chapter title, headings, boldface terms, and graphics. Next, **make a plan.** Decide what kind of notes you will take.

Boldface terms

VOCABULARY

set your purpose—ask yourself questions to make clear why you are reading
preview—look at ahead of time
make a plan—think about which way of reading and kind of note-taking might be best for what you are reading

Photo and caption

· LESSON ·

2

MAIN IDEA
Read to learn what some people did to try to end slavery.

WHY IT MATTERS
As conflict over slavery grew, divisions between the North and the South became deeper.

VOCABULARY
emancipation
resist
code
fugitive
underground
abolitionist
equality

Chapter title

Slavery and Freedom

1820–1860

By 1860 there were nearly 4 million slaves in the United States, an increase from 900,000 in 1800. This growth of slav was due chiefly to the growing importance of cotton as a ca crop in the South. The worldwide demand for cotton had m many Southern planters rich. It had also created a demand more enslaved workers.

Heading

The Slave Economy

Slavery had been a part of American life since colonial da Some people thought that slavery was wrong. Other people could not make money using enslaved workers. The cost of feeding, clothing, and housing slaves was too great.

In the South, however, slavery continued because owners come to depend on the work of enslaved people. Slaves wer made to work as miners, carpenters, factory workers, and ho servants. Some, however, were taken to large plantations. Th they raised many acres of cotton and other cash crops, such rice, tobacco, and sugarcane.

Many slaves had to wear identification badges (above). This scene (right) shows a plantation on the Mississippi River.

DURING READING

Your next step is to **read with a purpose.** In your notebook, take notes as you read. Summary Notes are one good way to keep track of your reading for school. Summary Notes are a list of key facts, terms, or ideas for each chapter or section.

One of the most important steps in using the reading process is **connecting.** Reading is not much fun if it doesn't mean anything to you. Take time to think about what you are reading and connect it to your life and what you know.

The best way to connect to your reading is by asking yourself questions like these.

> **Summary Notes**
> The Underground Railroad
>
> 1. Thousands of slaves tried to escape to freedom.
>
> 2. The people who helped slaves and the places where the slaves stayed were called the Underground Railroad.

How does this fit in with what I already know?

What do I think of this?

Language Notes

Verb Phrases
These phrases have special meanings.

- **take time:** give yourself the time to finish something

- **connect to:** link your life to something or think about why something is important to you

What does this remind me of?

VOCABULARY

read with a purpose—as you read, look for details and information that help you answer the question: "Why am I reading this?"

connecting—thinking about how the reading is important to you or related to your life and how you feel about it

AFTER READING

When you finish, **pause and reflect** on what you learned. This is really important with your reading for school. Ask yourself questions like these:

- Did I understand everything I read?

- Can I summarize the information in my own words?

If you're not sure you've fully understood the text, go back and **reread.** Skim for key information. Fill in any blanks in your notes or add more notes.

Last of all, try to **remember** what you've read. The best way to do this is to talk or write about it. Tell your partner or a friend what you learned. Put the ideas in your own words, and you will remember them.

(**TALK AND SHARE**) **Talk to a partner about how the reading process can help you read a textbook. Make Summary Notes about it.**

VOCABULARY
pause and reflect—stop and think about what you have just read. When you reflect, ask yourself if you learned what you needed.
reread—read again
remember—bring back into your mind

Ways of Taking Notes

After reading pages in a textbook, you probably won't remember everything. Textbooks have *a lot* of information in them. One good way to remember what you read is by taking notes. There are many different ways you can take notes. Here you'll learn about 3 ways.

CHAPTER NOTES

Chapter Notes are helpful with all kinds of textbooks. First, write the name of the chapter at the top of the page. Then, write the first heading. Below the heading write 2 to 4 important details, terms, or events you learned in that part. Chapter Notes give you a good summary of the chapter and can help you study for the chapter test.

▲ Slaves were often taken away from their families when they were sold.

Chapter Notes

Chapter 2: Slavery and Freedom
—The Slave Economy
    -The owners of plantations used slaves to work in the fields.
    -1 in 4 families in the South owned slaves.
—Slavery and the Law
    -The law said slaves were property, not people.
    -The law said runaway slaves had to be returned to their owners.

Reading Tip

Using an Index

An index can help you find terms, people, or subjects. Look in the back of a textbook for the index. It will list the most important terms and the page numbers where you can read about them. Look in the index to help you find a person, place, or term again or to learn more about a subject.

Forward Together by Jacob Lawrence shows Tubman leading slaves to freedom. ▼

SEQUENCE NOTES

Sequence Notes are another useful note-taking tool. They help you track the order of events and when they happened. When you make Sequence Notes for history textbooks, write the date and the description of the events in order. Look at the example below.

Sequence Notes

In 1820, Harriet Tubman was born.

↓

In 1849, she ran away from her owner.

↓

In 1850, the Fugitive Slave Act made it against the law to help runaway slaves.

↓

In 1865, slavery ended.

WEB

A Web is a great way of taking notes for any type of text. Write the main idea or topic in the center circle. Then write details in the circles around it. A Web helps you collect the ideas about one subject and remember them.

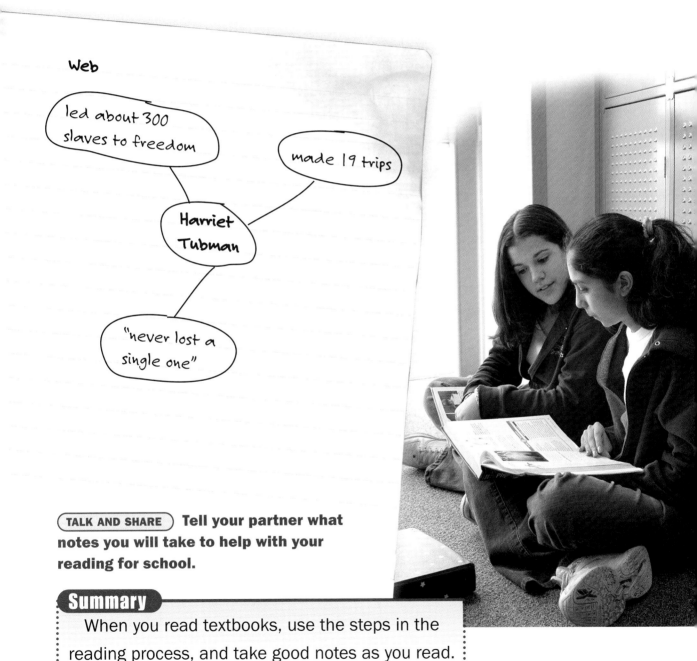

Web

led about 300 slaves to freedom

made 19 trips

Harriet Tubman

"never lost a single one"

TALK AND SHARE Tell your partner what notes you will take to help with your reading for school.

Summary

When you read textbooks, use the steps in the reading process, and take good notes as you read.

Comparing and Contrasting

Comparing and Contrasting Textbooks

In school, you will often be asked to compare and contrast ideas, people, or events. When you *compare* two things, you look for ways they are the same. When you *contrast* two things, you look for ways they are different. The Venn Diagram below compares and contrasts information about Harriet Tubman found in two textbooks.

Venn Diagram

American History textbook
- Tubman was the most famous "conductor" on the Underground Railroad.
- She escaped from slavery herself.

Both
- Tubman was born in 1820.
- She made 19 journeys to free slaves.
- She led around 300 slaves to freedom.

Literature textbook
- Tubman was one of America's greatest heroes.
- Tubman was never caught and never lost a slave.

Practice Comparing and Contrasting

1. Tell Think about an important event that has changed your life. Get together with a partner. Tell each other about the events. Then make a Venn Diagram to compare and contrast your stories.

2. Write Now compare two people, two places, or two things from school. Create a Venn Diagram. Then write a paragraph in which you compare and contrast the two things. Use words from the Word Bank in your writing.

Word Bank

same
different

bigger
smaller

easy
difficult

Activities

Grammar Spotlight

Comparing Two or More Things Use *more than* or *less than* when comparing two or more things.

		Use *more* or *less* + the adjective	Followed by *than*	
Tubman	had	more courage	than	many slaves.
Runaways	were	less afraid of her	than	of their owners.

Now compare two things you can see. Use *more than* in one sentence and *less than* in the next.

Partner Practice

Teacher, Teacher Prepare a lesson to teach a partner the parts of a textbook. First, explain where you find these 4 parts of a textbook: table of contents, boldface terms, chapters and headings, and graphics and captions. Then, tell how they can help you in your reading for school. Last, explain how you would use the reading process and what the main steps are.

Hands On

Kinds of Note-taking With a partner or in a small group, create a series of posters that shows the 5 different ways of taking notes presented in this lesson. Label each kind and give an example of it.

- Summary Notes
- Sequence Notes
- Chapter Notes
- Venn Diagram
- Web

Oral Language

Preview with a Partner With a partner, pick any textbook from your classroom library. Preview a chapter in the book. Look at the chapter title, first paragraph, last paragraph, any boldface words, and any pictures or graphics. As you look at each item, discuss with your partner what the chapter might be about.

Reading

Tests

Here you'll learn about reading and taking tests. You'll also learn how to draw conclusions and practice evaluating an issue.

▲ I don't get so nervous taking tests when I prepare ahead of time.

■ **What do you think is happening in this picture?**

■ **How do you think these students feel?**

■ **How do you feel about taking tests? Why?**

To do your best on tests, plan ahead and get ready for them. Learn about the different kinds of questions and how to read and respond to them.

1 **Prepare for the test.**

2 **Answer fact questions by recalling the information that is "right there" in the text.**

Who is Harriet Tubman?

What do you think was the main reason that Lincoln decided to free the slaves?

3 **Use what you already know to answer inference questions.**

Explain the major causes of the Civil War.

4 **Plan your response for essay questions.**

Key Concepts

Fact or recall questions ask for a detail that can be found and proven true.

Fact or Recall

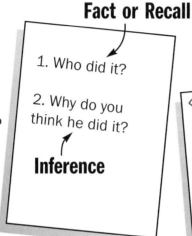

1. Who did it?

2. Why do you think he did it?

Inference

An **inference** question asks you to put together what you learned from your reading and what you already know from life.

Skimming

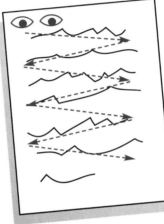

With both kinds of questions, you need to skim for key words. **Skimming** means moving your eyes quickly down a page to look for key words or phrases.

Tips for Taking Tests

1 Prepare ahead of time.

2 Preview the test questions before you start to answer them.

Name _____ Date _____

──────────── **History Test** ────────────
Unit 6: The Civil War

1. What was the major turning point of the Civil War?
   - Ⓐ The Battle of Antietam
   - Ⓑ The death of President Lincoln
   - Ⓒ The Union victory at Gettysburg
   - Ⓓ The bombing of Fort Sumter

2. Which amendment ended slavery in the United States in 1865?
   - Ⓐ 13th
   - Ⓑ 14th
   - Ⓒ 15th
   - Ⓓ 16th

Read the passage below and answer the next two questions.

"That on the first day of January, A.D. 1863, all persons held as slaves within any State or designated part of a State, the people whereof shall then be in rebellion against the United States, shall be then, thenceforward, and forever free. . . ."

3. This is the opening to what American speech?

4. Which slaves were still not fr after the speech?

Skill Building

Drawing Conclusions

When you draw conclusions, you put together two or more facts and decide what they mean. On some tests, you will be asked to read a timeline and draw a conclusion.

Look at the timeline at the right. What conclusions can you draw about the journey of African Americans over the last century?

You might conclude that the journey of African Americans has been a constant struggle, from slavery to the struggle for their civil rights.

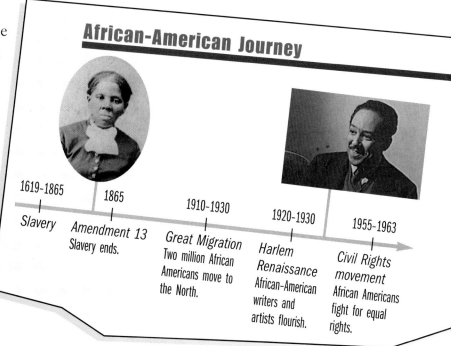

African-American Journey

1619–1865	1865	1910–1930	1920–1930	1955–1963
Slavery	Amendment 13 Slavery ends.	Great Migration Two million African Americans move to the North.	Harlem Renaissance African-American writers and artists flourish.	Civil Rights movement African Americans fight for equal rights.

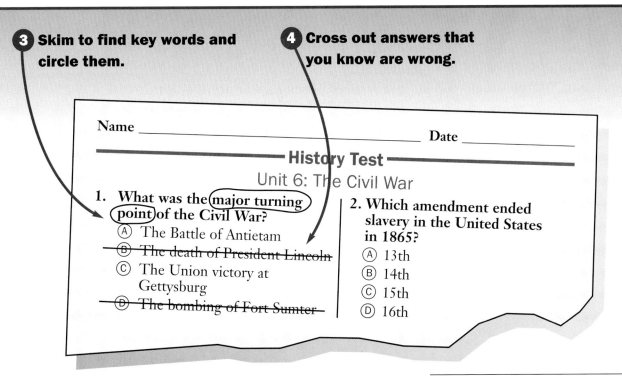

3 Skim to find key words and circle them.

4 Cross out answers that you know are wrong.

Name _____

Date _____

History Test
Unit 6: The Civil War

1. What was the (major turning point) of the Civil War?
   - Ⓐ The Battle of Antietam
   - ~~Ⓑ The death of President Lincoln~~
   - Ⓒ The Union victory at Gettysburg
   - ~~Ⓓ The bombing of Fort Sumter~~

2. Which amendment ended slavery in the United States in 1865?
   - Ⓐ 13th
   - Ⓑ 14th
   - Ⓒ 15th
   - Ⓓ 16th

Reading Tests

Y ou will have to answer many different kinds of test questions, from multiple choice to essay. In order to do well, you need to prepare for the test ahead of time. Then, when you take the test, read each question carefully.

Prepare for the Test

Think of a test as a long race. You wouldn't just start running. You would learn what the track is like. You might practice running it. You would get ready. It's the same with taking a test. You need to prepare ahead of time.

ASK QUESTIONS

As soon as your teacher tells you about an **upcoming** test, begin asking questions.

• What **material** will be covered? • What should I study?

• What will the test questions be like?

STUDY AND REVIEW

Next, begin to study and review the material. Do a little each night. There are 5 things you can do.

History Test

Unit 6: The Civil War

Date _____

major turning
ivil War?

of Antietam

of President Lincoln
victory at

g of Fort Sumter

2. Which amendment ended slavery in the United States in 1865?
    A 13th
    B 14th
    C 15th
    D 16th

ow and answer the next two questions.

of January, A.D. 1863, all persons held as slaves within any
t of a State, the people whereof shall then be in rebellion
es, shall be then, thenceforward, and forever free. . . ."

g to what

Address
on
Act

4. Which slaves were still not free after the speech?
    A Slaves in border states who fought for the Union
    B Slaves in southern areas fighting for the Union
    C Slaves in southern areas who were not fighting
    D All of the above

---

1. Take a careful look at your notes and textbook.

2. Make a list of 5 to 10 things you think will be on the test.

3. Make lists, flash cards, and **rhymes** to help you remember important terms and facts.

4. "Teach" the material to someone else. This can help you remember it.

5. Work with a partner. **Quiz** each other on the questions you think will be on the test.

VOCABULARY

upcoming—expected to happen in the future
material—the specific information covered

rhymes—groups of words that have the same ending sounds
quiz—test what someone knows by asking questions

GET READY FOR THE TEST DAY

Tests can be hard. You may get nervous and want to give up. Tests will **challenge** you, so get ready.

- A day or so before the test, go over your notes with a friend. Ask each other questions.

- Don't wait to do all of your studying at the last minute.

- On the day of the test, be sure you have what you need to take the test. Are you supposed to bring a pencil or calculator?

PREVIEW THE TEST

When your teacher hands you the test, do a quick preview of it. During your preview, answer these questions.

How much time will I have?	How many questions are there?	What do I have to read, and what are the questions like?	Which questions are easiest?	Do wrong answers count against me?

Once you have an idea of what the test is, you can begin answering the questions. Answer the easy questions first. Save the hard ones for later. If wrong answers count against you, leave questions you can't answer blank. Don't make wild guesses.

(TALK AND SHARE) **Explain to your partner how you will get ready for a test.**

VOCABULARY
challenge—make you work hard; require special effort

Language Notes

Multiple Meanings
These words have more than one meaning.

■ **last**
1. after all others; final
2. most recent; just happened
3. happen over a period of time

■ **hands**
1. gives something to someone
2. the parts of the arms below the wrists that include the fingers and palms

Standardized Tests

Many tests have an answer sheet with little circles, called bubbles. You show your answer by filling in the circle that matches the answer you think is right.

Ⓐ Ⓑ Ⓒ Ⓓ

If you think that **C** is the right answer, you fill in the circle marked **C**. Fill in *all* of the bubble.

Ⓐ Ⓑ ● Ⓓ

You also need to be careful. Check that you fill in the bubble that *goes with* your answer.

Skim for Fact Questions

Fact or recall questions can be the easiest kind of all to answer. The answer is usually "right there" in the reading **passage.** First, mark the key words in the question. Look at the example below.

Question from a **Multiple-choice Test**

1. **Who wrote the novel** *Uncle Tom's Cabin?*
   Ⓐ Sojourner Truth
   Ⓑ Frederick Douglass
   Ⓒ Harriet Beecher Stowe
   Ⓓ William Lloyd Garrison

Then go back to the reading passage and **skim** it. Look for the same key words. Read the sentences around them. That's where you'll find the answer.

Passage from a **Multiple-choice Test**

In 1852, one novel about the **cruelties** of slavery helped turn the whole nation against slavery. Harriet Beecher Stowe's *Uncle Tom's Cabin* quickly became a bestseller. People everywhere now knew how slaves suffered.

By reading the sentences around the key words, you know that **C** is the correct answer.

TALK AND SHARE **Explain to your partner how to answer fact or recall questions.**

▲ An 1859 ad is for *Uncle Tom's Cabin.*

VOCABULARY
passage—a part of a text or reading
skim—read quickly, skipping over parts that aren't important
cruelties—things that cause pain or suffering

Read Closely for Inference Questions

Inference questions are harder to answer. The answer is not always right there in the passage. You come up with the answer by putting together what you read with what you already know.

First, read the passage and the inference question carefully. Then read the answer choices.

▲ This is a theater poster for a play based on *Uncle Tom's Cabin*.

Question from a **Multiple-choice Test**

1. **Why was *Uncle Tom's Cabin* important to the outcome of the Civil War?**
   - (A) The novel was a bestseller and made a lot of money.
   - (B) The president knew about the novel.
   - (C) The novel made slaves hope they would be freed.
   - (D) It helped show people why slavery was wrong.

Now put together what you learned from the passage with what you already know. The passage tells you that the novel helped turn people against slavery. From history class, you probably know that the end of slavery was an **outcome** of the war. If you put both of those items together, you can cross out several answers.

A) Money made from the novel wasn't important.

B) Lincoln knowing about the novel didn't matter.

C) What slaves hoped didn't affect the outcome of the war.

The fact that it showed people why slavery was wrong was probably important to the outcome of the war.

(**TALK AND SHARE**) **With a partner, talk about what an inference question is and how you can answer it.**

VOCABULARY
inference—a conclusion made by putting together facts and ideas
outcome—an event that happens as a result

Three Steps for Essay Questions

Essay questions also have to be read very carefully. Here are 3 important steps that can help you answer them.

STEP 1: LOOK CLOSELY AT THE QUESTION

First, read the question several times. Be sure you understand the **assignment.** Highlight the words that tell you what to do. Then retell the assignment in your own words.

1 **Type of essay**

2 **Topic of the essay**

3 **Key instructions**

4 **Check for correctness**

Sample Essay Question

DIRECTIONS: Explain how Frederick Douglass was important to the outcome of the Civil War. Provide two or more examples of his role in the war. Be sure to proofread your writing when you finish.

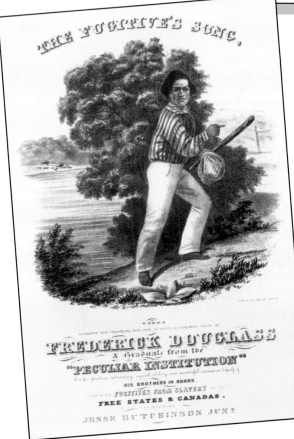

A careful reading of this question tells you:

1. Write an **expository** paragraph.

2. Make Frederick Douglass the topic.

3. Provide at least two examples of his role.

4. Check your paragraph for spelling and correctness.

◄ A sheet music cover shows Frederick Douglass, the famous runaway slave.

VOCABULARY

assignment—the work you are told or asked to do for school

expository—the type of writing that gives information. Explanations, directions, and how-to articles are examples of expository writing.

STEP 2: PLAN YOUR RESPONSE

Once you understand the essay question, your next step is to plan your response. Make a graphic organizer to help you organize your thoughts and keep you focused on the most important points.

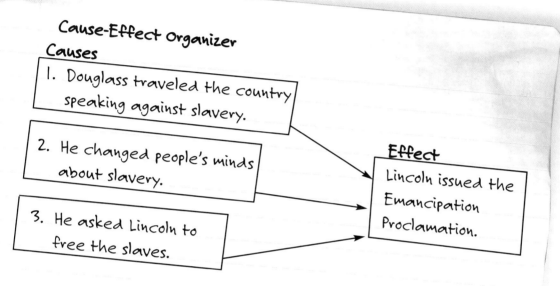

Cause-Effect Organizer

Causes

1. Douglass traveled the country speaking against slavery.

2. He changed people's minds about slavery.

3. He asked Lincoln to free the slaves.

Effect

Lincoln issued the Emancipation Proclamation.

STEP 3: WRITE YOUR ANSWER

After you finish planning, begin writing your essay. Remember, with any essay you need to state a main idea clearly and use two or more details to support it. Then, when you finish writing, check your answer for mistakes in spelling and grammar.

(TALK AND SHARE) **Make a list of what you need to remember when writing a response to an essay question. Then explain your list to your partner.**

Summary

Test questions may ask you to recall information, to make inferences, or to plan and write an essay. To do well on any kind of test, you need to prepare ahead of time. Always read the questions carefully. With essay questions, plan and then write your answer. Check for mistakes when you're finished.

Evaluating

Evaluating an Issue

In class or on a test, you may be asked to evaluate an issue. When you evaluate an issue, you tell how important, how good, or how bad an idea is. Here's an example: *Evaluate the importance of the antislavery movement.* Use an Evaluation Chart to plan your answer.

Evaluation Chart

Subject: Evaluating the Antislavery Movement

Detail	Detail	Detail
Former slaves such as Frederick Douglass spoke out against slavery.	Uncle Tom's Cabin helped people understand how terrible slavery was.	Newswriters told what happened to runaway slaves. Readers thought it was awful.

My Evaluation: The antislavery movement was very important. It united people in understanding the evils of slavery.

Practice Evaluating

1. Draw   Evaluate your ideas about treating people equally. Should *all* people *always* be treated the same? Make a picture showing the ideas you think are most important. Then tell your group what you think.

2. Write   Evaluate the issue of slavery in the United States. Make an Evaluation Chart to show details about what slavery was like. Be sure to write your main idea. Then use it to begin a paragraph telling what you think. Finally, check your writing with this checklist.

◄ Frederick Douglass (center) fought for the rights of African Americans.

Check Your Writing

Make sure you

- Use complete sentences.
- Use a period at the end of each sentence.
- Spell all the words correctly.

Grammar Spotlight

Questions with *where*, *when*, and *why* These important words signal how you should answer a test question.

Question that begins with	Answer with	Example
Where	a place	*Where did the Civil War start?*
When	a date a day a time	*When did the antislavery movement begin?*
Why	reasons	*Why did the Civil War end?*

Now write 3 questions. Use *where* in one, *when* in the next, and *why* in the last.

Hands On

Test-Buster Tips In a small group, talk about 3 or 4 tips you can follow to score better on tests. Then put the tips on index cards and display them around the classroom.

Oral Language

Test-Taking Tutor Quiz your partner on the practice test below. Keep asking each other the questions until you both can answer them. Look back at the lesson for help, if necessary.

> **Question:** *How can you prepare to take a test?*
>
> **Question:** *How do you answer fact or recall questions?*
>
> **Question:** *How do you answer inference questions?*
>
> **Question:** *What should you do for essay questions?*

Partner Practice

Draw a Conclusion Discuss with a partner these facts. Then draw a conclusion from them.

- Slavery began in the United States in the 1600s.

- Slaves were freed in the 1860s.

- African Americans fought for civil rights in the 1950s and 1960s.

Writing

Reports

Here you'll learn about writing a report. You'll also learn how to narrow a topic and practice synthesizing information from many sources.

Building Background

▲ My family moved from a small town to a big city when my dad found a new job. It was our "migration."

- **What do you see here?**
- **How could this be about moving, or migration?**
- **How does this picture make you feel?**

When you write a report, first gather information about your topic. Then organize the information and draft the report. Later, come back and revise your report. Next, edit and proofread it. Finally, create a bibliography.

1 **Get Started**
- Choose a Topic
- Gather Information
- Organize Details

2 **Write the First Draft**
- Beginning
- Middle
- Ending

3 **Finish Your Report**
- Revise
- Edit and Proofread
- Prepare a Bibliography

Key Concepts

research   references   cite   bibliography

When you **research** a report, you gather information on a topic from **references.** These can include books, atlases, magazines, encyclopedias, the Internet, and interviews. In your report, you **cite,** or name, the references from which you took information. The references come in a list at the end called a **bibliography.**

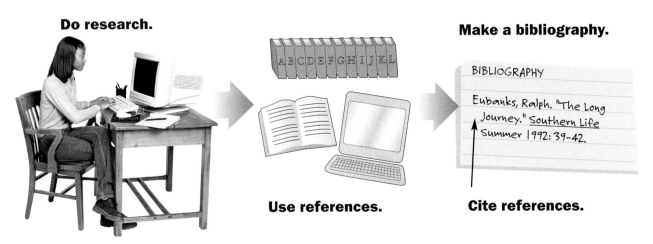

Do research.

Use references.

Make a bibliography.

BIBLIOGRAPHY

Eubanks, Ralph. "The Long Journey." Southern Life Summer 1992: 39-42.

Cite references.

Tips for Doing Research

1 Check the library.
Look in the *Readers' Guide* for magazine articles on your topic.

2 Check out books on your topic.
Look in the library catalog.

3 Ask friends and family what they know.
Interview people who know about your topic.

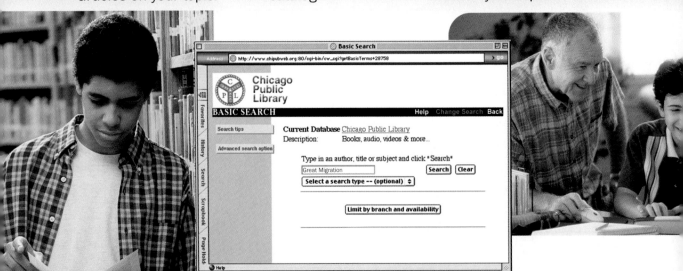

Narrowing a Topic

How do you find a good research topic? How will you get started? Here are two tips.

1. Use a Web to help you narrow your topic. Write the idea in the center of the Web. Then brainstorm ideas that spring from that.

2. Next, write a list of questions about the smaller topic you chose. Ask such questions as *Who? Where? What? When? Why?* and *How?* For a long report, choose several questions to answer. For a short paper, choose only one question.

Once you have your questions, you're ready to begin researching your topic.

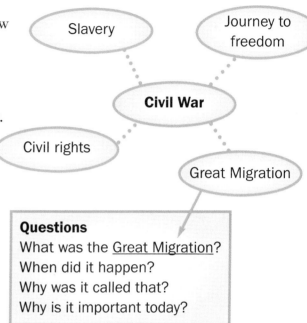

Questions

What was the Great Migration?

When did it happen?

Why was it called that?

Why is it important today?

4 Find encyclopedia articles about your topic.

Ask a librarian for encyclopedias to look up your topic.

5 Search on the Internet for your topic.

Enter the name of your topic in a search engine to find websites.

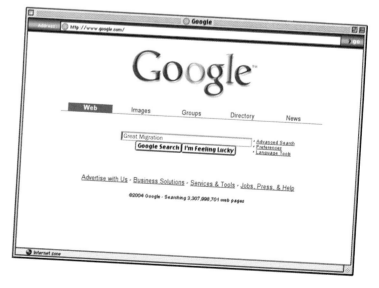

Writing Reports

When you write a report, begin by gathering and organizing information about a topic. Next, draft the report, revise it, edit it, and then proofread it. Last, create a bibliography.

Getting Started

The secret to writing a **report** is to go step by step. You will not be able to do it right in a day or two. Do a little bit each day, and you'll finish it with **ease.**

CHOOSE A TOPIC

You will find report writing more fun if you pick a topic you're interested in. Take time to do a little **brainstorming.** List 10 topics that interest you. Circle the best ones.

GATHER INFORMATION

Next, make a new list of questions you'd like to answer in your report. Ask such questions as:

- Who was involved?
- When did it occur?
- Where did it happen?
- Why is it important?

Use these questions to guide your research. The library and the Internet are both excellent places to do research. Make **note cards** with the question at the top. Then **paraphrase** what you learned below.

Question: What was the Great **Migration?**
- African Americans left the South after World War I.
- They could find jobs in cities in the North.
- They found a better way of life than they had in the South.

World Book Encyclopedia, p. 324

report—words said or written to tell about something
ease—without any problem
brainstorming—thinking of many possible ideas

note cards—cards used to record and keep track of information
paraphrase—put in your own words
migration—a movement of people from one country or region for settlement in another

ORGANIZE DETAILS

Good writing is well organized. A report usually has a beginning, middle, and end.

Before you write your report, make an **outline.** Use your note cards and questions to help you organize the report. Look at this outline.

The Great Migration
 I. What was it?
 II. When and where did it happen?
 III. What caused it?
 IV. Why was it important?

A family is ready to move from the South to Chicago during the Great Migration. ▼

Once you have an outline and have organized the information you found, you're ready to begin writing.

(TALK AND SHARE)
Discuss with your partner the steps you would take to start a report.

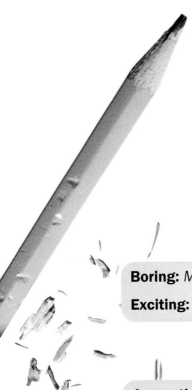

Writing the First Draft

Now that you have done research and made an outline, it is time to write your rough draft. Keep in mind that you will revise and edit your work later. The goal now is to get your ideas down on paper. You can fix spelling or grammar mistakes or even add missing information later.

THE BEGINNING

A good report begins with a powerful opening sentence or paragraph. Note the difference between these two opening lines.

Boring: *My report is about the Great Migration.*

Exciting: *After World War I, African Americans left the South by the thousands.*

Here are two more ways to make the start of a paragraph interesting.

A question: *Why did African Americans leave the South after World War I?*

A surprising fact: *From 1910 to 1930, the number of African Americans in Chicago more than tripled.*

However you begin your report, make sure you stick to the main idea in the opening paragraph.

A family packs and leaves to head North. ▼

The Long Journey

After World War I, African Americans left the South by the thousands. Their lives in the South had been hard during the war. After World War I, things began to change. African Americans heard about jobs in the North, and they talked about taking the long journey north to find a better life. Their journey was called the Great Migration.

THE MIDDLE

In the middle of your report, include the information you have gathered during your research. Be sure each paragraph supports and develops the main idea. Keep your writing focused by answering one question at a time about your topic. Remember to follow the outline you made.

The paragraphs in the middle of the report explain what you learned about the topic. Use your note cards as you draft the report. Include only the details you found interesting or that support the main idea.

THE ENDING

The closing paragraph summarizes the main points of your report. Try to answer the question, "Why is this important?" The person reading your report probably wants to know why you chose this topic. Explain your reasons. If you can, end with one final interesting fact or statement or give your opinion on the subject.

Good closing: *The Great Migration was a fascinating event in American history. It brought about two million African-American Southerners to cities in the North. At last, African-American business and culture boomed.*

(TALK AND SHARE) **Explain to your partner the 3 main parts of a research report and what they include.**

Finishing Your Report

After you finish the rough draft, you need to spend time revising and editing it. To stop after the rough draft would be like taking a shower but not drying off. Use proofreader's marks to **polish** your report.

REVISE

The purpose of revising is to make the content of your writing better. Ask questions about your ideas, **organization,** and **voice.** Make changes based on your answers.

Ideas	Organization	Voice
• Is the report interesting? • Have I left anything out? • Should I take anything out?	• Do I have a strong opening paragraph? • Is the main idea stated clearly in the first paragraph? • Is each paragraph clear? • Does the ending summarize my main points?	• Does my report sound interesting? • Does the writing show my ideas?

EDIT AND PROOFREAD

When you edit and proofread, you look at the writing style and the language you used. Ask questions about the words, sentences, and use of correct English.

Word Choice	Smooth Sentences	Correct English
• Did I use clear, specific words?	• Did I start my sentences in different ways? • Did I use different kinds of sentences?	• Have I spelled all of the words correctly? • Do all of my sentences start with a capital letter and have end punctuation?

VOCABULARY

polish—make last changes in order to make something look better and shine

organization—the way something is put together or arranged

voice—the way a piece of writing reflects the writer. The voice of a piece of writing should sound like the writer.

PREPARE A BIBLIOGRAPHY

For a report, you need to list your **sources** in a **bibliography.**
That means you must make an **alphabetical** list of the books,
magazines, encyclopedias, and websites you used.

Here are examples of different kinds of materials and the
way you would **cite** them in a bibliography.

Encyclopedia
"Great Migration." The World Book Encyclopedia.
    1993 ed.

Book
Halpern, Monica. The Great Migration. Washington,
    D.C.: National Geographic Society, 2002.

Article
Eubanks, Ralph. "The Long Journey." Southern Life
    Summer 1992: 39–42.

Internet
"From Slavery to Freedom: The African-American
    Pamphlet Collection." African-American Odyssey.
    31 Oct. 2003. <http://memory.loc.gov/ammem/
    aapchtml/aapchome.html>

Writing Tip

Using a Computer Catalog

A *computer catalog* is an
online list of all the books
a library owns. You can
find information in 3 ways.

1. Enter the *title* if you
   know it.

2. If you know the author
   but not the title, enter
   the *author's last name.*

3. If you only know the
   subject you want to
   learn about, enter the
   subject, or key word—a
   word related to the
   subject. If you have
   trouble with your
   subject search, ask a
   librarian for help.

TALK AND SHARE With a partner, list 3 things to check
for when you finish your report.

Summary

To write a report, first gather and organize information about
your topic. Then, draft the report. Next, revise the report, edit it,
and then proofread it. Finally, create a bibliography.

VOCABULARY
sources—books, magazines, and other places the writer found information
bibliography—a list of sources used to write a book or report
alphabetical—arranged in the order of the letters of the alphabet
cite—make a reference

Synthesizing

Synthesizing Information from Many Sources

The hard part of writing a report is pulling together, or synthesizing, the information you find. A Gathering Grid can help. Make a chart like the one below. Put your questions on the side and list your sources on the top.

Gathering Grid

Subject: The Great Migration	The Great Migration (Halpern)	1910–1930: Bound for Glory (Candaele)
Why did African Americans leave the South?	• hard life in the South • sharecroppers • Black Codes	• extreme racism in the South • hoped to find better jobs and respect in the North
When did it happen?	1910–1930	1910–1930
What was life like?	worked in factories in the North	• more schools in North • less poverty

My synthesis: During the Great Migration, African Americans left a hard life in the South to find better jobs in the North.

Practice Synthesizing

1. Tell Get together in a small group with 4 or 5 others. Talk about how each of you travels to school. Then think of one or two sentences that tell about how students travel to school. Write this on a sheet of paper. That's your synthesis.

2. Write Now get ready to do some research on your own. With a partner, choose a topic to research. Begin with brainstorming. Then narrow your topic. Make a Gathering Grid like the one above. First, write at least 3 questions about your topic. Next, research at least two sources, such as a book, encyclopedia, or the Internet. Last, write in the details that answer your questions. Share your grid with other groups. The Word Bank can help you.

Word Bank

who
what
when
where
why
how

Grammar Spotlight

Adjective Clauses with *that* and *which* An *adjective clause* is a group of words that describes a noun. A clause has a subject and a predicate.

That is used to give necessary information about the main subject. It does not take commas. Use *that* to refer to people or things.

Which is used in clauses that add extra information about the subject. *Which* is separated from the main part of the sentence by commas. Use *which* to refer to things.

Use	Example
	SUBJECT ADJECTIVE CLAUSE
that	*The journey **that** we made last summer was long.*
	SUBJECT ADJECTIVE CLAUSE
which	*The film, **which** was about the Great Migration, was interesting.*

Write two adjective clauses on your own. Use *that* in one sentence and *which* in the other. Model your sentences on the ones above.

Hands On

Narrowing a Topic In a small group of 3 or 4, decide on a research topic. Together, brainstorm ideas for narrowing the topic. Start by making a Web on the chalkboard or a large sheet of paper. Then decide on a research topic.

Partner Practice

Peer Editing With a partner, decide on a research topic. Remember to narrow your topic. Then write 3 questions about the topic and draft an opening sentence for a report. Have your partner draft questions and an opening sentence too. Then use the Proofreader's Marks on page 224 to edit each other's work. When you're finished, give the edited questions and sentence back to your partner and talk about the changes you suggested.

More About

Verbs

Here you'll learn about different kinds of verbs and their principal parts. You'll also learn how to revise your writing by using strong verbs and practice demonstrating how verbs are used.

Building Background

▲ I started playing the trumpet in our school band. My favorite kind of music is jazz.

■ **What do you think is happening here?**

■ **What does this make you think about?**

■ **How does music teach you about life?**

Some verbs express action. Others link words in a sentence. Some verb tenses are formed by using a helping verb and adding an ending like *ed*. But some verbs have irregular forms that you simply have to learn.

1 Action Verbs
Duke Ellington played the piano.

2 Linking Verbs
Ellington was a bandleader.

3 Helping Verbs
They <u>are playing</u> one of Ellington's songs.

4 Regular and Irregular Verbs
He tapped the drums.
They blew their horns.

Key Concepts

regular verbs   irregular verbs   helping (or auxiliary) verbs

walk + ed

Regular verbs use *ed* to form the past tense and past participle.

run ran

Irregular verbs do not follow the usual pattern of adding *ed*. Some examples of irregular verbs in the past tense include *spoke*, *ran*, and *caught*.

have run

Helping (or auxiliary) verbs are verbs that go with a main verb to express an action or condition. *Has, had, have, do, did,* and forms of *be* (*am, is, are, was, were*) are examples of **helping verbs**.

Learning About Verbs

◀ Duke Ellington played at the Apollo Theater in Harlem, New York.

1. Verbs in statements

Subject + Verb

Langston Hughes lived in New York City.

Subject + Helping + Verb
          Verb

Langston has lived in many places.

Revising: Using Strong, Vivid Verbs

When you revise your writing, choose strong, vivid verbs to bring your writing to life. For example, you might write in a first draft:

*Duke Ellington never **said** much.*

You could choose a stronger, more vivid verb for *said* and revise your sentence:

*Duke Ellington never **complained**.*

Verbs such as *complain, grumble, whine, gripe,* and *squawk* have similar meanings. Each one is strong and vivid. You can picture someone grumbling or complaining, but *said* is not very descriptive.

When you revise your writing, try to include as many strong, vivid verbs as you can.

2. Verbs in questions

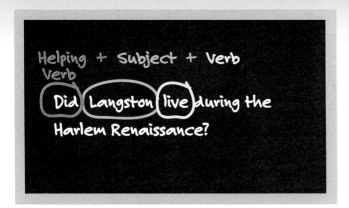

Langston Hughes was one of the African-American writers who joined artists and musicians in Harlem in the 1920s. That time is known as the Harlem Renaissance. ▶

More About Verbs

Some verbs show action, and some link words in a sentence. Other verbs "help" the main verb. Many verbs (called regular verbs) change by adding *ed* to form the past tense. But irregular verbs do not follow any single pattern.

Kinds of Verbs

Verbs sometimes change form to show when something happens and who is doing the action.

Present	*I help.*
	He, she, or it helps.
Past	*I helped.*
	He, she, or it helped.
Present Perfect	*I have helped.*
	He, she, or it has helped.

ACTION VERBS

Action verbs show someone or something doing something. The verbs *play*, *break*, *skate*, *fly*, and *sing* all show action. They tell what someone or something is doing.

who   what they did
People *danced* all night.

Harlem jazz clubs were popular places to dance in the 1940s. ▼

LINKING VERBS

Linking verbs connect, or link, the subject to another part of the sentence.

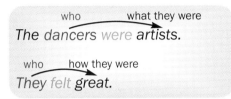

who → what they were
The dancers were artists.

who → how they were
They felt great.

Try to learn these main kinds of linking verbs.

Common Linking Verbs

Forms of *be*
am, is, are, was, were, been, being

Verbs of Condition
look, feel, smell, become, seem, grow, appear

▲ Sheet music told people to move to Harlem.

HELPING VERBS

Helping (or **auxiliary**) verbs are used with main verbs. They help to form some verb tenses, such as the **present perfect.**

Common helping verbs are *am, is, are, was, were* and *has, have,* and *had.* Note the helping verbs in these examples.

Duke Ellington wrote over 1,000 songs and performed all over the world. ▼

helping verb   main verb
Louis Armstrong is playing.

helping verb   main verb
Duke Ellington has played.

Helping verbs are used to show *when* an action occurs (*is playing, has played*).

(**TALK AND SHARE**) **With a partner, think of 3 sentences. In your sentences, give examples of 1) an action verb, 2) a linking verb, and 3) a helping verb.**

VOCABULARY

auxiliary—something that helps or gives support to something else

present perfect—a verb form that describes an action that started in the past but continues or is completed in the present. *A storm has passed* means a storm started in the past but has ended in the present.

Principal Parts of Verbs

English verbs have 4 **principal** parts.

1. The base, or **present**, tense: *wonder*

2. The present **participle:** (is) *wondering*

3. The past tense: *wondered*

4. The past participle: *(had) wondered, (has) wondered, (have) wondered*

PRESENT TENSE

The present tense of a verb states *an action that is happening right now.*

> People everywhere love Duke Ellington's songs.

PRESENT PARTICIPLE

The present participle of a verb states *an action that is happening right now and that goes on for a long time.* The present participle is used with a helping verb, such as *am, is,* or *are.* You form the present participle by adding the **suffix** *ing* to the present form of the verb.

> Radio stations are <u>playing</u> Duke Ellington's songs.

A jazz band performs in New Orleans. ▼

Forms of Verbs

Present	Present Participle
sing	singing
play	playing
understand	understanding
dance	dancing

VOCABULARY

principal—main
present—right now, at this very moment
participle—a verb form. Many present participles end in *ing*.
suffix—a word ending. For example, *ing* is a suffix that can be added to the word *play* to make *playing*.

PAST TENSE

The **past tense** of a verb states *an action that happened in an earlier time.* For regular verbs, add the suffix *ed* to form the past tense.

> *Duke Ellington liv<u>ed</u> during the Big Band era.*

PAST PARTICIPLE

The past participle is the form of a verb that can be used with a helping verb to show that the *action has already been completed in the past.*

> *He had <u>moved</u> to New York in 1923 for his music.*

The past participle is used with a helping verb, such as *has* or *have.* Use *has* with *he, she,* or *it: She has played.* Use *have* with *I, you, we,* or *they: I have danced. They have moved.* Here are the principal parts of some common regular verbs.

Principal Parts of Verbs

Present	Present Participle	Past	Past Participle
play	(is) playing	played	(has) played
dance	(is) dancing	danced	(has) danced
move	(is) moving	moved	(has) moved

Note that when the suffix *ed* or *ing* is added to a verb that ends in *e,* the final *e* is dropped.

(**TALK AND SHARE**) **With your partner, write the principal parts of these 4 verbs: *watch, listen, pass, believe.* Compare your charts, and talk about how they are alike and different.**

Miles Davis plays the trumpet. ▼

Grammar Tip

Active and Passive Verbs

In your own writing, try to use active verbs to make your sentences more clear and interesting. A verb is **active** if the subject is doing the action in the sentence.

subject   verb
Miles Davis <u>played</u> the
object
trumpet.

A verb is **passive** if the action is done *to* the subject. In passive sentences, the subject receives the action.

subject   verb
The trumpet <u>was played</u> by
object
Miles Davis.

VOCABULARY

past tense—tells about something that happened before or previously
active—showing action
passive—not active; allowing things to happen

Irregular Verbs

Many verbs in English do not follow a simple **pattern** to form their past tenses and past participles. They are **irregular verbs.** Regular verbs add the suffix *ed* to form the past tense. But irregular verbs have special forms for the past and past participle. This chart shows the difference between regular and irregular verbs.

	Present	Present Participle	Past	Past Participle
REGULAR VERBS	turn	(is) turning	turned	(has) turned
	watch	(is) watching	watched	(has) watched
IRREGULAR VERBS	see	(is) seeing	saw	(has) seen
	go	(is) going	went	(has) gone

The past and past participle of irregular verbs are not formed by adding *ed*. With irregular verbs, sometimes a vowel changes.

	Present	Present Participle	Past	Past Participle
IRREGULAR VERB	sing	(is) singing	sang	(has) sung

Sometimes the word stays the same, and other times the spelling changes for the past and past participle.

	Present	Present Participle	Past	Past Participle
IRREGULAR VERBS	set	(is) setting	set	(has) set
	teach	(is) teaching	taught	(has) taught

The chart on the next page lists some of the more common irregular verbs.

VOCABULARY

pattern—something that is regular and that you can predict. You know what letters come next in this pattern: abcd, abcd, _ _ _ _.

irregular verbs—verbs that do not change in ways you can predict. You have to learn how to form them.

Principal Parts of Irregular Verbs

Present	Present Participle	Past	Past Participle
sit	(is) sitting	sat	(has) sat
get	(is) getting	got	(has) gotten
bite	(is) biting	bit	(has) bitten
break	(is) breaking	broke	(has) broken
ring	(is) ringing	rang	(has) rung
begin	(is) beginning	began	(has) begun
make	(is) making	made	(has) made
say	(is) saying	said	(has) said
swim	(is) swimming	swam	(has) swum
build	(is) building	built	(has) built
bring	(is) bringing	brought	(has) brought
buy	(is) buying	bought	(has) bought
catch	(is) catching	caught	(has) caught

You can use a dictionary to find the correct spelling of the past and past participle of irregular verbs. Dictionary entries show the spelling changes for irregular verb forms.

TALK AND SHARE With a partner, say the forms of 3 or 4 irregular verbs above. Then try to tell them to your partner from memory. Finally, try to use them in sentences.

Summary

Verbs express action or a state of being. Helping verbs are used to form some verb tenses. Regular verbs add *ed* to create the past tense. But many verbs in the English language are not formed that way. They are called irregular verbs.

Demonstrating

Demonstrating How Verbs Are Used

When you demonstrate, you show something. Demonstrate your understanding of different kinds of verbs. Imagine you have to teach someone about the different kinds of verbs in English. Make a chart like the one below to help you organize all you have learned about verbs.

Verb Chart

Action Verb	Example
talk	I talked about Duke Ellington.
march	He marched in the band.
press	They pressed the button.
Helping Verb	Example
am	I am reading about Langston Hughes.
are	He and Duke Ellington are remembered today.
is	Juanita is recording his music.

Practice Demonstrating

1. Draw   With a partner, draw or find pictures of people doing things. Then work together to list all the words you know that tell about their actions. Share your list with other pairs of partners. Choose the vivid verbs and make a giant list for the class.

2. Write   Now demonstrate that you understand the principal parts of verbs. Look back at the charts on pages 235 and 237. Make one chart with the principal parts of regular verbs. Then make another with the principal parts of irregular verbs. Include at least 3 examples in each chart. Use words from the Word Bank if you can.

Word Bank

drop
lower
laugh
describe
blow
feel
break
become

◀ Louis Armstrong was a popular jazz musician.

Grammar Spotlight

Using *have* and *has* The verb *have* (or *has*) acts as a helping verb when it is placed before a main verb in the past tense. When *have* or *has* is a helping verb, it tells you that the action started in the past and continues in the present or is completed in the present.

Subject	Verb	Example
I	have	I <u>have</u> heard Duke Ellington's records.
you	have	You <u>have</u> listened to them, too.
he	has	He <u>has</u> lived on through his music.
she	has	She <u>has</u> listened to all his records.
it	has	It <u>has</u> made me want to learn more.
we	have	We <u>have</u> studied about his life.
you	have	You <u>have</u> heard his band.
they	have	They <u>have</u> become famous.

Now practice using *have* and *has* as helping verbs in two sentences of your own. Use the sentences above as models.

Partner Practice

Vivid Verbs With a partner, brainstorm a list of strong, vivid verbs that could be used in this sentence to replace *went*.

Raul <u>went</u> down the street.

Start your list this way:

went
ran
jogged
skied

Oral Language

Flash Cards With a partner, make flash cards with the principal parts of irregular verbs. Put the verb in the middle of one side of the card. On the other side, write the present participle, past, and past participle forms. Here is an example. ⟶

strike

(is, are) striking
struck
(has, have) struck

After you and your partner have both created 3 to 8 cards, give your cards to your partner. Ask your partner to quiz you. Then you quiz your partner.

Theme 5
Our Place

Sometimes a dream or a job takes people far from home. Wherever they are, people want a place to call their own.

- What is happening here?
- How do you think the people feel?
- Which photograph do you like best? Why?

Understanding Theme

Most fiction writers have a *theme*, or message, for their readers. As you read, find the "big ideas." Look at what characters do and say. Decide what the clues mean and what statement they make about the author's message.

1. Look for "big ideas."

2. Find out what characters say or do related to those ideas.

3. Come up with a statement that tells the author's message about life.

Before Reading Activities

Partner Practice

K-W-L Chart   With a partner, make a K-W-L Chart like the one here. In "The Circuit," you will read about migrant workers. In the first column, write or draw what you already know about this subject. In the second column, write what you want to know about migrant workers. After you read, fill in the last column with things you and your partner learned.

Migrant workers

What I Know	What I Want to Know	What I Learned
• in California	• What happened?	
• hard work	• Do they still work hard there?	

Oral Language

Work and Jobs   In a small group, share your ideas about working. Discuss these questions to learn what others know about jobs.

• What different jobs do you know about?

• What kind of work is done by people in your city or area?

• What are the good things about these jobs? What are the bad things?

• What kind of education do you need for these jobs?

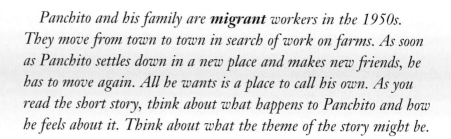

The Circuit

by Francisco Jiménez

*Panchito and his family are **migrant** workers in the 1950s. They move from town to town in search of work on farms. As soon as Panchito settles down in a new place and makes new friends, he has to move again. All he wants is a place to call his own. As you read the short story, think about what happens to Panchito and how he feels about it. Think about what the theme of the story might be.*

It was that time of year again. Ito, the strawberry **sharecropper,** did not smile. It was natural. The **peak** of the strawberry season was over and the last few days the workers, most of them **braceros,** were not picking as many boxes as they had during the months of June and July.

As the last days of August disappeared, so did the number of *braceros.* Sunday, only one—the best picker—came to work. I liked him. Sometimes we talked during our half-hour lunch break. That is how I found out he was from Jalisco, the same state in Mexico my family was from. That Sunday was the last time I saw him.

When the sun had tired and sunk behind the mountains, Ito **signaled** us that it was time to go home.

VOCABULARY

migrant—traveling. Migrant workers move from one place to another to get jobs doing farm work.
sharecropper—a farmer who gives part of his crops to the owner of the land in place of rent
peak—the busiest point

braceros—Spanish for Mexican migrant workers
signaled—gave a command or other information using signs or gestures

"Ya esora," he yelled in his broken Spanish. Those were the words I waited for twelve hours a day, every day, seven days a week, week after week. And the thought of not hearing them again saddened me.

As we drove home Papá did not say a word. With both hands on the wheel, he stared at the dirt road. My older brother, Roberto, was also silent. He leaned his head back and closed his eyes. Once in a while he cleared from his throat the dust that blew in from outside.

Yes, it was that time of year. When I opened the front door to the **shack,** I stopped. Everything we owned was neatly packed in cardboard boxes. Suddenly I felt even more the weight of hours, days, weeks, and months of work. I sat down on a box. The thought of having to move to Fresno and knowing what was in store for me there brought tears to my eyes.

That night I could not sleep. I lay in bed thinking about how much I hated this move.

A little before five o'clock in the morning, Papá woke everyone up. A few minutes later, the yelling and screaming of my little brothers and sister, for whom the move was a great **adventure,** broke the silence of dawn. Shortly, the barking of the dogs **accompanied** them.

Cardboard boxes ▼

(**TALK AND SHARE**) **Talk to a partner about why Panchito and his family might be moving.**

> **VOCABULARY**
>
> **ya esora**—Spanish for "it's time"
> **shack**—a small, poorly built house, often with only one or two rooms
> **adventure**—an unusual or exciting experience
> **accompanied**—went along with or happened together with

▲ Houses of migrant
workers, 1941

from "The Circuit"

While we packed the breakfast dishes, Papá went outside to start the "Carcachita." That was the name Papá gave his old black Plymouth. He bought it in a used-car lot in Santa Rosa. Papá was very proud of his little jalopy. He had a right to be proud of it. He spent a lot of time looking at other cars before buying this one. When he finally chose the Carcachita, he checked it **thoroughly** before driving it out of the car lot. He examined every inch of the car. He listened to the motor, tilting his head from side to side like a **parrot,** trying to detect any noises that spelled car trouble. After being satisfied with the looks and sounds of the car, Papá then insisted on knowing who the **original** owner was. He never did find out from the car salesman, but he bought the car anyway. Papá figured the original owner must have been an important man because behind the rear seat of the car he found a blue **necktie.**

Papá parked the car out in front and left the motor running. **"Listo,"** he yelled. Without saying a word Roberto and I began to carry the boxes out to the car. Roberto carried the two big boxes and I carried the two smaller ones. Papá then threw the **mattress** on top of the car roof and tied it with ropes to the front and rear **bumpers.**

Everything was packed except Mamá's pot. It was an old large **galvanized** pot she had picked up at an army **surplus store** in Santa Maria. The pot had many **dents and nicks,** and the more dents and nicks it acquired the more Mamá liked it. **"Mi olla,"** she used to say proudly.

I held the front door open as Mamá carefully carried out her pot by both handles, making sure not to spill the cooked beans. When she got to the car, Papá reached out to help her with it. Roberto opened the rear car door and Papá gently placed it on the floor behind the front seat. All of us then climbed in. Papá sighed, wiped the sweat from his **forehead** with his sleeve, and said **wearily: "Es todo."**

As we drove away, I felt a **lump** in my throat. I turned around and looked at our little shack for the last time.

At sunset we drove into a labor camp near Fresno. Since Papá did not speak English, Mamá asked the camp **foreman** if he needed any more workers. "We don't need no more," said the foreman, **scratching** his head. "Check with Sullivan down the road. Can't miss him. He lives in a big white house with a fence around it."

When we got there, Mamá walked up to the house. She went through a white gate, past a row of rose bushes, up the stairs to the house. She rang the doorbell. The porch light went on and a tall **husky** man came out. They **exchanged a few words.**

Sullivan's house was a big white house with a fence. ▼

(**TALK AND SHARE**) **How did Panchito feel about moving to a new place? Talk to a partner about it.**

VOCABULARY

surplus store—a place where leftover items are sold to the public, often at cheap prices
dents and nicks—small holes and scratches
mi olla—Spanish for "my pot"
forehead—the part of the face above the eyes
wearily—in a tired way
es todo—Spanish for "that's everything"

lump—a bump or piece of something. The narrator is sad about moving. This makes him feel like he has something caught in his throat.
foreman—someone in charge of a group of workers
scratching—rubbing or scraping with fingernails
husky—big and strong
exchanged a few words—had a very short talk

from "The Circuit"

After the man went in, Mamá clasped her hands and hurried back to the car. "We have work! Mr. Sullivan said we can stay there the whole season," she said, gasping and pointing to an old garage near the **stables.**

The garage was worn out by the years. It had no windows. The walls, eaten by **termites, strained** to support the roof full of holes. The dirt floor, **populated** by **earth worms,** looked like a gray road map.

That night, by the light of a **kerosene** lamp, we unpacked and cleaned our new home. Roberto swept away the loose dirt, leaving the hard ground. Papá plugged the holes in the walls with old newspapers and tin can tops. Mamá fed my little brothers and sister. Papá and Roberto then brought in the mattress and placed it on the far corner of the garage. "Mamá, you and the little ones sleep on the mattress. Roberto, Panchito, and I will sleep outside under the trees," Papá said.

Early the next morning Mr. Sullivan showed us where his crop was, and after breakfast, Papá, Roberto, and I headed for the **vineyard** to pick.

Around nine o'clock the temperature had risen to almost one hundred degrees. I was completely soaked in sweat and my mouth felt as if I had been chewing on a handkerchief. I walked over to the end of the row, picked up the jug of water we had brought, and began drinking. "Don't drink too much; you'll get sick,"

A migrant boy picks cranberries. ▼

Roberto shouted. No sooner had he said that than I felt sick to my stomach. I dropped to my knees and let the jug roll off my hands. I remained motionless with my eyes **glued** on the hot sandy ground. All I could hear was the **drone** of **insects.** Slowly I began to recover. I poured water over my face and neck and watched the dirty water run down my arms to the ground.

I still felt dizzy when we took a break to eat lunch. It was past two o'clock and we sat underneath a large **walnut tree** that was on the side of the road. While we ate, Papá jotted down the number of boxes we had picked. Roberto drew **designs** on the ground with a stick. Suddenly I noticed Papá's face turn pale as he looked down the road. "Here comes the school bus," he whispered loudly in alarm. **Instinctively,** Roberto and I ran and hid in the vineyards. We did not want to get in trouble for not going to school. The neatly dressed boys about my age got off. They carried books under their arms. After they crossed the street, the bus drove away. Roberto and I came out from hiding and joined Papá. ***"Tienen que tener cuidado,"*** he warned us.

(TALK AND SHARE) **Talk to a partner about why Panchito and Roberto hid in the vineyards.**

VOCABULARY

glued—stuck to something, as if with glue
drone—a humming sound
insects—animals with 6 legs, a body, and usually wings. Flies, bees, and butterflies are all *insects.*

walnut tree—a tall tree with nuts you can eat
designs—drawings, sketches, or patterns
instinctively—done without thinking
tienen que tener cuidado—Spanish for "you have to be careful"

from **"The Circuit"**

After lunch we went back to work. The sun kept beating down. The buzzing insects, the wet sweat, and the hot dry dust made the afternoon seem to last forever. Finally the mountains around the valley reached out and swallowed the sun. Within an hour it was too dark to continue picking. The vines blanketed the grapes, making it difficult to see the bunches. ***"Vámonos,"*** said Papá, signaling to us that it was time to quit work. Papá then took out a pencil and began to figure out how much we had earned our first day. He wrote down numbers, crossed some out, wrote down some more. ***"Quince,"*** he murmured.

When we arrived home, we took a cold shower underneath a **water hose.** We then sat down to eat dinner around some wooden **crates** that served as a table. Mamá had cooked a special meal for us. We had rice and **tortillas with *"carne con chile,"*** my favorite dish.

The next morning I could hardly move. My body **ached** all over. I felt little control over my arms and legs. This feeling went on every morning for days until my muscles finally got used to the work.

It was Monday, the first week of November. The grape season was over and I could now go to school. I woke up early that morning and lay in bed, looking at the stars and **savoring** the thought of not going to work and of starting sixth grade for the first time that year. Since I could not sleep, I decided to get up and join Papá and

VOCABULARY

vámonos—Spanish for "let's go"
quince—Spanish for 15
water hose—a long tube used to carry water
crates—boxes used for packing and shipping

tortillas with *"carne con chile"*—cornmeal pancakes with meat and peppers
ached—hurt
savoring—enjoying very much

Roberto at breakfast. I sat at the table across from Roberto, but I kept my head down. I did not want to look up and face him. I knew he was sad. He was not going to school today. He was not going tomorrow, or next week, or next month. He would not go until the cotton season was over, and that was sometime in February. I rubbed my hands together and watched the dry, **acid** stained skin fall to the floor in little rolls.

When Papá and Roberto left for work, I felt **relief.** I walked to the top of a small **grade** next to the shack and watched the *Carcachita* disappear in the distance in a cloud of dust.

Two hours later, around eight o'clock, I stood by the side of the road waiting for school bus number twenty. When it arrived I climbed in. Everyone was busy either talking or yelling. I sat in an empty seat in the back.

When the bus stopped in front of the school, I felt very **nervous.** I looked out the bus window and saw boys and girls carrying books under their arms. I put my hands in my pant pockets and walked to the principal's office. When I entered I heard a woman's voice say: "May I help you?" I was startled. I had not heard English for months. For a few seconds I remained speechless. I looked at the lady who waited for an answer.

(TALK AND SHARE) **How did Panchito feel about going to school? Talk to a partner about it.**

VOCABULARY

acid—a liquid that can burn. Grape juice has an acid in it; the narrator's skin is burned and stained from the acid in grapes he picks.

relief—an easing of pain or worry
grade—a hill or rise in the ground
nervous—anxious or fearful

from "The Circuit"

My first **instinct** was to answer her in Spanish, but I held back. Finally, after struggling for English words, I managed to tell her that I wanted to **enroll** in the sixth grade. After answering many questions, I was led to the classroom.

Mr. Lema, the sixth grade teacher, greeted me and **assigned** me a desk. He then introduced me to the class. I was so nervous and scared at that moment when everyone's eyes were on me that I wished I were with Papá and Roberto picking cotton. After **taking roll,** Mr. Lema gave the class the **assignment** for the first hour. "The first thing we have to do this morning is finish reading the story we began yesterday," he said **enthusiastically.** He walked up to me, handed me an English book, and asked me to read. "We are on page 125," he said **politely.** When I heard this, I felt my blood rush to my head; I felt dizzy. "Would you like to read?" he asked **hesitantly.** I opened the book to page 125. My mouth was dry. My eyes began to water. I could not begin. "You can read later," Mr. Lema said understandingly.

During recess I went into the rest room and opened my English book to page 125. I began to read in a low voice, pretending I was in class. There were many words I did not know. I closed the book and headed back to the classroom.

Mr. Lema was sitting at his desk correcting papers. When I entered he looked up at me and smiled. I felt better. I walked up to him and asked if he could help me with the new words. "Gladly," he said.

The rest of the month I spent my lunch hours working on English with Mr. Lema, my best friend at school.

One Friday during lunch hour Mr. Lema asked me to take a walk with him to the music room. "Do you like music?" he asked me as we entered the building. "Yes, I like **corridos,**" I answered. He then picked up a trumpet, blew on it, and handed it to me. The sound gave me goose bumps. I knew that sound. I had heard it in many *corridos.* "How would you like to learn how to play it?" he asked. He must have read my face because before I could answer, he added: "I'll teach you how to play it during our lunch hours."

That day I could hardly wait to get home to tell Papá and Mamá the great news. As I got off the bus, my little brothers and sister ran up to meet me. They were yelling and screaming. I thought they were happy to see me, but when I opened the door to our shack, I saw that everything we owned was neatly packed in cardboard boxes.

(**TALK AND SHARE**) **With a partner, make a list of 3 words that describe Mr. Lema.**

VOCABULARY

corridos—Spanish word for songs that tell a story

Responding to Literature

Explore the Reading

Talk with a partner about each question below.

1. Why does the family in the story move so often?

2. How do the family members show respect for each other?

3. Compare Mr. Sullivan's house to the place where Panchito's family lives.

4. How would you describe Mr. Lema?

5. What changes in Panchito's life occur in the story?

6. How do you think Panchito feels at the end of the story?

7. What are the "big ideas" of the story?

8. What do you think is the theme of this story?

Learn About Literature

Irony

Irony describes a difference, or contrast, between what is expected and what actually happens. In "The Circuit," the narrator has just begun to feel at home in the new school. Then something happens that he didn't expect.

In a small group, talk about these questions to understand the irony in the story.

• How does Panchito feel when Mr. Lema offers to teach him to play the trumpet?

• Why does the narrator rush home that day?

• What does he see when he opens the door to the shack?

• What difference, or contrast, makes this ending ironic?

Activities

Oral Language

Buddy Reading Choose a favorite part from the story. Read it silently first to make sure you know all of the words. Read one line aloud to a partner. Then have your partner read the next line. Continue that way through the part you chose. Then talk with your partner about why you liked that part.

Partner Practice

Travel the Circuit The word *circuit* means "the route," or way, around. The names of the places in this story tell where the family traveled. On index cards, write the names of places given in the story: Jalisco, Fresno, Santa Rosa, and Santa Maria. Mix up the cards. Show one to your partner. Ask your partner to tell what happened in that place.

Hands On

Draw Your Place Think about a place you have called home. It can be a place you live now or a place you lived before. First, draw a descriptive picture of that place. For ideas, reread the part of the story where Panchito tells about the garage where they lived in Fresno. Then, write about or describe your place to a partner.

Know the Author
Francisco Jiménez

Francisco Jiménez arrived in California from Mexico when he was just 4 years old. He wrote "The Circuit" from his own experiences growing up in a family that traveled around to harvest crops. He liked school because it made his life better. Jiménez also wrote *Breaking Through* and *The Christmas Gift*.

Reading a
Story

Here you'll learn how to read a story. You'll also learn how to make inferences and practice synthesizing parts of a story.

Building Background

▲ Sometimes I help my grandparents on their farm.

■ **What is happening here?**

■ **What are these children doing?**

■ **What kind of work have you done?**

A story has a setting, characters, and a plot. Through these parts of a story, the author tells a message about life. That message is the theme.

Story = "The Circuit"

1 Setting

Near Fresno, California
Late August through November

Characters 2

Panchito (the narrator); his parents; Mr. Lema

3 Plot

Has to do with moving

4 Theme Moving to a new place is hard, but things get better when you meet new people.

Key Concepts

genre   fiction   realistic fiction

Genre means a type of literature. **Fiction** is one genre. It includes made-up stories. **Realistic fiction** is a kind of fiction with believable characters and events. Poetry and nonfiction are other genres.

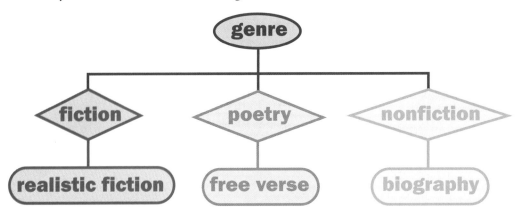

Parts of a Plot

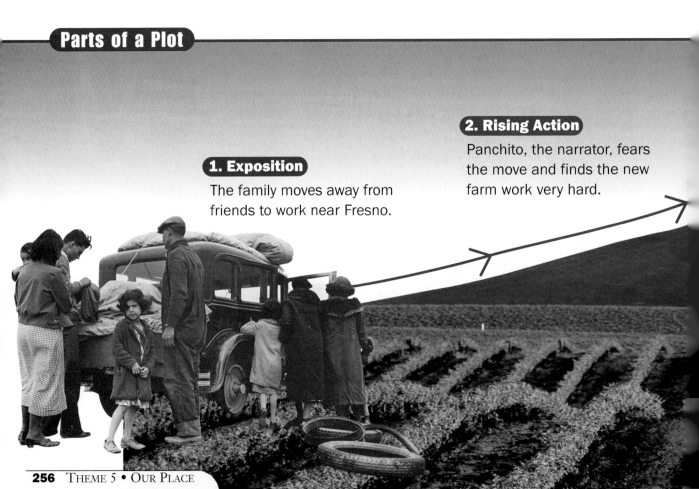

1. Exposition

The family moves away from friends to work near Fresno.

2. Rising Action

Panchito, the narrator, fears the move and finds the new farm work very hard.

Making Inferences

Good writing doesn't always tell you everything. It has little gaps in the story for readers to fill in from their own experience. When you fill in the gaps, you are making inferences.

As you read, write down key lines and sentences. Put together what you learned with what you already know. Then write in your own words what you think the key lines mean. That's making an inference.

What the Character Said or Did	What I Infer
"When we arrived home, we took a cold shower underneath a water hose."	The family doesn't have a bathroom or shower. They are very poor.

3. Climax
Panchito struggles at school to read English aloud.

4. Falling Action
A teacher gives Panchito hope that his life will be better.

5. Resolution
Panchito discovers his family will be moving again.

Reading a Story

When you read a story, keep track of the setting, characters, and plot. Look for what changes. That will help you find the theme, or the author's message about life.

Understand the Parts of a Story

To understand a story, you need to follow the details about the setting, characters, and plot. Watch what changes. How does the character **respond** to change? This can be a clue to understanding the theme, or the author's message about life.

SETTING

The setting in a story is where and when it happens. A story takes place at a **specific** time and place. Often, the setting gives a mood. For example, it could be hope or fear.

CHARACTERS

Characters are people, animals, or **imaginary** beings that take part in the action of a story. The action in a story usually focuses on a **main character.** The others are called **minor characters.** What the characters say and do in the setting helps tell you the author's message.

PLOT

The plot is the action or what happens in a story. Usually the plot centers around a conflict, or problem. Authors often describe the problem early in the story. The plot is the series of events in which the characters try to solve the problem.

CHARACTER
Migrant worker ▼

▲ **SETTING**
Vineyard in California

PLOT
The whole story is about moving. ▶

(**TALK AND SHARE**) **Tell your partner about the setting, the characters, or the plot of a story you know.**

VOCABULARY

respond—act as a result of, or because of, something
specific—clearly stated; definite
imaginary—made-up, not real. An *imaginary* character is not a real person.

main character—the most important character
minor characters—less important characters

How to Read a Story

You can read a story many different ways, but you always need to understand the setting, characters, and plot.

KEEP TRACK OF THE SETTING

Authors often describe the setting in the first few paragraphs of a story. Look carefully for **clues** about when and where the story occurs. Read the beginning of "The Circuit" once more.

---

from "The Circuit"
by Francisco Jiménez

It was that time of year again. Ito, the strawberry sharecropper, did not smile. It was natural. The peak of the strawberry season was over and the last few days the workers, most of them *braceros*, were not picking as many boxes as they had during the months of June and July.

As the last days of August disappeared, so did the number of *braceros*. Sunday, only one—the best picker—came to work.

▲ The sun kept beating down.

These first paragraphs have many words that tell about time, such as *June*, *July*, and *August*. You also learn the strawberry season was over. That's the reason Panchito, the **narrator,** and his family move. The setting tells you where Panchito lives and when the events happen.

VOCABULARY

clues—hints; facts that help solve a problem
narrator—the person or character who tells the story

▲ Basket of strawberries

NOTE WHAT CHARACTERS ARE LIKE

In "The Circuit," the main character, Panchito, is telling the story. He is called the *narrator.* Watch how the main character changes throughout a story. You can also learn a lot about characters by watching for these things:

- What they say

- What they do

- What others think about them

You can make a Character Map to help you learn about characters. Here is an example of a Character Map for the narrator in "The Circuit."

Character Map

What the character says and does	How others act toward the character
• He works hard in the fields.	Mr. Lema is nice to him.
• He opens the book but can't read.	

Panchito, the narrator

How the character looks and feels	How I feel about the character
• He hates moving.	I feel sad for him.
• He wants to go to school.	

You learn about characters just like you learn about your friends. First, you watch what they say and do and what others think about them. Then, you decide what you think about them.

KEEP TRACK OF THE PLOT

The plot is the action, or series of events, in a story. The plot usually begins with a problem, or **conflict.** The conflict then leads to a series of events, often in an **attempt** to **solve** it. The turning point, or **climax,** comes at the point when the conflict is most serious or **intense.**

During your reading, make a Story String to help you keep track of what happens in the plot. Look at this Story String for "The Circuit."

Story String

1. Panchito leaves his friends when he moves from Ito's farm.

2. moves where he doesn't know anyone (conflict)

3. goes to school and struggles to read

4. Mr. Lema becomes a friend.

5. Mr. Lema offers to teach him to play the trumpet (climax).

6. learns he has to leave again

If you take notes on the plot as you read, it will help you better understand and remember what happens in the story.

(**TALK AND SHARE**) **With your partner, talk about how you can keep track of the setting, characters, and plot in a story.**

VOCABULARY

conflict—a problem, or struggle between two things or two people

attempt—an effort or try

solve—find an answer to

climax—the turning point of a story, or when the problem or struggle is the greatest

intense—very strong

Understand the Theme

The theme of a story is a message about life. It is a message or idea that the writer wants readers to remember. Stories can have one or several themes. Here's how you find a theme.

1. FIND THE "BIG IDEAS"

Themes are often about "big ideas," such as:

growing up	loyalty	unhappiness	childhood
hope	friendship	**prejudice**	**courage**
family	**justice**	**success**	**identity**

Repeated words, symbols, and events in the plot are clues to theme. As you read, watch for ideas that come up again and again. Sometimes the theme is stated directly, but usually it is up to the reader to make an **inference** about theme.

2. FIND OUT WHAT THE CHARACTERS SAY AND DO RELATED TO THE "BIG IDEAS"

One character may make a statement about life. Something might happen that changes a character. Or, you might see a symbol that comes up again and again, like the packed boxes in "The Circuit." Changes or repeated words give you clues about the theme.

Reading Tip

Symbol

A *symbol* is a person, place, action, or object that has a meaning in itself but also stands for something greater. For example, the dove is often used as a symbol for peace. In "The Circuit," the cardboard boxes become a symbol of moving. When Panchito sees them, he is sad because he knows his family is going to move again.

VOCABULARY

justice—fairness; getting what is deserved

prejudice—a strong feeling or opinion formed unfairly or without knowing all the facts

success—getting what was wanted after working for it. Someone who has success in life reaches his or her goals.

courage—bravery; not being afraid

identity—the traits and characteristics that make a person who he or she is

inference—a conclusion you come to by putting together facts or ideas

3. MAKE A STATEMENT ABOUT THE AUTHOR'S MESSAGE

To find the theme, you need to state what you think it is and support your thinking. Make a Topic and Theme Organizer to help you find the theme in a story.

First, list the main topic, or "big idea." Then, tell what the characters say, do, or think that relates to the main topic. Finally, write a theme statement about an important lesson you learned from the story.

Topic and Theme Organizer

Topic

(Moving)

What Characters Say, Do, and Think

The family is sorry to leave friends they made.	Panchito is nervous about going to a new school.	Panchito is happy when he makes friends with Mr. Lema.	Panchito is excited about learning to play the trumpet, but it's time to move.

Theme (message about life)

It's hard to always move from place to place.

(**TALK AND SHARE**) **Explain to your partner the steps you can take to understand the theme in a story.**

Summary

As you read a story, look closely at the setting, characters, and plot. Take notes to help you keep track of what happens. Then think about the author's message about life, or the theme.

Synthesizing

Synthesizing Parts of a Story

When you synthesize, you look at the parts and pull them together. You can look at the setting, characters, and plot to find the theme and understand the story. Here one reader used a Fiction Organizer to synthesize the different parts of "The Circuit."

Fiction Organizer

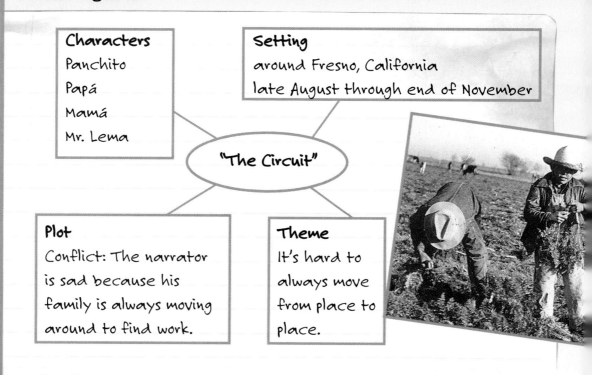

Characters
Panchito
Papá
Mamá
Mr. Lema

Setting
around Fresno, California
late August through end of November

"The Circuit"

Plot
Conflict: The narrator is sad because his family is always moving around to find work.

Theme
It's hard to always move from place to place.

Practice Synthesizing

1. Tell With a partner, talk about a story or movie you both know. First, make a Fiction Organizer like the one above. Then, fill in the information in each box.

2. Write Think about the story of your own life. First, make a Fiction Organizer for your life story. Then, use your organizer to write a paragraph that tells your story. Finally, exchange paragraphs with your partner and check each other's writing using the Check Your Writing tips.

Check Your Writing

Make sure you

- Use complete sentences.
- Use a period at the end of each sentence.
- Spell all the words correctly.

Grammar Spotlight

Possessive Pronouns A *possessive pronoun* shows who or what owns something. Some possessives are pronouns, and some are adjectives.

Pronouns	Adjectives
The car is mine.	Mi Carcachita, my little jalopy, he called it.
Are these boxes yours?	Are these your boxes?
The desk was his.	Mr. Lema was sitting at his desk correcting papers.
The old pot was hers.	It was her old pot.
The shack was ours.	I looked at our little shack for the last time.
The books were theirs.	They carried their books under their arms.
	Papá got the car and threw the mattress on its roof.

Write two sentences. Use a possessive pronoun in one and a possessive adjective in the other.

Oral Language

What Did They Talk About? The narrator spent his lunch hours working on English with Mr. Lema. With a partner, talk about what each character might say and how he would say it. Each partner plays the role of a character. Start this way:

> Mr. Lema: *Hi. Do you want to have lunch?*
> Narrator: *Yes, I'm hungry.*

Partner Practice

Make an Inference Talk with a partner about the sentences below from "The Circuit." Infer how you think Roberto feels about moving.

> As we drove home Papá did not say a word. With both hands on the wheel, he stared at the dirt road. My older brother, Roberto, was also silent. He leaned his head back and closed his eyes. Once in a while he cleared from his throat the dust that blew in from outside.

Writing a
Narrative Paragraph

Here you'll learn how to write a narrative paragraph about an event or experience in your life. You'll also learn how to give your writing voice and practice describing an experience.

Building Background

▲ My cousins pick grapes in California. It's really hard work!

■ **What words would you use to describe this picture?**

■ **How do you think the people feel?**

■ **What story does this picture suggest to you?**

A narrative tells the story of an event or experience. Good writers plan, write a draft, and revise and edit their writing.

1 **Choose an interesting story that you want to share.**

2 **Gather details.**

from **"One Last Time"**
by Gary Soto

Grandfather worked in the fields, as did his children. Mother also found herself out there when she separated from Father for three weeks. I remember her coming home, dusty and so tired that she had to rest on the porch before she trudged inside to wash and start dinner. I didn't understand the complaints about her ankles or the small of her back, even though I had been in the grape fields watching her work. With my brother and sister I ran in and out of the rows; we enjoyed ourselves and pretended not to hear Mother scolding us to sit down and behave ourselves. A few years later, however, I caught on when I went to pick grapes rather than play in the rows.

Details

All day Mother worked hard in the fields. ▼

3 **Write a clear beginning, middle, and end. Use time order.**

4 **Revise and edit.**

Key Concepts

narrative   chronological order

A **narrative** tells a story or describes an event. In a narrative, events are often told in **chronological order.** That is, they are told in time order, or the order in which they happened.

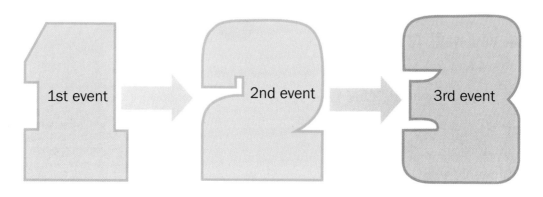

1st event → 2nd event → 3rd event

Organizers for Chronological Order

Timeline

1. List what happens first and the date here.

2. List what happens next here, along with the date.

3. Continue listing events and dates until the end.

Story String

1. Write the first thing that happens here.

2. Tell what happens next here.

3. Tell what happens next here.

4. Finally, end with the last event here.

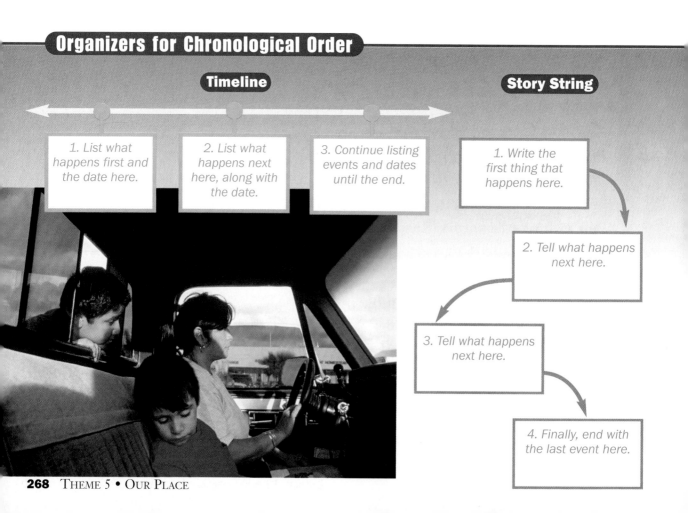

Skill Building

Writing with Voice

Voice is the writer's special way of sharing ideas about an experience. Your writing should sound like you, not like someone else.

Here are some tips for writing with voice.

1. Let your feelings show.

2. Write as if you were having a conversation.

3. Read your writing out loud to be sure it sounds like you.

from **"One Last Time"**
by Gary Soto

Personal

I remember her coming home, dusty and so tired that she had to rest on the porch before she trudged inside to wash and start dinner.

Caring

Story Organizer

Beginning	Middle	End
Write what happens first here.	*Write what happens in the middle of the story here.*	*Write what happens at the end of the story here.*

Storyboard

Draw what happened first here.	*Then draw what happened next.*	*Keep adding sketches until you have included all of the major events.*
Make a note about the drawing.	*Make a note about the drawing.*	*Make a note about the drawing.*

Writing a Narrative Paragraph

To write a narrative paragraph, start by choosing a subject and gathering interesting details. Then write a draft using time order. Later, revise and edit using the 6 Traits Checklist.

Starting Your Paragraph

The first steps for writing a narrative paragraph:

> **1. Choose a subject.**

> **2. Gather details.**

CHOOSE A SUBJECT

Subjects for narrative paragraphs come from your **experience.** How do you decide what to write about? We all have hundreds of stories to tell. Here are some tips to help you pick a subject.

1. Make a List Write down 5 things that happened to you in the last year. Choose the most interesting one.

2. Keep a Writing Journal Writers often keep a writing journal with ideas in it. That way they always have a ready list of things to write about.

3. Talk with a Partner Work with a partner to find out about one or two events that have happened recently in your partner's life. Ask for details about what happened, where it happened, and what your partner thought about it.

4. Look at Photos If every picture tells a story, you should be able to find an idea by looking at photos in a magazine or photo album. What happened around the time of the photo? Why is that time so **memorable?**

5 Things That Happened to Me in the Last Year
1. moved to Miami
2. started at a new school
3. made the soccer team
4. went to professional baseball game
5. met my friend Kyla

VOCABULARY

experience—what happens in a person's life
memorable—important or something you cannot forget.
Something is *memorable* if it is vivid and likely to be remembered.

GATHER DETAILS

Once you have your subject, the next step is to gather the details you want to include. Be **selective.** Try not to tell everything. Leave out any boring parts that have little to do with the story. Start right where the story gets exciting.

Use a Story String to fill out the details of your paragraph. Organize the details before you begin to write.

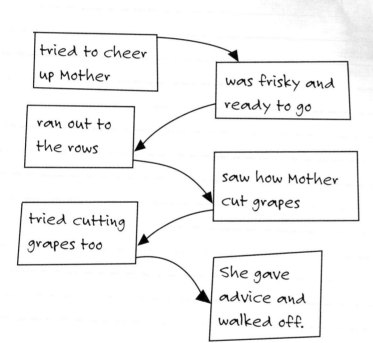

Story String

- tried to cheer up Mother
- ran out to the rows
- tried cutting grapes too
- was frisky and ready to go
- saw how Mother cut grapes
- She gave advice and walked off.

Note that the events are listed in the order in which they happened. That will make telling the story easier to do when you begin drafting.

TALK AND SHARE For a partner, create a Story String for something that happened to you today. Then compare yours with the one your partner did.

VOCABULARY

selective—careful in choosing only what is important or necessary

Writing Your Paragraph

When you are writing your narrative paragraph, tell a story. Think of your paragraph as a tale with a beginning, middle, and end.

ORGANIZE THE DETAILS

One way to keep your paragraph organized is to use a Story Organizer. It has 3 parts and makes it easy to tell the events of your experience in order.

Story Organizer

Beginning	Middle	End
The narrator and his mother get up before dawn.	His mother shows him how to cut grapes.	She gives one last suggestion and goes off to her row.

DRAFT YOUR PARAGRAPH

When it is time to write your first draft, keep the order of events clear. Use signal words, such as *first*, *next*, *then*, and *finally*. They will help the reader know the order of events. You may also need to add clues about time. For example, you might write, "after breakfast" or "just before dinner." Clues about time help the reader know when something happened.

As you draft your paragraph, keep in mind these important tips.

• Start with a strong beginning.

• Leave out any unimportant details.

• End the paragraph in a memorable way.

Now read the narrative paragraph on the next page. Look for clues that signal time.

from "One Last Time"
by Gary Soto

Beginning

Mother and I **got up** before dawn and ate quick bowls of cereal. She drove in silence while I **rambled** on how everything was now solved, how I was going to make enough money to end our **misery** and even buy her a beautiful copper tea pot, the one I had shown her in Long's Drugs.

Middle

When we arrived I was **frisky** and ready to go, **self-consciously** aware of my grape knife **dangling** at my wrist. I almost ran to the row the foreman had **pointed out**, but I returned to help Mother with the grape pans and jug of water. She told me to **settle down** and reminded me not to lose my knife. I walked at her side and listened to her explain how to cut grapes; bent down, hands on knees, I watched her **demonstrate** by cutting a few bunches into my pan.

End

She stood over me as I tried it myself, tugging at a bunch of grapes that pulled loose like beads from a necklace. "Cut the stem all the way," she told me as last advice before she walked away, her shoes sinking in the loose dirt, to begin work on her own row.

Note that the paragraph has 3 parts: a beginning, a middle, and an end. Clues about the time help you see the order of events.

TALK AND SHARE **Tell your partner how to write a good beginning, middle, and end of a narrative paragraph.**

VOCABULARY
rambled—talked without staying on the topic
misery—great pain or suffering
frisky—playful and full of energy
self-consciously—in a shy or embarrassed way
dangling—hanging and swinging loosely
demonstrate—show how to do something

Revising and Editing Your Paragraph

To improve your **draft,** you need to revise and edit. Here are 4 ways to help you improve narrative paragraphs.

> **1. Add details.**
>
> **2. Tell the story in time order.**
>
> **3. Give voice to your writing.**
>
> **4. Use the 6 Traits Checklist.**

ADD DETAILS

Add colorful or specific details where you can.

> Our hike began on a
> dirt
> ∧path in the ~~woods.~~
>   ∧
>   forest by the river.

TELL THE STORY IN ORDER

Write the events in the order they happened. Try not to skip around or jump back and forth. Cut out any sentences that you don't need.

> Our hike began on a path in the
> woods. ~~We got up at 7 to get going~~
> ~~early. My mom drove us to the~~
> ~~woods.~~ As we started up the path
> to the mountain, we saw
> something in the trees.

GIVE YOUR WRITING VOICE

Read your writing out loud. Be sure it sounds like you do when you are talking to a friend.

> buddy
> ~~Once upon a time,~~ my
> ∧~~friend~~ Hector and I went
> on a hike in the woods.

VOCABULARY

draft—the quick, rough
  writing done to get
  ideas down on paper

USE THE 6 TRAITS CHECKLIST

When you revise your writing, read it aloud to yourself. It will help if you look for some of the 6 traits of good writing. Use the 6 Traits Checklist. Ask yourself these questions as you revise and edit your paragraph.

6 Traits Checklist

1. Ideas

Are my ideas clear, and do they flow **smoothly?**

2. Organization

Can I move around or reorder sentences to improve my paragraph?

3. Voice

Does my writing sound like I do when I'm speaking to a friend?

4. Word Choice

Did I choose just the right words to give the reader a clear picture?

5. Sentence Fluency

Did I use signal words like *first, next,* and *then* to connect my ideas and sentences?

6. Correctness

Are all of the words spelled correctly? Did I start each sentence with a capital letter and end with a period?

Writing Tip

Keeping a Writing Journal

A *journal*, or diary, is a record of your experiences. In a journal, you can tell what you have seen or what you did. Journal writers often include their thoughts on what happened during the day. A journal is an excellent place to write down things that happen to you so you can write about them later. Writers use their journals for finding subjects to write about. Make a place in your journal called "Ideas to Write About." Then look there when you need to find a subject.

TALK AND SHARE **Talk to your partner about what you look for when you revise and edit your writing. Together think of ways you can both make your writing even better.**

Summary

A narrative paragraph tells a story about an event or experience. Start by choosing a good subject. Then gather and organize the details. Write a clear beginning, middle, and end using time order. Finally, be sure to revise and edit your paragraph.

VOCABULARY

smoothly—not roughly; evenly
fluency—ease; smoothness; easy flow of ideas from one to the next

Describing

Describing an Experience

When you describe an experience, you tell exactly what happened, how it made you feel, and what the results were. When you describe a personal experience, you have an opportunity to tell your story. You can use a 5 W's and H Organizer like the one below to plan your writing.

5 W's and H Organizer

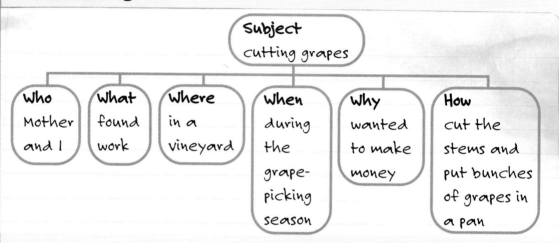

Subject
cutting grapes

Who
Mother and I

What
found work

Where
in a vineyard

When
during the grape-picking season

Why
wanted to make money

How
cut the stems and put bunches of grapes in a pan

Practice Describing

1. Draw Choose an experience from your own life. Draw a picture to show what it is. Then complete a 5 W's and H Organizer like the one above to add details to your drawing. Use your picture to describe your experience to a partner.

2. Write Write a narrative paragraph about an experience you have had. First, plan your paragraph. Then, write a draft of your paragraph. Be sure it has a beginning, middle, and end. Afterward, revise and edit using the 6 traits of good writing. The words in the Word Bank can help you.

Word Bank

work
play

wanted
felt

first
next
last

thought
remembered

Prepositions of Direction and Location A *preposition* is a word or group of words that shows how two things or ideas are related. Prepositions of direction and location show where things are. They usually come right after a verb.

Prepositions of Direction

away from	in	into	off	on	out of	to

Examples: *He almost ran to the row.*
Her shoes sank in the loose dirt.

Prepositions of Location

between	in	in back of	near	next to	on	over	under

Examples: *They worked between the rows.*
She stood over him while he tried cutting the stem.

Now write a sentence using a preposition of direction and another sentence using a preposition of location.

Partner Practice

Story Time Think of a subject for a narrative paragraph. It might be an experience with someone, an adventure you had, or an interesting place you visited. Talk about your experience with a partner. Then listen to your partner's story.

Hands On

Start a Writing Subjects Box Make a "subject box." Put in pictures, news clippings, photographs, and anything else that would be an interesting subject to write about. For example, you might include a lucky penny or the ticket stub from a movie. Share your ideas with others.

Oral Language

Writing with Your Own Voice With a partner, think about an event you both went to, something you both did, or a story you both know about. Then separately write a paragraph about it. Take turns reading your paragraphs aloud. Describe the voice in your partner's writing. How is it different from your own?

Writing
a Story

Here you'll learn how to write a story. You'll also learn how to write dialogue and practice explaining what happens in a story.

Building Background

▲ My grandfather is one of my favorite people. I wish he lived closer to me!

- **What do you think is the story behind these people?**
- **What words would you use to describe this man and boy?**
- **What does this remind you of?**

When you write a story, you need to create 3 main parts: plot, setting, and characters. Then, you plan and draft the story. Later, you revise, edit and proofread, and publish and present it.

1 Create the 3 parts of a story.

Plot

Setting

Characters

2 Write your story.

Plan

Draft

Revise

Edit and Proofread

Publish and Present

Key Concepts

Characterization is the way writers bring characters to life and make them seem real. **Plot development** is the problem, or conflict, in a story. It is the series of events in a story.

Characterization
❐ What character says
❐ How character looks
❐ What character does

Plot Development
❐ A problem is introduced.
❐ The problem gets worse.
❐ One way or another, the problem is solved.

How to Develop a Character

1. Tell how a character looks.

Use sensory details.

2. Tell what a character does.

Describe actions he or she does.

Writing Dialogue

The words that characters speak are called *dialogue*. Dialogue brings characters to life by giving them words and making them sound real. Put dialogue in quotation marks to show it is the words of the speaker.

1. Use dialogue to help you develop characters and show how characters relate to each other.

2. When you write dialogue, read it out loud. See if it sounds natural and believable.

3. Use a comma and quotation marks to set off words in dialogue. See the highlighted marks in the example on the right.

---

from **"The Medicine Bag"**
by Virginia Driving Hawk Sneve

My buddies passed in a single file and shook his hand as I introduced them. They were so polite I almost laughed. "How, Grandpa," and even a "How . . . do . . . you . . . do, sir."

"You look fine, Grandpa," I said as the guys sat down.

---

3. Tell what a character says.

Make his or her words sound realistic.

4. Tell what others say about the character.

Show how the character makes other people feel.

Writing a Story

Before you write a story, you need to create the plot, setting, and characters. Then you write your story using the writing process.

Developing Parts of a Story

What's in a good story? Through reading, you learn that most good stories have several **characteristics.** As this story begins, note how it introduces the characters, setting, and conflict.

Characters

A problem or conflict

Setting

from "The Medicine Bag"
by Virginia Driving Hawk Sneve

My kid sister, Cheryl, and I always **bragged** about our **Lakota** grandpa, Joe Iron Shell. Our friends, who had always lived in the city and only **knew** about Indians from movies and TV, were impressed by **our** stories. Maybe we **exaggerated** and made Grandpa and the reservation sound **glamorous,** but when we returned home to Iowa after **our** yearly summer visit to Grandpa, we always had some exciting tale to tell.

Characteristics of Good Stories
- ❑ Strong characters, interesting plot, and clear setting
- ❑ Characters who seem real and believable
- ❑ Clear series of events
- ❑ Interesting details

"The Medicine Bag" seems to have all of the characteristics of a good story: good characters, a clear setting, and an interesting plot.

VOCABULARY
characteristics—qualities or traits that make something what it is
bragged—talked about how good something was
Lakota—a group of Native Americans who live in the West
exaggerated—spoke or wrote about something as if it were greater than it was
glamorous—fascinating, wonderful

THE PLOT

What makes a great plot? Usually the main character has a problem, or **conflict,** of some kind. The plot is a series of events that shows the problem and how it is solved.

Developing a Plot

Beginning
The problem is introduced.

→

Middle
The characters try to solve the problem.

→

End
One or more characters solve the problem.

Here is the way the plot develops in the story "The Medicine Bag." Martin's Grandpa from the reservation comes to visit him in Iowa.

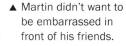

▲ Martin didn't want to be embarrassed in front of his friends.

---

from "The Medicine Bag"
by Virginia Driving Hawk Sneve

I stared just as my friends did, and I heard one of them murmur, "Wow!"

Grandpa looked up, and when his eyes met mine they twinkled as if he were laughing inside. He nodded to me, and my face got all hot. I could tell that he had known all along I was afraid he'd **embarrass** me in front of my friends.

What is the problem, or conflict, here? Look at the highlighted words. Grandpa isn't really glamorous, and he knew his grandson was afraid he would embarrass him.

Language Notes

Homophones
These words sound alike, but they have different spellings and meanings.

☐ **our:** belongs to us
☐ **hour:** 60 minutes

☐ **knew:** had the facts; was familiar with
☐ **new:** not old or used yet

VOCABULARY
conflict—a problem or struggle
embarrass—make uncomfortable or ashamed

THE SETTING

The setting of a story refers to the time and place it occurs. The more specific and detailed you can make the setting, the better your story will be.

Consider these kinds of questions as you plan your setting.

- *Where* does the story take place?
- *What* does this place look like?
- *What* sounds and smells are in the air?
- *When* does the story take place?

Note the details that are highlighted in this description of Grandpa's arrival in Iowa.

from "The Medicine Bag"
by Virginia Driving Hawk Sneve

I never thought that Grandpa would be lonely after our visits, and none of us noticed how old and weak he had become. But Grandpa knew, so he came to us. He had ridden on buses for two and a half days. When he arrived in the city, tired and stiff from sitting for so long, he set out walking to find us.

He had stopped to rest on the steps of some building downtown, and a policeman found him. The officer took Grandpa to the city bus stop, waited until the bus came, and then told the driver to let Grandpa out at Bell View Drive. After Grandpa got off the bus, he started walking again. But he couldn't see the house numbers on the other side when he walked on the sidewalk, so he walked in the middle of the street. That's when all the little kids and dogs followed him.

THE CHARACTERS

Characters can be real people or imaginary creatures. They are who the story is about. Often the action of a story is mostly about one character. That is the **main character.** The characters who are less important to the story are called **minor characters.**

When you write a story, put in only as many characters as you need. If you add too many, the story may be confusing.

Writers provide a lot of details about characters. They tell how the characters look, what they say, and what people think about them. That's called **characterization.** Through these details, readers learn about a character. Look at what you know so far about Joe Iron Shell.

Web

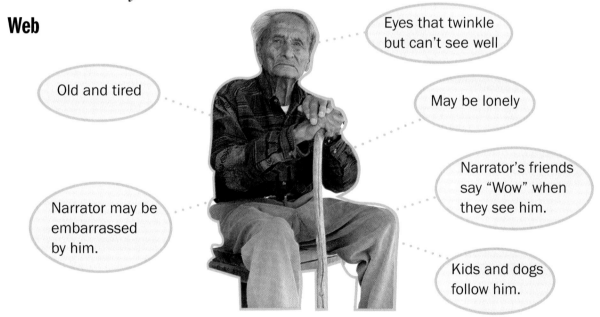

Old and tired

Eyes that twinkle but can't see well

May be lonely

Narrator's friends say "Wow" when they see him.

Narrator may be embarrassed by him.

Kids and dogs follow him.

Besides finding out about Joe Iron Shell, you learn about several other characters: Martin the narrator, his sister Cheryl, and his friends.

(TALK AND SHARE) **Discuss with your partner 3 parts of a story you know. Then talk about a story you could write.**

Developing Characters

Here are some things you can use to describe the *characters* in your story:

- **Physical Appearance** hair color, age, how they look, or the way the characters are dressed
- **Personality** shy, bold, grumpy, loving, and so on
- **Goals** finding a part-time job, getting along with a difficult person

Writing Your Story

To write a story, use the writing process. The steps below will help you to plan and write a good story.

PLAN YOUR STORY

To plan a story, create a Story Map like the one below. Make notes about the setting, who the characters are, and what the problem or conflict in the story will be. Then list the main events in your plot. End by telling how the characters finally solve the problem.

Story Map

Setting	
Time	today
Place	small town in Iowa

Characters

narrator	Joe Iron Shell
sister Cheryl	narrator's friends

Problem or Conflict

The narrator is afraid his Lakota grandfather will embarrass him in front of his friends.

Events in the Plot

1. The narrator tells everyone how great his Lakota grandpa is.
2. Grandpa Joe visits the narrator's small Iowa town.
3. The narrator brings his friends to meet Grandpa Joe.

DRAFT YOUR STORY

Now, you draft your own story. One way to write a story is to follow a plan, such as the Story Map. Begin writing, and do not stop until you have reached the end. You can fix your draft later when you revise.

physical appearance—the way someone looks
personality—how someone acts or behaves. For example, a person may have a shy, bold, or mean personality.
goals—aims, objectives, or purposes

REVISE

Once you have written your story, put it aside for a day. Think about other things for a while. Then, come back and read it again. Ask yourself these questions.

- What is missing? Is there anything I should take out?

- What parts aren't clear?

- What details can I add?

EDIT AND PROOFREAD

After you revise, go back over your story one more time. Look carefully at each sentence. You might even want to read your draft out loud to a partner. Ask yourself:

- Does each sentence begin with a capital letter?

- Does each sentence end with some punctuation?

- Do any sentences have any words that are misspelled?

Use proofreader's marks to show your changes. Here is an example.

my grandfather once gave me a gift

PUBLISH AND PRESENT

The last step in writing a story is to create a clean copy. Write the story again. Be careful to put in all of your changes. Then, add a title and cover page. Read your story to the class or to a partner.

TALK AND SHARE **With your partner, list 3 different things you need to look for when you revise and edit a story.**

Proofreader's Marks

≡ Capitalize a letter.
／ Make the letter lowercase.
⊙ Put in a period.
∧ Insert a word or letter.
℘ Delete or take out.
SP. Correct spelling error.
¶ Start a new paragraph.

Summary

To write a story, first create the plot, setting, and characters. Then, draft your story, revise and edit it, proof it, and publish and present it.

Explaining

Explaining a Story

When you explain, you tell about something in a way that helps people understand it. When you write, be sure to explain how the events connect in your story. You can explain the events in a story more clearly if you create a Story String. It will help you explain how events in the story connect.

Story String

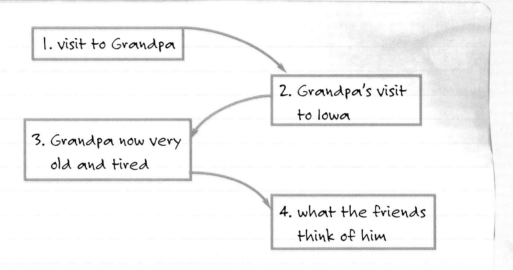

1. visit to Grandpa

2. Grandpa's visit to Iowa

3. Grandpa now very old and tired

4. what the friends think of him

Practice Explaining

1. Tell   Talk with your partner about a story you want to tell. Create a Story String like the one above. Describe or draw the setting, characters, and major events in the plot. Then explain your story to your partner.

2. Write   After talking with your partner about a story you can tell, create a Story Map like the one on page 286. Explain to your partner what your story will be. Then, write a draft of your story. Exchange papers with your partner and check each other's work using this checklist.

Check Your Writing

Make sure you

- Use complete sentences.

- Use a period at the end of each sentence.

- Spell all the words correctly.

Grammar Spotlight

Subject Pronouns The subject tells who or what a sentence is about. A *subject pronoun* stands for a noun and is used as the subject of a sentence. Note that the verb isn't always next to the subject pronoun.

Subject Pronoun	Example
I	*I wanted to run and hide.*
you	*You told me about the conflict in the story.*
he, she, it	*After Grandpa got off the bus, he started walking.*
we	*We always had some exciting tale to tell.*
you (plural)	*You, the readers of my story, will learn the truth.*
they	*Did they laugh at Martin?*

Now write 3 sentences using subject pronouns.

Hands On

Story Poster Work with a partner to make a poster telling how to create a story. Use the "Big Idea" on page 279 as a model. Add details or illustrations. Then explain your poster to the class and display it in the room.

Oral Language

Describe Characters Draw a picture of how you think one of these characters may have looked: Grandpa, Cheryl, or Martin, the narrator. Ask your partner to describe the character you drew. Then tell something about what the character does or says.

Partner Practice

Write Dialogue Martin and Cheryl bragged about their Lakota grandpa. Make up a dialogue that tells what they might have said to their friends. Be sure to use quotation marks around the words of each speaker. Also put a comma between the speaker and what he or she says. You might begin this way:

> "My grandpa made these moccasins! They are beautiful," Cheryl said.
>
> Martin replied, "Grandpa gave me this drum with a painting of a warrior on a horse. He taught me a real Lakota chant!"

Understanding
Adjectives and Adverbs

Here you'll learn how adjectives and adverbs describe other words. You'll also learn how to improve your writing by combining sentences and practice interpreting text.

Building Background

▲ A lot of kids live on my street, so there's always someone to play with.

■ **What words would you use to tell about these buildings?**

■ **What would you say to explain how the children are playing?**

■ **What does this place remind you of?**

Big Idea

Adjectives and adverbs modify, or tell about, other words. Phrases, or groups of words, can also be modifiers. Adjectives and adverbs have comparative and superlative forms.

1 Adjectives and Adverbs

ADJECTIVE
red car
tall fence

ADVERB
carefully stood
looked ahead

2 Adjective and Adverb Phrases

ADJECTIVE PHRASE
sidewalk by the rusting fence

ADVERB PHRASE
walked in a playful way

3 Comparative and Superlative Forms

COMPARATIVE
busier neighborhood

SUPERLATIVE
busiest neighborhood
built the most solidly

Key Concepts

modify   comparative   superlative

To *modify* means to change or limit the meaning of a word in some way. The **comparative** form of a word compares two things. The **superlative** form of a word compares 3 or more things.

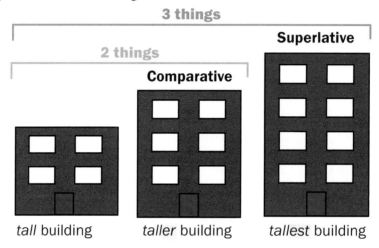

tall building   taller building   tallest building

Placing Adjectives and Adverbs

An adjective can come before a noun.

An adjective can come after a linking verb.

Combining Sentences

You can improve your writing by using sentences of different lengths. For example, you can combine two short sentences to make one longer, smoother sentence. One way to do this is to combine your ideas with adjective and adverb phrases. Study these examples.

Combining Sentences with Phrases

Two Sentences	Combined Sentence
We took a taxi to the apartment. The taxi went through the streets of Brooklyn.	We took a taxi through the streets of Brooklyn to the apartment.
The taxi wove in and out of traffic. It was speeding through the streets.	The taxi, speeding through the streets, wove in and out of traffic.

An adverb that modifies an adjective comes before it.

adverb adjective

His street was very busy.

Some adverbs can also come after an adjective.

adjective adverb

The sun was bright today.

Understanding Adjectives and Adverbs

Adjectives and adverbs describe other words. A phrase, or group of words, can also act like an adjective or an adverb. Comparatives and superlatives are forms of adjectives and adverbs used to compare things.

Adjectives and Adverbs

Adjectives modify **nouns** and **pronouns.** Adverbs modify **verbs,** adjectives, or other adverbs.

ADJECTIVES

An adjective is a word used to change or modify a noun or a word that takes the place of a noun. For example, in the phrase "a hard test," the adjective hard describes the noun *test.* Note the adjectives in this paragraph.

1. medical—adjective describing *care*

2. youngest—adjective telling which *brother*

3. bicycle—adjective modifying *chain*

4. red and **swollen**— adjectives modifying *foot*

> from *Almost a Woman*
> by Esmeralda Santiago
>
> We came to Brooklyn in 1961, in search of [1]medical care for my [2]youngest brother, Raymond, whose toes were nearly **severed** by a [3]bicycle chain when he was four. In Puerto Rico, doctors wanted to **amputate** the often [4]red and swollen foot, because it wouldn't heal. In New York, Mami hoped, doctors could save it.

Adjectives answer questions such as *what kind? how much? which one?* and *how many?*

VOCABULARY

nouns—words that name a person, place, thing, or idea

pronouns—words that take the place of a noun. For example: *She* had a book and then lost *it. She* and *it* are pronouns.

verbs—words that show action or link parts of a sentence

severed—cut off

amputate—cut off a part of the body

Adjectives

How They Describe	Example
What kind?	*The family came to find medical care for Raymond.*
Which one?	*Esmeralda had just had her thirteenth birthday.*
How many?	*Raymond had an accident when he was four years old.*

ADVERBS

Adverbs are another kind of describing word. They modify verbs, adjectives, or other adverbs. For example, the adverb *slowly* modifies the verb *drove* in this sentence:

> The taxi drove <u>slowly</u> down the **block**.

Here the adverb *very* modifies the adjective *peaceful:*

> She seemed <u>very</u> peaceful.

Here the adverb *too* modifies the adverb *softly:*

> She spoke <u>too</u> softly to be heard.

Finding an adverb in a sentence can be very easy because many adverbs end in *ly.* Adverbs answer the questions *when? where? how?* or *to what extent?*

Adverbs

What They Tell	Example
When?	*I will see my brother tomorrow.*
Where?	*We can sit here on the steps and talk.*
How?	*She speaks kindly about everyone.*
To what extent?	*It is always warm in this city.*

(TALK AND SHARE) **Talk with your partner about how adjectives and adverbs are different. Give 3 or 4 examples of each.**

Language Notes

Multiple Meanings
These words have more than one meaning.

☐ **hard**
1. difficult
2. solid and firm
3. with great force

☐ **foot**
1. a part of the body
2. the bottom of something
3. 12 inches long

☐ **block**
1. an area in a city or town
2. a cube of wood
3. put things in the way of
4. prevent or stop from happening

Adjective and Adverb Phrases

A **phrase** is a group of words. Adjective and adverb phrases are groups of words that act just like adjectives and adverbs. They describe other parts of the sentence.

UNDERSTANDING ADJECTIVE AND ADVERB PHRASES

An adjective phrase describes a person, place, thing, or idea. An adverb phrase describes an action. It often tells where the action happens. Note the phrases in this paragraph.

1. Adverb phrase
describes *where* I leaned

2. Adjective phrase
describes *which* wall

3. Adjective phrase
describes *what* the buildings are like

4. Adverb phrase
describes *how* the playground is surrounded

from *Almost a Woman*
by Esmeralda Santiago

Two days later, I leaned **¹**against the wall **²**of our apartment building on McKibbin Street wondering where New York ended and the rest of the world began. It was hard to tell. There was no **horizon** in **Brooklyn.** Everywhere I looked, my eyes met a **vertical maze** of gray and brown straight-edged buildings**³**with sharp corners and deep shadows. Every few blocks there was a cement playground surrounded **⁴**by **chain-link fence.** And in between, weedy lots mounded with garbage and rusting cars.

Can you find another adverb phrase in the last sentence?

VOCABULARY

phrase—a group of words that has meaning but no subject or predicate and is not a complete sentence
horizon—the line where Earth and the sky seem to meet

Brooklyn—a part of New York City
vertical—straight up and down
maze—a path that is hard to find the way through
chain-link fence—a fence of metal rings

USING ADJECTIVE AND ADVERB PHRASES

An adjective modifies a noun or pronoun. An adverb modifies a verb, an adjective, or another adverb. Adjective and adverb phrases modify words in the same way. Good writers use them to add details to their writing and create pictures in the reader's mind.

Adjective and Adverb Phrases

Phrase	Word the Phrase Modifies
1. against the wall	leaned (a verb)
2. of our apartment building	wall (a noun)
3. with sharp corners and deep shadows	buildings (a noun)
4. by chain-link fence	surrounded (a verb)

The same phrase can be used in two different ways. Look at these examples.

> I leaned against the wall.
>
> The broom against the wall fell down.

In the first example, "against the wall" is an adverb phrase. In the second example, "against the wall" is used as an adjective phrase. You can tell because it describes *which* broom.

Grammar Tip

Misplaced Modifiers

Modifiers such as *adjective phrases* and *adverb phrases* need to be as close as possible to the word they describe. Otherwise, the reader may become confused about what you mean. A *misplaced modifier* says something you don't mean. For example, in this sentence, who has the large rooms?

Misplaced modifier: *We have <u>apartments</u> for big families <u>with large rooms</u>.*
To correct this sentence, put the adjective phrase (*with large rooms*) right after the word it modifies (*apartments*).
Correct: *We have apartments with large rooms for big families.*

(**TALK AND SHARE**) **Think of a sentence with an adjective phrase and a sentence with an adverb phrase. Then tell your sentences to a partner.**

Comparatives and Superlatives

Some modifiers compare two things. Other modifiers compare 3 or more things.

MAKING COMPARISONS WITH ADJECTIVES

Comparative adjectives compare two persons, places, things, or ideas. Superlative adjectives compare 3 or more persons, places, things, or ideas.

Comparative and Superlative Adjectives

COMPARATIVE ADJECTIVES	This apartment is *larger than* mine.
	In the city, I will be *more careful than* usual.
	You need to get some *better* shoes for walking.

SUPERLATIVE ADJECTIVES	The *largest* apartment was perfect for us.
	I am the *least careful* person in our family.
	These are the *best* shoes for walking.

To make comparative and superlative forms, remember these things.

- Some short comparative adjectives end in *er* (*smaller*). Longer words often have *more* or *less* (*more colorful*).

- Add *est* to short adjectives to make them superlative (*boldest*). The word *most* or the word *least* is used with longer words (*most beautiful*).

- Some words are **irregular.** You need to memorize these forms. For example, the comparative adjective for *good* is *better*; and the superlative is *best*.

▲ These are the *best* shoes for walking.

VOCABULARY
irregular—not normal or following a pattern

COMPARING WITH ADVERBS

Comparative adverbs compare two actions. Superlative adverbs compare 3 or more actions.

Comparative and Superlative Adverbs

COMPARATIVE ADVERBS	José drives faster than I do.
	People talk more quietly in the library.
	Carmen sings better than Judy.

SUPERLATIVE ADVERBS	Taxi drivers drive fastest of all.
	People talk most quietly when someone is sleeping.
	Maya sings best of anyone I know.

Remember these tips when forming the comparative and superlative forms of adverbs.

• Short comparative adverbs usually end in *er* (*faster*). For longer words, use the word *more* or the word *less* (*more quietly*).

• Add *est* to short adverbs to make them superlative (*fastest*). The word *most* or the word *least* is used with longer words (*most quietly*).

• Some words are irregular. You need to memorize the comparative and superlative forms of these words. For example, the comparative adverb for *badly* is *worse*, and the superlative form is *worst*.

(TALK AND SHARE) **Tell your partner a sentence comparing two things. Have your partner change it to compare 3 or more things.**

▲ Taxi drivers drive *fastest* of all.

Summary

Adjectives and adverbs modify other words. Phrases are groups of words in a sentence. They, too, sometimes act as adjectives and adverbs. The comparative and superlative forms of adjectives and adverbs are used to make comparisons.

Interpreting

Interpreting Text

When you interpret something, you figure out what it means. When you read, you try to interpret the writer's meaning. Writers use adjectives and adverbs to add details. Look closely at the highlighted details in the example below. They will help you interpret the text.

> #### from *Almost a Woman*
> #### by Esmeralda Santiago
>
> Everywhere I looked, my eyes met a vertical maze of gray and brown straight-edged buildings with sharp corners and deep shadows. Every few blocks there was a cement playground surrounded by chain-link fence.

How does the writer describe the buildings and the playground? Which details help you see that the writer thinks this place is dark, hard, and confusing?

Practice Interpreting

1. Draw   With a partner, look at the two sentences below.

> The playground had a fence. (no modifiers)
>
> The cement playground was surrounded by a high chain-link fence. (with modifiers)

Now make up your own sentences. In one, leave out all adjectives and adverbs. In the other, add adjectives and adverbs or even a phrase. The words in the Word Bank may help you. Then draw the picture shown by each sentence and compare them to those of your partner.

Word Bank	
good	more
better	less
best	
bad	most
worse	least
worst	

2. Write   Now find a paragraph with lots of adjectives and adverbs. Make two columns on a piece of paper. Copy the paragraph in the left column. Circle all of the adjectives and adverbs in the paragraph. Then, in the right column, interpret what you think the paragraph means. Use the adjectives and adverbs to help you interpret it.

Activities

Grammar Spotlight

Spelling Adverbs Most adverbs end in *ly*. Here are some rules you can follow when forming *ly* adverbs.

Rules for Spelling Adverbs

Word	Adverb	Rule
quick	quickly	Add *ly*.
sure	surely	Add *ly*.
angry	angrily	If the word ends in *y*, change the *y* to *i* and add *ly*.
terrific	terrifically	If the word ends in *ic*, add *ally*.
remarkable	remarkably	If the word ends in *le*, drop the *e* and add *y*.

Use the rules to add *ly* to each of these words: *happy, agreeable, usual, realistic.*

Hands On

Adjective and Adverb Hunt With a partner, search the room to find two different objects. Use adjectives and adjective phrases to describe the objects. Then think of how to talk about the same objects using adverbs. Look at the examples below.

Adjective and Adjective Phrase

> ADJECTIVE ADJECTIVE PHRASE
> *I will water the tall plant with the big green leaves.*

Adverb and Adverb Phrase

> ADVERB
> *I will carefully water the plant and then move*
>
> ADVERB PHRASE
> *it to the desk.*

Partner Practice

Combine Sentences With a partner, write short sentences on several index cards. Then combine the sentences into one long sentence. Here is an example.

> *My dog is big.*
> *She is red.*
> *She barks when she's outside.*
> **Combined Sentence:** *My big, red dog barks a lot when she's outside.*

Theme

6

Making a Difference

People make a difference every day. You can make a difference by helping one person or by helping to make the world a better place.

- Who are these people?
- What are they doing?
- What kind of difference would you like to make?

BOYCOTT GRAPES

FARM WORKERS OF AMERICA

WORLD PEACE MARCH

SAVE OUR WORLD

Understanding Author's Purpose

An author's purpose is the reason why he or she wrote something. There are 3 general reasons why an author writes: to explain, entertain, or persuade. As you read, look for clues to help you figure out the author's purpose. The chart below can help you.

Purpose and Clues Chart

Purpose	Clues
To explain or inform	• Definitions or instructions • Facts or details
To entertain	• Funny, lively language • Friendly, casual
To persuade	• Strong language • Argues a point

▲ A girl *persuades* people to stop being unfair.

Before Reading Activities

Partner Practice

Who Made a Difference? Think about someone who made a difference. Who was the person? What did he or she do? Where? When? Why did the person do it? How was it done? Answer the questions in a 5 W's and H Organizer. Share it with a partner.

```
          ┌──────────────┐
          │     Name     │
          └──────┬───────┘
      ┌──────────┼──────────┐
┌─────────┐ ┌─────────┐ ┌─────────┐
│   Who   │ │  When   │ │  Where  │
└─────────┘ └─────────┘ └─────────┘
┌─────────┐ ┌─────────┐ ┌─────────┐
│  What   │ │   Why   │ │   How   │
└─────────┘ └─────────┘ └─────────┘
```

Oral Language

Tell Me About It Tell a partner about something that happened to you. First, think about what you want to share. Is it a funny story or a serious message about life? Do you want to tell about something you heard on the news? Or, do you want to convince your partner to think like you? Look at the Purpose and Clues Chart at the top of this page. Use clues as you tell your story. Then have your partner guess your purpose.

Lessons of
Dr. Martin Luther King, Jr.

César Chávez

▲ Dr. Martin Luther King, Jr., 1968

*César Chávez knew firsthand about the unfair working conditions of migrant workers. He organized farm workers to fight for better safety and pay. He organized **nonviolent** protests, such as marches, speeches, strikes, and **boycotts**. In this speech, Chávez talks about the lessons we can learn from another civil rights leader, Dr. Martin Luther King, Jr.*

My friends, today we honor a giant among men: today we honor the **reverend** Martin Luther King, Jr.

Dr. King was a powerful figure of **destiny,** of courage, of **sacrifice,** and of vision. Few people in the long history of this nation can rival his **accomplishment,** his reason, or his **selfless dedication** to the cause of peace and social justice.

Today we honor a wise teacher, an inspiring leader, and a true **visionary,** but to truly honor Dr. King we must do more than say words of praise.

We must learn his lessons and put his views into practice, so that we may truly be free at last.

Who was Dr. King?

Many people will tell you of his wonderful qualities and his many accomplishments, but what makes him special to me, the truth many people don't want you to remember, is that Dr. King was a great **activist,** fighting for **radical social change** with radical methods.

VOCABULARY

nonviolent—using peaceful methods; not using force
boycotts—not using or buying something as an act of protest
reverend—someone with religious duties in a church
destiny—future events that are already decided
sacrifice—the giving up of something valuable for an important cause

accomplishment—great things he's done
selfless dedication—the unselfish support of a cause
visionary—someone who has a dream and wants to make it real
activist—someone who works to make changes in society
radical social change—a large, sudden change

from **"Lessons of Dr. Martin Luther King, Jr."**

While other people talked about change, Dr. King used direct action to **challenge the system.** He welcomed it, and used it wisely.

In his famous letter from the Birmingham jail, Dr. King wrote that "The purpose of direct action is to create a situation so **crisis-packed** that it will **inevitably** open the door to **negotiation."**

Dr. Martin Luther King, Jr., speaks in Selma, Alabama. ▼

Dr. King was also radical in his beliefs about violence. He learned how to successfully fight hatred and violence with the unstoppable power of nonviolence.

He once stopped an armed mob, saying: "We are not **advocating** violence. We want to love our enemies. I want you to love our enemies. Be good to them. This is what we live by. We must meet hate with love."

Dr. King knew that he very probably wouldn't survive the struggle that he led so well. But he said, "If I am stopped, the movement will not stop. If I am stopped, our work will not stop. For what we are doing is right. What we are doing is just, and God is with us."

My friends, as we enter a new **decade,** it should be clear to all of us that there is an unfinished **agenda,** that we have miles to go before we reach the **promised land.**

(**TALK AND SHARE**) **Ask a partner what he or she thinks about Dr. King. Talk about how he made a difference.**

VOCABULARY

challenge the system—point out the wrongs in business and government and fight to change them
crisis-packed—full of problems
inevitably—surely; certainly. When something will happen inevitably, it is impossible to stop it from happening.

negotiation—a discussion to come to an agreement
advocating—supporting; speaking in favor of
decade—a period of 10 years
agenda—a list of goals. An "unfinished agenda" is one where the goals are not yet achieved.
promised land—refers to a story in the Bible. Here it means "our goal."

Responding to Literature

Explore the Reading

Talk with a partner about each question below.

1. Who was Dr. Martin Luther King, Jr.? Why was he honored?

2. What does César Chávez say about Dr. King?

3. How would you describe Dr. King?

4. How did Dr. King make a difference in the world?

5. What can you tell about Chávez from his speech?

6. What do you think is Chávez's purpose for the speech?

Learn About Literature

Connotation and Denotation

Writers often choose words that stir emotions in their readers. The *connotation* is the emotional feelings that a word carries. The *denotation* is the dictionary meaning of the word. Read the sentence below.

> "I was profoundly moved that someone facing such a tremendous struggle himself would take the time to worry about a struggle taking place on the other side of the continent."

▲ César Chávez and Dr. King's wife, Coretta Scott King, march for migrant workers' rights.

The denotation of *profoundly* is "coming from a great depth." The definition of *tremendous* is "extremely large or enormous." The message these words send is different from saying that Chávez was *seriously* moved or that the struggle was *big*. Those words have different connotations. Sometimes words have negative connotations. To say "I was foolishly moved" would have a negative connotation.

With a partner, reread Chávez's speech. Find one word with a positive connotation and one word with a negative connotation. Then look up the denotation for each word in a dictionary.

Activities

Tell Your Partner Why   Think about why César Chávez might have written the speech. Then tell your reasons to a partner. Ask your partner what he or she thinks. Then complete the sentence: "Chávez wrote his speech because . . ."

Partner Practice

Author's Purpose   Below is an excerpt from the speech. Read it with a partner. Talk about what the excerpt means. Then talk about what the author's purpose might be.

> "He once stopped an armed mob, saying: 'We are not advocating violence. We want to love our enemies. I want you to love our enemies. Be good to them. This is what we live by. We must meet hate with love.'"

Hands On

Write About Making a Difference   Think about how you can make a difference. Think about something in the world, at school, or in your life that seems unfair to you. Make a poster about it. First, describe the problem in a sentence or show a picture. Then tell why it's unfair. Finally, say what you could do to change it.

Know the Author

César Chávez

César Chávez grew up in California. He was a migrant farm worker who founded the United Farm Workers (UFW). In the 1970s, the UFW helped get better working conditions for farm workers. Chávez led protests against companies that didn't treat workers fairly.

Reading
Real-world Writing

Here you'll learn about reading real-world writing. You'll also learn how to skim and practice comparing and contrasting information.

Building Background

▲ We have a mural of César Chávez in our school.

- **What do you see in this picture?**
- **Which symbols can you find? What do you think they stand for?**
- **What does this picture have to do with real-world writing?**

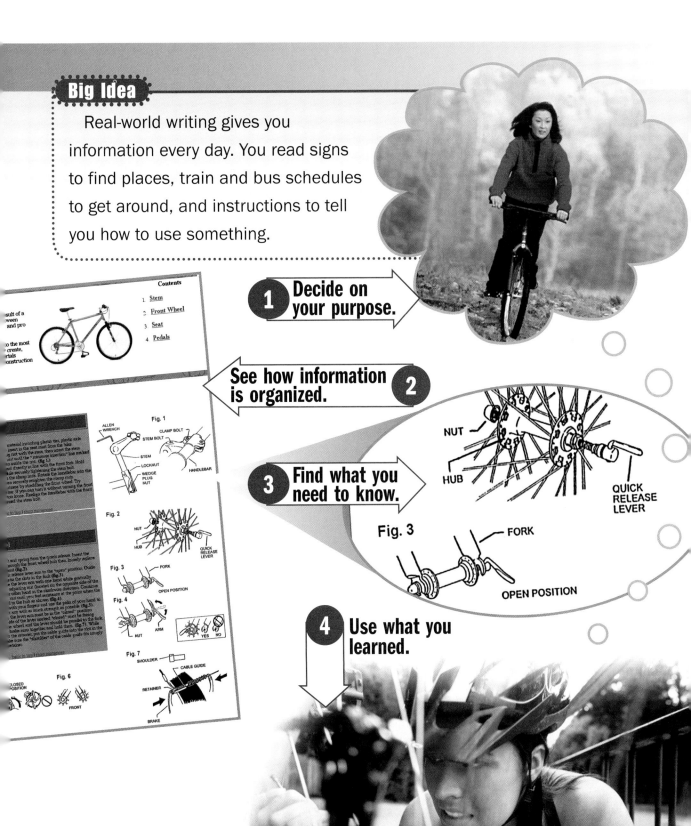

Big Idea

Real-world writing gives you information every day. You read signs to find places, train and bus schedules to get around, and instructions to tell you how to use something.

1 Decide on your purpose.

2 See how information is organized.

3 Find what you need to know.

4 Use what you learned.

Key Concepts

When you read real-world writing, figure out how the information is **organized,** or put together. Most real-world writing uses **labels,** or text that names the main parts. **Skimming,** or reading for key words, helps you find the information you need quickly.

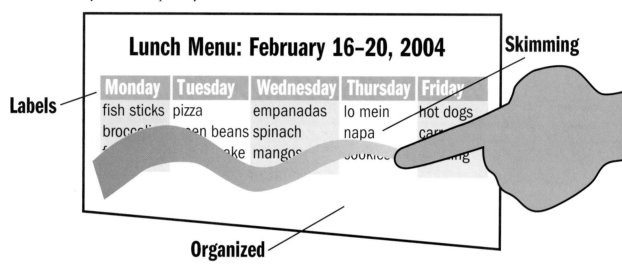

Types of Real-world Writing

A bus schedule

A street sign

Skimming

Most of the time you won't read real-world writing word for word. Instead, you will skim for the information you need. *Skimming* is moving your eyes quickly over the material, looking for headings or key words as you go. In the poster below, one reader highlighted the key words.

Paint *for* Peace

Join this fun great club for students who want to make a difference. We'll work with teachers and artists to paint murals in our school and in our community.

When: Tuesdays after school

Where: Art Room 215

Bring your friends and your ideas!

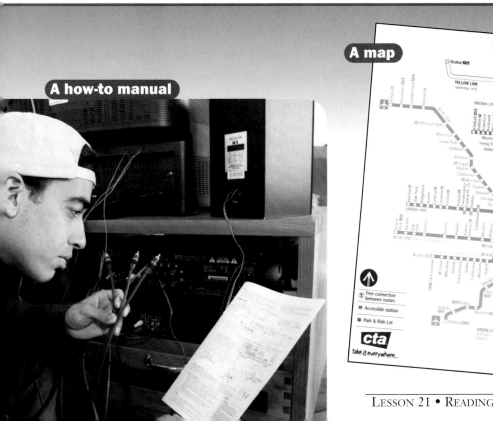

A how-to manual

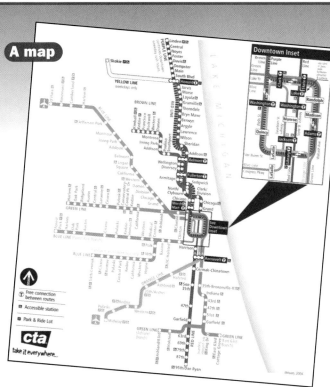

A map

Reading Real-world Writing

Real-world writing includes schedules, maps, and instructions. When you read real-world writing, first decide on your purpose. Then, see how the information is organized. Next, find the information you need. Finally, apply what you learned.

Four Steps for Reading Real-world Writing

You read real-world writing every day, whether it's a lunch **menu,** web page, bus **schedule,** or telephone book. Usually you don't need to read the entire thing. You just look for the information you need. Follow the steps below to get the most out of real-world writing.

STEP 1. DECIDE ON YOUR PURPOSE FOR READING

First, think about *why* you are reading. Are you reading to find out when a bus **arrives** or when it **departs?** Knowing your **purpose** will make it easier to find the information you need.

Reading Purpose

Real-world Writing	Reading Purpose
1. Train Schedule	To find out when the next train arrives
2. Instructions	To learn how to put something together

VOCABULARY

menu—list of food served or available for a meal
schedule—a list of arrival and departure times. A bus schedule lists when the buses arrive and leave.
arrives—gets there
departs—leaves
purpose—a reason for doing something

STEP 2. SEE HOW THE INFORMATION IS ORGANIZED

Once you figure out your reading purpose, see how the writing is **organized.** First, read the heading or title. Then, skim the entire text. Look for any of these **features:**

Words in large or boldface type	Bulleted items	Headings	Numbered lists (1, 2, 3, . . .)	Diagrams or graphics	Rows or columns

Once you know how the information is organized, you can find what you're looking for quickly.

STEP 3. FIND WHAT YOU NEED TO KNOW

Real-world writing often contains more information than you need. When you're searching for **specific** information, you don't have to read the entire text. You can skim to help you quickly find the information you need. When you skim, you skip what you don't need and focus only on the information you do need. To skim, follow these steps.

- Let your eyes roam down the page.
- Watch for titles, headings, and repeated words.
- Look at diagrams or sketches. They, too, can give key information.

STEP 4. USE WHAT YOU LEARNED

As a final step, *use* what you learned. Catch the train, bake the cake, or put together the bike. Keep the text handy in case you need to reread a detail or step you missed.

(TALK AND SHARE) **Review with a partner the 4 steps for reading real-world writing. Quiz each other to see if you know the steps.**

> **Language Notes**
>
> **Verb Phrases**
> These phrases have special meanings.
>
> ☐ **find out:** learn about or discover
>
> ☐ **figure out:** work to understand. As you *figure out* something, you think about it and begin to understand it.

Reading a Train Schedule

Follow the 4 steps when you read a train schedule.
1) Figure out what you want to find. For example, imagine that you're **volunteering** at an animal shelter on Howard Street. You need to find out when the next train is leaving for Howard after 3:15 P.M. on a Monday.

2) See how the schedule is organized. The largest heading at the top says "Weekday." There are also two large headings above each part. The schedule is organized by rows that show the times trains leave each hour.

3) Skim to find the information you need. Go to the "To Howard" heading. Then skim down to the 3 P.M. row. You'll find that the next train after 3:15 leaves at 3:17 P.M. Check the time again just to be sure that you read it correctly.

4) Now you can use what you learned to catch the 3:17 P.M. train to Howard Street.

Headings

Information for reading purpose

WEEKDAY

To Howard

Trains leave at minutes shown past each hour.

Midn	Tue-Fri: 06 12 20 26 33 41 48 57 / Mon only: 00 07 14 20 27 34 42 49 58
1am	Tue-Fri: 06 16 26 36 46 56 / Mon only: 07 17 27 37 47 57
2am	Tue-Fri: 06 16 26 36 48 / Mon only: 09 24 39 54
3am	Tue-Fri: 03 18 33 48 / Mon only: 09 24 39 54
4am	03 18 28 35 43 50 58
5am	05 13 20 28 35 43 50 58
6am	05 13 20 28 35 43 50 56
7am	04 12 19 25 31 37 42 48 53 58
8am	03 08 13 18 23 28 33 38 42 47 51 56
9am	01 06 11 16 21 26 31 36 41 46 51 57
10am	03 09 15 20 25 31 37 43 49 55
11am	03 10 18 25 33 40 48 55
Noon	03 10 18 25 33 40 48 55
1pm	03 10 18 25 33 40 48 55
2pm	03 10 18 25 33 40 48 55
3pm	03 10 17 25 32 39 46 52 58
4pm	04 10 16 22 28 34 39 45 50 55
5pm	01 06 10 15 19 24 28 32 36 39 42 45 48 51 54 57
6pm	00 03 07 10 14 17 21 25 29 34 38 43 47 52 56
7pm	01 05 10 15 20 25 30 35 41 47 51 56
8pm	01 07 14 21 29 36 44 51 59
9pm	06 14 21 29 36 44 51 59
10pm	06 14 21 29 36 44 51 59
11pm	06 14 21 29 36 44 51 59

To 95/Dan Ryan

Trains leave at minutes shown past each hour.

Midn	06 13 21 28 36 43 51 58
1am	06 14 21 29 36 44 55
2am	05 17 30 45
3am	00 15 32 47
4am	02 17 32 47
5am	02 14 26 38 49
6am	00 10 20 30 40 50
7am	00 10 20 30 40 50
8am	00 10 20 30 40 50
9am	00 08 15 23 30 38 45 53
10am	00 08 15 23 30 38 45 53
11am	00 08 15 23 31 38 46 53
Noon	01 08 16 23 31 38 46 53
1pm	01 08 16 23 31 38 46 53
2pm	01 08 16 23 31 38 46 53
3pm	01 08 16 23 31 38 46 53
4pm	01 08 16 23 31 38 46 53
5pm	01 08 16 23 31 38 46 53
6pm	01 08 16 26 36 46 56
7pm	06 16 26 36 46 56
8pm	06 16 26 36 46 56
9pm	06 16 26 36 46 56
10pm	06 16 26 36 46 56
11pm	06 16 26 33 38 44 50 58

For trains after midnight on weekday nights, see Saturday schedule.

Tips for Reading Schedules

Schedules contain a lot of information—more than you probably need to know. For example, the train schedule includes trains leaving at 5 A.M. You probably will never need to ride a train that early in the morning! But, the writer of the schedule doesn't know who is going to read it and puts in all of the information so anyone can use it.

Here are some useful tips for finding what you need.

Tip #1: Use a Highlighter
Use a highlighter to mark information that meets your purpose. Remember to ignore any information that has nothing to do with what you need.

Tip #2: Pay Attention to Headings
Headings point out the key parts. Pay attention to headings that have to do with the information you need. Skip over any lists, columns, or rows that aren't what you need.

Tip #3: Learn the Jargon
Sometimes real-world writing contains a lot of jargon. *Jargon* is the special language of different professions. Use **context clues** to help you find the meaning.

(TALK AND SHARE) **Look at the train schedule again. Come up with a new reading purpose. Then complete each step with a partner.**

VOCABULARY
context clues—words or phrases that surround a word and help you know what the word means

Reading Instructions

Instructions are another common type of real-world writing. If you buy a new cell phone, bicycle, or bookshelf, it will probably come with instructions. Read the instructions slowly and carefully.

Before you start reading them, figure out your reading purpose. If your printer ran out of ink, your purpose would be to learn how to change the ink.

Look to see how the information is organized. The instructions here are in a list numbered 1 and 2.

Next, find the information you need to know. Here steps 1 and 2 show you how to change the ink. Now use what you learned. Note that *protective cap* is jargon. You may not know what it is, but the labeled picture will help you.

❶ Peel back the orange tab and completely remove the plastic wrapper from the Yellow Ink Tank (BCI-6Y).

❷ Twist off and discard the orange protective cap.

📖 **NOTE:** To avoid spilling ink, never press on the sides of an ink tank.

Protective cap

Reading Tip

Following Instructions

Sometimes instructions are hard to follow. When you begin, make sure you *read the instructions all the way through* before you start to follow them. Also, make sure you have the instructions and all the parts before you start. If you weren't able to finish what you set out to do, go back and see where you went wrong. Try doing these two things.

1. Ask Someone for Help

Sometimes it's easier to put something together when someone reads the instructions aloud to you. Ask a friend or teacher to read each step aloud as you do it. Or give them the directions and ask them to look at what you did. They might be able to see what you missed.

2. Check Off the Steps

When there are a lot of steps, it's easy to skip one or do them in the wrong order by accident. You can avoid skipping steps by checking them off as you complete them.

VOCABULARY
instructions—steps that explain how to do something

Tips for Reading Instructions

Instructions can be hard to understand if you read through them quickly. It's important to read instructions very closely, step by step and line by line. Here are some tips to follow.

1. Highlight or Mark
Use a highlighter or pencil to mark important words and phrases.

2. Think Aloud
Think about each step as you read it aloud. It helps to put the instructions in your own words.

3. Reread
Rereading is something you should do often with instructions. Go back and reread the steps as often as you need.

4. Go Step by Step
Steps are there for a reason—you need to do them one by one and in order. Read each step carefully. Make sure you finish it before moving on to the next step.

5. Read the Diagrams
Sometimes instructions will include diagrams or pictures. The labels point to important parts and steps so that you know what to do.

6. Ask Yourself Questions
As you carry out each step, ask yourself such questions as, "Did it work?" or "Did I do that step correctly?"

(TALK AND SHARE) **With a partner, read the 6 tips above for reading instructions. Then take turns trying them out on some instructions.**

Summary

Schedules, maps, and instructions are all types of real-world writing. To read real-world writing, first know your purpose. Then, figure out how the writing is organized. Next, find the information you need. Last, use what you learned.

Comparing and Contrasting

Comparing and Contrasting Information

Sometimes you may need to compare one piece of real-world writing to another. For example, you might need to compare two sets of instructions to see which makes more sense. A Venn Diagram like the one below can help.

Venn Diagram

Recycling Instructions "A"
Label each bin.

Both
• Separate paper, plastic, and glass.
• Put each kind in its own recycling bin.
• Take the bins out on trash day.

Recycling Instructions "B"
• Wash out bottles before placing them in the bin.
• If your city doesn't pick up recycled products at your home, take the bins to the nearest recycling center.

"B" gives more complete instructions.

Practice Comparing and Contrasting

1. Tell Make a list of all the real-world writing you've read today. Read aloud your list to a partner. Then put both of your lists in a Venn Diagram. Talk about how the kinds of real-world writing are alike and different.

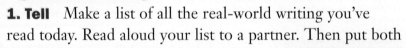

2. Write Compare two kinds of real-world writing. Fill out a Venn Diagram. Then write 3 to 4 sentences comparing how they are alike and different. Exchange papers with a partner and check each other's writing.

Check Your Writing

Make sure you

☐ Use complete sentences.

☐ Use a period at the end of each sentence.

☐ Spell all the words correctly.

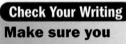

Activities

Grammar Spotlight

Questions with *how* *How* has many uses. It is often used with describing words, such as *funny*, *pretty*, *quickly*, *useful*, and *carefully*. When you use *how* and a describing word in a question, keep the two words together.

Examples

How useful were the instructions?

How carefully did I recycle?

Now write two questions of your own using *how*. Use the sentences above as models.

Oral Language

Say a Chant to Remember   With your partner, chant these lines.

Real-world writing, like a menu or a map,
Is easy to read if you follow a plan.
First, decide what you want to find.
Then, look at how the text is organized.
Skim to find what you need.
Use what you learned, and you'll succeed.

Partner Practice

Write Instructions   Choose something you know how to use, such as a bike or TV. Write instructions for it. Make sure you draw a picture with each step. Then give your instructions to your partner. Did the instructions make sense? What could you add to make them clearer?

Hands On

Skimming   With a partner, collect one or two sets of instructions. Read them and highlight the most important parts in them. Then talk with your partner about what you were skimming for when you highlighted the instructions.

Persuasive

Writing

Here you'll learn about persuasive writing. You'll also learn how to support an opinion and practice persuading others to your viewpoint.

Building Background

▲ I gave a great speech once. When I finished, a lot of people agreed with me!

■ **How would you describe this person and what he's doing?**

■ **What do you think he's saying?**

■ **If you gave a speech, what would you say?**

Persuasive writing is meant to change the way a reader thinks or acts. First, the author states a viewpoint, or opinion, about a topic. Then, the author supports it with facts and details and answers opposing viewpoints.

1 **The author states a viewpoint, or opinion.**

from *Malcolm X: By Any Means Necessary*
by Walter Dean Myers

Topic

Malcolm scared America. The fear he generated might well have cost him his life. But in scaring America, in bringing it face-to-face with the realities of our society in the sixties, he left it a better place.

Viewpoint

2 **The author supports the opinion.**

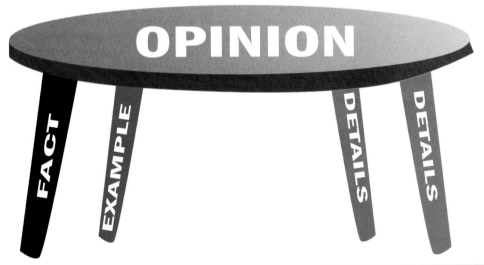

OPINION

FACT EXAMPLE DETAILS DETAILS

Key Concepts

persuasive   **persuasive writing**   **opinion**   **fact**

The word **persuasive** comes from *persuade*. To persuade means "to cause someone to believe something." **Persuasive writing** tries to change the way a reader thinks or acts. It starts with an **opinion,** or personal judgment or belief. Then it supports the opinion with evidence, facts, examples, and details. A **fact** is something that can be proved true or real.

Not persuasive writing

Persuasive writing

Propaganda Techniques

Watch out for the ways some writers try to persuade you.

Jumping on the Bandwagon

These words give you the idea that since everyone else does or thinks something, it must be good.

Loaded Words

These strong words make people feel strong emotions or reactions.

Supporting an Opinion

Every time you give an opinion in writing, you should give good, strong details to support it. Choose details that convince the reader that your opinion is correct.

Note how 4 details here support Myers's opinion: Malcolm X made America a better place.

from *Malcolm X: By Any Means Necessary*
by Walter Dean Myers

Malcolm showed that one person, riding the crest of social discontent, could still [1] inspire great masses of people. He [2] displayed the awesome potential of a portion of black America that many thought would sleep forever and [3] proved that black docility was a thing of the past. Malcolm and the Nation of Islam drove the civil rights movement, gave it the dark side that many feared it might have. It was Malcolm who said to black Americans that they did not always have to hide their pain, or their outrage. It was Malcolm who [4] claimed the imagination of young black men as no one had since Frederick Douglass had called them to fight in the Civil War.

Exaggeration

This way of saying something makes things seem much better or worse than they really are.

Straw Man

This kind of argument makes another opinion or point of view so simple that it seems stupid. It becomes as easy to knock down as a man made of straw.

Persuasive Writing

Persuasive writing tries to convince you to do, say, or think something. Usually persuasive writing has 3 parts: a viewpoint, supporting details, and an opposing viewpoint.

The most beautiful thing that ever happened to horsepower

It steals the show wherever you go—the long, clean, powerful 1958 Edsel

1958 **EDSEL**

▲ Ads often persuade people to buy a product, such as a car.

Kinds of Persuasive Writing

Among other things, persuasive writing can ask you to

- Accept an opinion
- Support a cause
- Change your mind
- Spend money

To *persuade* means "to cause you to do something." To change someone's mind, a writer needs to give strong reasons that a reader will believe.

You might not always know when you read persuasive writing, but it is all around you. Here are some common kinds of persuasive writing.

AD

An ad persuades you to buy something.

SPEECH

A speech often persuades you to believe in a **cause,** person, or idea.

"I have a dream..."

Martin Luther King, Jr., gives a speech. ▶

VOCABULARY
cause—an idea or goal that many people want to see happen

EDITORIAL

An **editorial** is a newspaper or magazine article that persuades you to believe an opinion about events in the news.

LETTER OF COMPLAINT

A letter of **complaint** tries to persuade a company to fix a problem with a product.

All of these types of writing try to change what people think. They make an argument that starts with an opinion and then gives reasons to support it.

TALK AND SHARE With your partner, talk about types of persuasive writing you have seen and remember. Discuss what the writer was trying to persuade you to do.

September 25, 2003
The Hartford Post

Editorials

Once Again, It's Guns or Butter

As in past eras, the government must choose whether to spend money on the military or on things the people need. We believe Washington is making the wrong decision. It is spending too much money on the military and not enough on problems at home. More people are losing their jobs every day. More people are living in poverty. Look around you, Congress! Fix what needs fixing.

Sincerely,
John Lee

All-American Bicycles
6680 Hawthorne Ave.
Dayton, OH 45414

Dear Sir or Madam:

Your product, the GT500, does not work as promised in the instructions. The chain comes off every time I shift from 4th to 5th gear! Please tell me how to fix this problem, or refund my money.

Sincerely,
Stanislav Minsky
Stanislav Minsky

Three Parts of an Argument

A good argument has 3 parts.

1. Opinion or viewpoint   2. Supporting details

3. Opposing viewpoint

Good persuasive writing includes all 3 parts.

THE VIEWPOINT

The **viewpoint,** or opinion, is the author's statement of belief about the topic.

Topic	Viewpoint
Malcolm X	Malcolm X left America a better place than it was when he was born.

▼ Malcolm X waits to speak at a meeting in Washington, D.C.

SUPPORTING DETAILS

Supporting details are the facts, figures, and examples the writer uses to support his or her viewpoint. The supporting details help show or **convince** the reader that what the writer says is true. Organize your viewpoint and details in a Viewpoint and Evidence Organizer.

Viewpoint and Evidence Organizer

Topic
Malcolm X

Viewpoint
Malcolm X left America a better place than it was when he was born.

Detail
He inspired great masses of people.

Detail
He displayed the potential of the people.

Detail
He claimed the imagination of young African Americans.

VOCABULARY

viewpoint—an opinion or something a person believes

supporting details—examples or reasons that explain an opinion or viewpoint

convince—cause someone to believe or feel certain about

OPPOSING VIEWPOINT

Every argument has two sides. Good writers think about how readers might feel about their opinions. They try to answer any **objections** in advance. Then readers know the writers have thought carefully about their viewpoint because they consider opposing viewpoints.

For example, look at how the author here defends his viewpoint against **opposing** viewpoints that readers might have.

▲ An audience listens to Malcolm X's speech.

from *Malcolm X: By Any Means Necessary* by Walter Dean Myers

To select one person, or even one group of people, as being **pivotal** to the sixties is **risky.** There were many people who were important in that exciting time in American history. Who is best remembered? Whose words have best stood the test of time? Whose actions most defined the **temper** of the times as we remember that time, and that temper, from the present? For many it was a man named Malcolm X.

Opposing viewpoint

Author's response

Language Notes

Multiple Meanings
This word has more than one meaning.

■ **stood**
1. was in an upright position
2. put up with
3. continued to be true. "Malcolm X's words *stood* the test of time" because their importance and meaning did not change over time.

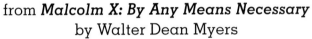

TALK AND SHARE **Explain the 3 parts of an argument to your partner.**

VOCABULARY
objections—reasons *not* to believe or support an opinion
opposing—against or on the other side; on the opposite side
pivotal—very important, central
risky—dangerous
temper—the feeling or attitude of a person or point in time

Writing a Persuasive Paragraph

Now you are ready to write a persuasive paragraph of your own. Follow these steps to plan your paragraph.

Topic

Martin Luther King, Jr.

STEP 1. CHOOSE YOUR TOPIC

First, figure out what you want to write about. Since your goal is to convince readers to accept your viewpoint, you'll want to choose a topic about which you have strong feelings.

STEP 2. FORM AN OPINION

Next, decide on your viewpoint. Ask yourself, "How do I feel about the topic?" This formula can help.

Topic
+
How I feel about the topic
=
My viewpoint

My Viewpoint

Dr. Martin Luther King, Jr.

+

I feel that he did more for people than anyone else.

=

Dr. Martin Luther King, Jr., was the most important leader of the 20th century.

STEP 3. SUPPORT IT

Your third step is to gather support for your argument. Try to support your viewpoint with facts and details and defend it against any opposing viewpoints.

Topic: Dr. Martin Luther King, Jr.

Viewpoint: Dr. Martin Luther King, Jr., was the most important leader of the 20th century.

Detail: He led amazing civil rights marches.

Detail: He showed America how important it is to have a dream.

Detail: His message of peace lives on today.

Detail: He worked for the rights of people everywhere.

STEP 4. DRAFT YOUR PARAGRAPH

After planning your paragraph, write a draft of it. State your viewpoint, or opinion, in the first sentence. Then support your opinion with two or more sentences that tell why you believe it. Finally, tell what the opposing viewpoint is, and give reasons why your reader should not believe it.

STEP 5. REVISE, EDIT, AND PROOFREAD

Put your writing aside once you have finished it. Come back to it another day. As you read it again, ask yourself what you can add to make it better.

- Did I give strong facts, details, and examples?

- Did I have an answer for people who don't agree with me?

- Did I end with a strong statement?

TALK AND SHARE With your partner, go over the steps to writing a persuasive paragraph. Make a chart or poster of the steps.

Summary

Persuasive writing tries to change the way a reader thinks or acts. As the writer, you first state your viewpoint, or opinion, about a topic. Then you support it with examples, facts, and details and answer an opposing viewpoint.

Writing Tip

Using the Computer to Write

Do you handwrite your first drafts, or do you write on the computer? If you write on the computer, here are some tips to keep in mind.

- Create an organizer before you begin writing your first draft.

- Get your ideas down first. Leave problems about how the paper looks for later.

- Save your work as you go.

- As a final step, print a copy of your work. Then read and proofread it with a pencil. Computer spell-check programs can be helpful, but they do not catch every error.

Persuading

Persuading Others to Your Viewpoint

Planning is key to persuading. Always begin by organizing your thoughts. Choose a topic, decide your viewpoint, gather details, and prepare for the opposing argument. An organizer like this one can help.

Persuasive Paragraph Organizer

Topic	Viewpoint	Support for Viewpoint
Model teacher	Mr. Bloom is a model teacher because he relates to us.	1. He helps all of his students who want to learn.
		2. He relates really well to young people.
	Opposing Viewpoint	3. He gives up a lot of free time to help us.
	Some people might say he is just too easy on us.	4. He is both a good friend and a good teacher.

Practice Persuading

1. Create Share with your partner one of your opinions about someone you know who makes a difference. First, give your viewpoint, or opinion. Then, give at least two reasons why you believe what you do. Include an answer to people who don't agree with you. Create an organizer like the one above.

2. Write How would you change your school? First, write your opinion. Then, write at least two reasons why you feel the way you do. Next, draft a persuasive paragraph. Ask your partner to read it after you are finished. Then check each other's paragraphs. Use the revising checklist to improve your paragraph.

Check Your Writing
Make sure you

- ☐ Use complete sentences.
- ☐ Use a period at the end of each sentence.
- ☐ Spell all the words correctly.

Activities

Grammar Spotlight

Count and Noncount Nouns *Count nouns* have both singular and plural forms. *Noncount nouns* have only one form. You don't have to make noncount nouns plural.

Count Nouns

Singular	Plural	Remember
a teacher	teachers	• Use *a*, *an,* or *the* with singular count nouns.
an advisor	advisors	• Add s or es to form plural count nouns.

Noncount Nouns

Examples	Remember
clothing	• Noncount nouns have only one form.
mail	• You don't use *a* or *an*.
homework	• You don't make them plural.

With a partner, try to think of one count noun and one noncount noun. Use each in a sentence.

Hands On

Create a Checklist Make a list of everything a good persuasive paragraph should have. Have your partner do the same. Then, compare your list with the list your partner made. Decide on the 4 or 5 best items. Then make a poster called "Checklist for Writing a Persuasive Paragraph." After you finish, hang your poster in the classroom. Talk together about what it shows.

Partner Practice

Support That Point With a partner, think of two of your strongest opinions on any subject. Write your opinions on strips of paper. Then, exchange your opinions with another group. Write two sentences in support of each opinion from the other group. Finally, explain the two opinions and support for them to the other group.

Writing
Letters

Here you'll learn about writing different kinds of letters. You'll also learn how to proofread and practice responding to a situation.

Building Background

▲ My grandmother lives in Ecuador. I write her letters.

■ **How would you describe what's happening here?**

■ **Have you ever written a letter?**

■ **What does this remind you of?**

You write different kinds of letters, depending on your purpose for writing. To friends, you write friendly letters or email. For serious purposes, you write business letters or formal emails.

Read this sample letter. How do you know it is a business letter?

Heading

1211 Central Ave.
Willow Grove, UT 84720
January 13, 2005

Inside address

Organization for a Better World
2321 King's Way
Salt Lake City, UT 84101

Salutation

Dear Organization for a Better World:

I am researching where our class might start a program to help students of different cultures get along better.

Could you please send information about your organization? Also, I wondered if you work with other school groups.

Thank you in advance for your help.

Body

Closing

Sincerely,

Jasel Trivedi

Signature

Jasel Trivedi

Key Concepts

Your **purpose** for writing is the reason you are doing it. The person you are writing to—your **audience**—often determines your purpose. Business letters are **formal**—they are proper and follow all the rules. Friendly letters are **informal**. They are freer and follow fewer rules.

Purpose = reason for doing something

1211 Central Ave.
Willow Grove, UT 84720
January 13, 2005

Organization for a Better World
2321 King's Way
Salt Lake City, UT 84101

Dear Organization for a Better World:

I am researching where our class might start a program to help students of different cultures get along better.

Could you please send information about your organization? Also, I wondered if you work with other school groups.

Thank you in advance for your help.

Sincerely,

Jasel Trivedi

Jasel Trivedi

Formal

Audience

377 Sepulveda Blvd.
Los Angeles, CA 90045
September 22, 2004

Dear Tia Carmen,

I am writing today from our new home! Mamá and Papá found us a nice house with three big bedrooms. Tomás and I can walk to school, and Mamá can walk to the grocery store. Everything is very close.

I like living in Los Angeles, but I miss you so much. Mamá says you will come for my birthday in December. That would be so great!

Love,

Rosario

Informal

Punctuating and Capitalizing Letters

1. Date
- This is the date you wrote the letter.
- Capitalize the month and put a comma between the day and the year.

2. Inside Address
- This is who you're writing to and their address. Capitalize the name of the street, city, and state.
- Put a comma after the city name.

3. Greeting, or Salutation
- Capitalize the first letter of the greeting and the name of the person or organization to which you are writing.
- End with a colon.

1. January 13, 2005

2. Organization for a Better World
2321 King's Way
Salt Lake City, UT 84101

3. Dear Organization for a Better World:

Skill Building

Proofreading Your Writing

Any letter you write should be free of spelling, grammatical, and punctuation errors. For business letters, this is especially true. A checklist like this one can help you proofread the letters you write.

When you proofread, touch each sentence with your finger. Ask yourself the questions in the checklist as you do.

Letter-writing Checklist
- ❏ Did I capitalize correctly in the heading, inside address, salutation, and closing?
- ❏ Did I use commas properly in the date and address?
- ❏ Did I capitalize the beginning of each sentence?
- ❏ Did I put a period, question mark, or exclamation mark at the end of each sentence?
- ❏ Did I spell every word correctly?
- ❏ Is my letter written as neatly as possible?

4. Body
- Add space between each paragraph.
- Capitalize the first word of each sentence and put punctuation at the end of each sentence.

4.

I am researching where our class might start a program to help students of different cultures get along better.

Could you please send information about your organization? Also, I wondered if you work with other school groups.

Thank you in advance for your help.

5. Closing
- Capitalize the first letter of the first word used to say goodbye.
- Put a comma after the last word.

5. Sincerely,

6. *Jasel Trivedi*

Jasel Trivedi

6. Signature
- Capitalize your first and last name.

Writing Letters

▲ From top: People who made a difference: César Chávez, Thurgood Marshall, and Zora Neale Hurston

You write different kinds of letters, depending on your purpose. You write friendly letters and email to friends. For business or important matters, you write a business letter or formal email.

Writing Friendly Letters

The purpose of a friendly letter is to share information with family and friends. A friendly letter has 5 parts.

1. HEADING

This is your address and the date. Capitalize the names of streets, cities, states, and countries.

2. GREETING

Here you address the person you are writing. You begin *Dear* with a capital letter and end with a comma after the person's name. The greeting is sometimes called the **salutation.**

3. BODY

This is the main part of your letter. It is the message and tells what you want to say. Indent each paragraph of the body of your letter. Unlike business letters, friendly letters don't need a space between each paragraph.

4. CLOSING

This part ends the letter. It usually includes a phrase like "Best wishes," "Your friend," or **"Sincerely."** Capitalize the greeting and put a comma after it.

5. SIGNATURE

This is where you sign your name.

Now read the friendly letter on the next page. Notice how the writer included each of the 5 parts of a friendly letter.

VOCABULARY
salutation—a greeting or hello
sincerely—really, honestly. *Sincerely* is a polite way to end a letter.

Friendly Letter

Heading

377 Sepulveda Blvd.
Los Angeles, CA 90045
September 22, 2004

Greeting

Dear Tia Carmen,

I am writing today from our new home! Mamá and Papá found us a nice house with three big bedrooms. Tomás and I can walk to school, and Mamá can walk to the grocery store. Everything is very close.

I like living in Los Angeles, but I miss you so much. Mamá says you will come for my birthday in December. That would be so great!

Body

Closing

Love,

Rosario

Signature

▲ Tia Carmen

TALK AND SHARE With your partner, talk about a friendly letter you could write. Then explain what you would write in each of the 5 parts of the letter.

Writing an Email

An **email** is sent with a computer over the **Internet.** It is called email because it is "electronic" mail. Like a letter, an email usually has a heading, greeting, body, closing, and signature.

Email

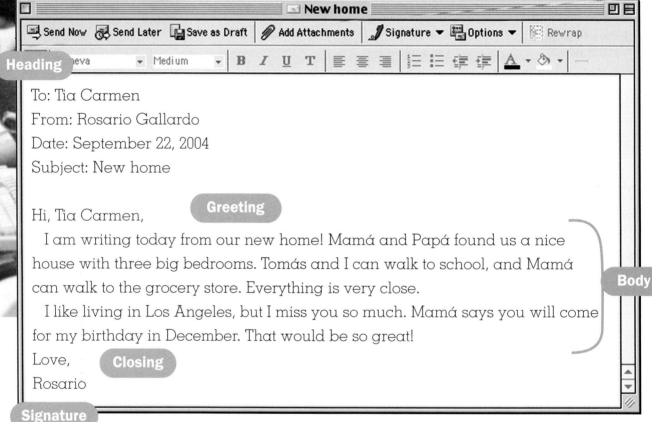

Heading

To: Tia Carmen
From: Rosario Gallardo
Date: September 22, 2004
Subject: New home

Greeting

Hi, Tia Carmen,

I am writing today from our new home! Mamá and Papá found us a nice house with three big bedrooms. Tomás and I can walk to school, and Mamá can walk to the grocery store. Everything is very close.

I like living in Los Angeles, but I miss you so much. Mamá says you will come for my birthday in December. That would be so great!

Body

Love,

Closing

Rosario

Signature

Whether you write a formal or an informal email depends on your audience and purpose. Your *audience* is the person or persons to whom you are writing. Your *purpose* is the reason you are writing. Together they help you know how formal your email needs to be. An email can be friendly, like the one above, or formal like a business letter. It depends on your purpose for writing.

TALK AND SHARE With a partner, talk about someone to whom you might write an email and why.

VOCABULARY

email—a letter sent by computer over the Internet
Internet—a system that connects computers around the world and allows them to send messages to each other

Writing Business Letters

For serious or important matters, you will want to write a formal kind of letter. The form of the letter lets people who read it see that your purpose is serious.

For example, when you are applying for a job, you write a formal business letter.

Job Application Letter

351 1st Street
Morrison, IL 61021
August 13, 2004

Rock River Food Service
120 River Drive
Rockton, IL 61043

Dear Food Services Manager:

I am replying to your ad last week in *The County Observer* for a bakery manager.

The position of manager is one I am well qualified to handle. My most recent position was working in the bakery at Rockton Foods. After two years there, I feel I'm ready to manage a bakery of my own.

Please consider my resume and application. I look forward to speaking with you more about this position.

Sincerely,

Hector Martínez

Hector Martínez

Language Notes

Homophones
These words sound alike, but they have different spellings and meanings.

- **here's:** here is
- **hears:** receives sound through the ears (third-person present tense)

- **would:** the past tense of *will*
- **wood:** a material that comes from trees

WRITING A LETTER OF COMPLAINT

You may also want to write to a company about a product. What if you bought a product and it broke right away? You might want to write to the company. Here's what you would do.

1. First, state the problem and what caused it.

2. Next, tell what you want the company to do about the problem. This is called the **recommendation.**

3. Then, check to be sure your letter is honest and nice. (This will show the reader that you are a fair person.)

Letter of Complaint

Heading

351 81st Street
New York, NY 11377
August 13, 2004

Inside address

Big Fun Adventure Park
100 Universal Drive
Trenton, NJ 08202

Salutation

Dear Park Manager:

Problem

Last week my family and I visited your theme park. We had a blast. But, I got stuck on two rides, the "Thriller" and the Ferris wheel.

The rides do not seem very safe if they keep breaking. I think you should have people fix the rides and then check them once or twice a day. Small children could get hurt.

Recommendation

Please make the rides at the park safe.

Sincerely,

Closing and signature

Amy Johnson
Amy Johnson

VOCABULARY
recommendation—a suggestion about what to do

WRITING A LETTER OF OPINION

Write a letter of opinion, or an editorial, when you want to share your feelings about an **issue.** Follow these steps.

1. First, explain the issue you are writing about.

2. Next, state your opinion or feelings about it.

3. Support your opinion with facts and examples.

4. Finish with your recommendation of what to do.

Letter of Opinion

To the Editors:

I am writing to tell about a problem in our neighborhood park. For the last two months, the trash has not been picked up. The garbage is piling up around the trash cans, and the playground is a mess.

I think the mayor should have the city pick up the trash at least once every week.

Sincerely yours,

Marvin Jones

Marvin Jones

Writing Tip

Using a Search Engine

Search engines are sites on the Internet that help you find information you need. You can use a search engine to find the name of a company or product. You can use it to learn about an issue or an organization. In fact, you can use a search engine to learn about almost anything.

Follow these steps when you use a search engine:

1. Type in a few key words about your topic.

2. The search engine will quickly list links to websites related to your topic. Look closely at the links before clicking on any.

3. Click on the links that look like they have the best information about your topic.

TALK AND SHARE **Talk about one kind of business letter you could write. Tell a partner what you would say in your letter.**

Summary

Whether you write a friendly letter, an email, or a formal business letter depends on your purpose and audience. For friends and family, write friendly letters. For serious purposes, write business letters.

VOCABULARY

issue—something that is discussed or argued about

Responding

Responding to a Situation

At some time, you will be asked to respond to some literature, an issue, or a situation. You probably will not have a lot of time to plan ahead. When you respond, you express your personal feelings about a subject. Use a Web like the one below to help you quickly gather your thoughts.

Web

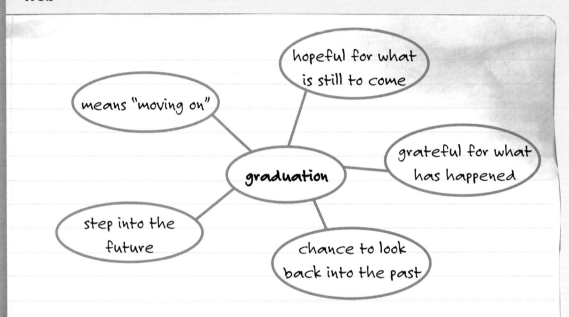

Practice Responding

1. Tell Get together with a small group. On a slip of paper, have each person write a topic about a new change, such as "graduation" or "new job." Put the topics into a bowl. Everybody reaches in and pulls out a topic. Then respond for one minute on what that topic means to you. Start by making a Web.

2. Write With a partner, think of an issue you care about. Then write a business letter of opinion about that issue. Have your partner read it and check it using the Check Your Writing checklist. After you have revised and edited each other's letters, send them to the school or local newspaper to share your opinion.

Check Your Writing
Make sure you

- Use complete sentences.
- Use a period at the end of each sentence.
- Spell all the words correctly.

Activities

Grammar Spotlight

Using *may*, *might*, and *will*   *May* and *might* mean the same thing. Use them to say something is possible in the future. Use *will* to show you are certain about the future.

Example	Using *may* or *might* or *will*	Meaning
My aunt	*will visit.*	The speaker is 100% sure.
My aunt	*might visit.* *may visit.*	The speaker says it's possible.

First, write a sentence using *will*. Then write a sentence using *may* and another sentence using *might*.

Oral Language

Read Aloud   With a partner, choose one of the letters in the lesson. Read aloud the letter to your partner. Then ask your partner to respond to the letter as if it were written to him or her. Switch roles and have your partner read aloud. Then you respond to the letter your partner reads.

Hands On

Model Letter Poster   With a partner, create a poster showing the parts of either a friendly letter or a business letter. First, write a model letter. Then, label the parts of the letter. Put the words that need to be capitalized in red. Add the punctuation in blue so it stands out. Then display the poster in the classroom to help everyone remember what to include.

Partner Practice

Be a Proofreader   Write part of a friendly letter or business letter. For example, write just the inside address. Put at least one mistake in what you write. Then ask your partner to proofread it using the checklist on page 335. Ask your partner to make the changes needed using proofreader's marks. Do the same for your partner's letter.

More
Parts of Speech

Here you'll learn about more parts of speech, or the ways that words work in sentences. You'll also learn how to build your vocabulary and practice persuading your audience.

▲ Someday I hope to do something important to help people, too.

■ **How would you describe what's going on here?**

■ **What words best tell what is happening?**

■ **How does this make you feel?**

The English language has 8 parts of speech. You already know 4 of them (nouns, verbs, adjectives, and adverbs). The other 4 are pronouns, prepositions, conjunctions, and interjections.

Parts of Speech

Part of Speech	Definition	Examples
1. Noun	a word that names a person, place, thing, or idea	*workers, California, grapes, fairness*
2. Verb	a word that shows action or links a subject to another word in a sentence	*lead, work, strike, dream, is*
3. Adjective	a word that describes a noun or pronoun	*one, green*
4. Adverb	a word that describes a verb, an adjective, or another adverb	*only, totally*
5. Pronoun	a word used in place of a noun	*I, you, he, she, it, we, they*
6. Preposition	a word that shows direction or location	*in, down, into, at*
7. Conjunction	a word that connects other words or groups of words	*and, but, so, because*
8. Interjection	a word (often set off by a comma or an exclamation mark) that shows strong emotion	*No! Wow!*

Key Concepts

parts of speech   function   gender   masculine   feminine

Parts of speech describe the ways words are used. The **function,** or use, of a word is called its part of speech. Some words also have **gender.** That means they show whether they are **masculine** (male) or **feminine** (female).

Gender

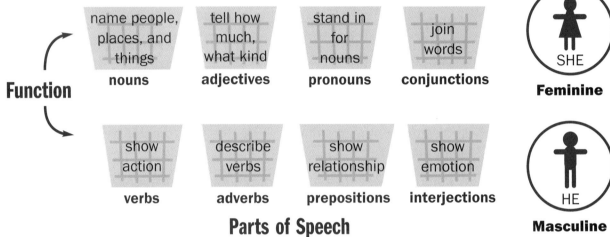

Function

name people, places, and things	tell how much, what kind	stand in for nouns	join words
nouns	**adjectives**	**pronouns**	**conjunctions**

show action	describe verbs	show relationship	show emotion
verbs	**adverbs**	**prepositions**	**interjections**

Parts of Speech

SHE
Feminine

HE
Masculine

Learning About Pronouns

Person
Refers to whether the person is speaking, is being spoken to, or is spoken about

1st person (I, we, me, us)

2nd person (you)

3rd person (he, she, it, him, her, his, they, them)

Case
Refers to the way the word is used

Subject (He gave a speech.)

Object (Dr. King gave him hope.)

Possessive (He gave his speech.)

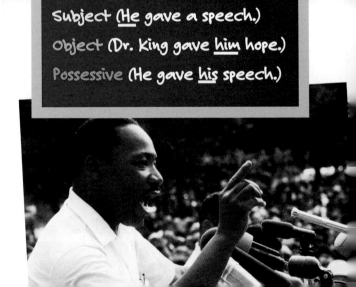

Building Vocabulary

Do you know ways to build your vocabulary? The best way to build vocabulary is to read a lot. Another good way is to start a vocabulary journal. Here's how to do it.

1. Read every day. Listen carefully as your teacher reads aloud too.

2. When you read or hear a new word, jot it down in your journal.

3. Look up the word in the dictionary, and write its meaning in your own words in your journal.

4. Write a sentence of your own using the new word.

5. Challenge yourself to use the new word at least once more that week. The more you use your new words, the sooner you will learn them.

> Vocabulary Journal
>
> **bountiful**—more than enough
>
> Example: The farmers hoped for a <u>bountiful</u> harvest.

Gender
Refers to whether it's male or female

> Masculine (<u>He</u> gave a speech.)
> Feminine (<u>She</u> gave a speech.)
> Neuter (<u>It</u> was moving.)

Number
Refers to singular (one) or plural (more than one)

> Singular (<u>She</u> gave her speech.)
> Plural (<u>They</u> gave their speeches.)

More Parts of Speech

Pronouns, prepositions, conjunctions, and interjections are 4 parts of speech you use every day. Learn about each of them. They can help you understand English.

Pronouns

A pronoun is a word used in place of a noun. There are a number of important types of pronouns.

Personal pronouns	Subject pronouns	Object pronouns	Possessive pronouns	Indefinite pronouns

PERSONAL PRONOUNS

When a personal pronoun replaces a noun, it must be just like the noun it replaces. A personal pronoun shows **number** (whether it's singular or plural). It shows **person** (whether it's first, second, or third person). It shows **gender** (whether it's masculine, feminine, or **neuter**). And, it shows **case** (whether it's used as a subject, object, or possessive).

she

he

VOCABULARY

number—how many of something; singular or plural

person—the point of view. The phrase "I think" is from a *first-person* point of view, and "you think" is from the *second-person* point of view. "He, she, or it thinks" is from the *third-person* point of view.

gender—whether something is masculine, feminine, or neuter

neuter—neither male nor female

case—the way a word functions, or works, in a sentence

PERSON, CASE, AND NUMBER

The case of a personal pronoun shows you that the pronoun is a subject pronoun, an object pronoun, or a possessive pronoun. Each of these pronouns works differently in a sentence, so each one has a different form.

Example

SUBJECT   OBJECT
Dr. King challenged Americans to work for America.

SUBJECT   OBJECT   POSSESSIVE
PRONOUN   PRONOUN   PRONOUN
He challenged us to work for our country.

In the second sentence, *he* replaces the noun *Dr. King*, the subject of the sentence. *He* is a subject pronoun. *Us* replaces *Americans*. *Us* is plural and an object pronoun because *Americans* is plural and a direct object. *Our* is a plural possessive pronoun, because it tells *whose* country.

Grammar Tip

Direct Objects

The *direct object* is the noun or pronoun that receives the action in a sentence *directly*. To find the direct object, ask yourself *what* or *who* received the action.

Example: *The marchers needed a leader.*

Whom did the marchers need? A *leader*. *Leader* is the direct object.

Personal Pronouns

Singular Pronouns

	SUBJECT PRONOUNS	OBJECT PRONOUNS	POSSESSIVE PRONOUNS	
FIRST PERSON	I	me	my	mine
SECOND PERSON	you	you	your	yours
THIRD PERSON	he	him	his	his
	she	her	her	hers
	it	it	its	its

Plural Pronouns

	SUBJECT PRONOUNS	OBJECT PRONOUNS	POSSESSIVE PRONOUNS	
FIRST PERSON	we	us	our	ours
SECOND PERSON	you	you	your	yours
THIRD PERSON	they	them	their	theirs

▲ People listen to Dr. King's speech in Washington.

TALK AND SHARE   **Explain to your partner what the terms** *number, person,* **and** *gender* **mean.**

▲ César Chávez asked Americans not to buy grapes until the farm owners agreed to make farm workers' lives better.

Common Indefinite Pronouns	
any	few
anybody	many
anyone	neither
anything	nobody
both	none
each	several
either	some
everybody	somebody
everyone	someone
everything	something

POSSESSIVE PRONOUNS

A possessive pronoun shows to whom or what something belongs. Possessive pronouns replace possessive nouns.

Examples

POSSESSIVE NOUN

1. *Maria's dream was to hear Chávez give a speech.*

POSSESSIVE PRONOUN

2. *Her dream was to hear Chávez give a speech.*

POSSESSIVE PRONOUN

3. *The dream [to hear Chávez give a speech] was hers.*

The possessive pronouns *my, your, her, his, its, our, your,* and *their* must be placed directly before the noun. The possessive pronouns *mine, yours, hers, his, its, ours, yours,* and *theirs* are used with a form of the verb *be.*

Examples

NOUN VERB POSSESSIVE PRONOUN

1. *The speech is ours.*

POSSESSIVE PRONOUN VERB NOUN

2. *Mine is the longest speech.*

INDEFINITE PRONOUNS

Indefinite pronouns are more general than personal pronouns. An indefinite pronoun does not tell you what it replaces.

Examples

INDEFINITE PRONOUN

1. *I have not seen any.*

INDEFINITE PRONOUN

2. *There were so many who came.*

INDEFINITE PRONOUN

3. *Chávez felt everyone could make a difference.*

(**TALK AND SHARE**) **To your partner, explain what personal pronouns are and what you know about them.**

Prepositions

A **preposition** is a word that shows direction, location, or how two things are related.

Example

As a child, César Chávez worked PREPOSITION *in the vineyards.*

The preposition *in* helps to show location. It tells where Chávez worked.

A **prepositional phrase** is made up of a preposition, the object of the preposition, and any **modifiers.** The object of a preposition is always a noun or pronoun. Modifiers tell more about the object.

Example

PREPOSITIONAL PHRASE
As a child, César Chávez worked in large vineyards.

PREPOSITION — OBJECT OF THE PREPOSITION

in large vineyards

MODIFIER

In the example, *in* introduces the prepositional phrase *in large vineyards. In* is the preposition, *vineyards* is the object of the preposition, and *large* is a modifier that limits the meaning of *vineyards.*

Common Prepositions

aboard	besides	out
about	beyond	over
above	by	past
across	down	through
after	during	throughout
against	for	to
along	from	under
at	in	until
before	inside	up
behind	into	upon
below	of	with
beneath	on	within
beside	onto	without

(**TALK AND SHARE**) **Give your partner one example of a preposition and one example of a prepositional phrase.**

VOCABULARY
preposition—a word that gives location, direction, or relationship
prepositional phrase—a group of words that includes a preposition, an object, and any modifiers
modifiers—words that limit the meaning of another word. In the sentence, *Chávez gave a strong speech*, the word *strong* limits the meaning of *speech* by telling what kind it was.

Common Conjunctions	
after	nor
although	or
and	since
as	so
as if	so that
as long as	that
as though	though
because	unless
before	until
but	**where**
for	whereas
if	while
in order	yet

Conjunctions

A **conjunction** connects words or groups of words. The most common conjunctions are *and*, *but*, and *or*.

> **Example**
> *Both Dr. King and César Chávez worked for workers' rights, but Dr. King was better known as a civil rights leader.*

A few conjunctions are always used in pairs: *either/or, neither/nor, not only/but also, both/and, whether/or,* and *as/so*.

> **Example**
> *Neither Dr. King nor César Chávez chose to use violence in their* **protests.**

Conjunctions help you put together two or more ideas or sentences. You can combine your sentences by using them.

> **Example**
> *Dr. King became famous as a civil rights leader. César Chávez led the farm workers' protests.*
>
> **Combined Example**
> *After Dr. King became famous as a civil rights leader, César Chávez led the farm workers' protests.*

Use conjunctions to help vary your sentences and make your writing more interesting to read.

(**TALK AND SHARE**) **First, explain to your partner what a conjunction is. Then, have your partner give you some examples of how to use conjunctions.**

Language Notes

Confusing Word Pairs
These words are easily mixed up.

- **where:** at, in, or to what place
- **wear:** have on the body

- **chose:** selected or picked out from a group (past tense)
- **choose:** select or pick out from a group (present tense)

VOCABULARY

conjunction—a word that connects words or groups of words in a sentence
protests—actions, such as marching and carrying signs, to persuade people that something is wrong

"Long live the Cause!" Chávez says in this poster. The cause was to help California grape workers. ▶

Interjections

An **interjection** is a word that shows emotion, such as *wow*, *gosh*, or *quiet!* Interjections sometimes interrupt a sentence, and they are usually followed by an exclamation mark.

> **Example**
> *Wow! That was a powerful speech.*
> *That's my coat you're standing on. Stop!*

TALK AND SHARE With a partner, make a list of 4 or 5 more interjections that you can think of. Then compare your list with those of others in your class.

A protester yells, "Strike!" ▼

Summary

Learn the parts of speech. The parts of speech can help you understand how the English language works. Pronouns, prepositions, conjunctions, and interjections are 4 of the 8 parts of speech.

VOCABULARY
interjection—a part of speech that interrupts or shows emotion

Persuading

Persuading Your Audience

Writing can be a powerful way to persuade, or convince, people to believe in your ideas. Good persuasive writing needs to be well organized. Use an Argument Chart to help you organize your writing. Note how this Argument Chart organizes the ideas needed to persuade someone.

Argument Chart

Viewpoint	Three Supporting Details	Opposing Viewpoint	Answer
Lincolnview needs more after-school programs for kids.	1. The programs help kids meet new people. 2. The programs help kids find new interests, such as art, sports, and music. 3. The programs are a way for older kids to become positive role models.	After-school programs cost a lot of money.	It costs more to fix the problems kids can get into when they have no place to go.

Practice Persuading

1. Tell   Get together with a small group of 3 or 4 people to talk about changes you would like to see made. Decide on one change that you all think is important. Then create an Argument Chart like the one above. First, talk through your viewpoint. Next, give 3 reasons as supporting details. Then, tell what the opposing viewpoint is. Last, tell how you would answer it.

2. Write   Write a paragraph about a change you would like to see. Begin by stating your viewpoint. Then list at least two supporting reasons. Think what the opposing viewpoint might be and be sure to include an answer to it. Use an Argument Chart to help you plan your writing. The words in the Word Bank may help you.

A poster persuades people to support farm workers. ▼

Word Bank

support

because

reason

but

disagree

Grammar Spotlight

Reflexive Pronouns Some pronouns refer back to the subject of the sentence. They are called *reflexive pronouns*. They end with *self* or *selves*.

Our nation continues to wage war upon its neighbors and upon <u>itself</u>.

In the example above, *nation* is the subject of the sentence. *Itself* is the reflexive pronoun. It reflects, or throws the action of the sentence back upon, the subject.

Reflexive Pronouns	Examples
myself	<u>I</u> introduced myself to Dr. King.
yourself	Listen to yourself as <u>you</u> speak.
himself	Did <u>he</u> hurt himself during the march?
herself	<u>She</u> taught herself to read.
itself	A <u>house</u> divided against itself cannot stand.
ourselves	<u>We</u> helped ourselves.
themselves	The <u>farm workers</u> stood up for themselves.

Now write 3 sentences of your own using reflexive pronouns.

Partner Practice

Pick a Pronoun With a partner, write all of the personal pronouns on file cards. Write the possessive pronouns, too. Then take turns drawing a card. Think of a sentence that uses the pronoun. Say the sentence to your partner. Then try to tell your partner what kind of pronoun you used.

Hands On

Get Involved In a small group, create a poster for a cause you believe should be supported. On your poster, include at least two pronouns and two resources that other people can use to get involved, such as websites, phone numbers, or the addresses of people they can write to. Present your poster to the class. Have each person in your group say why the cause is interesting, why it's important, or what others can do to help.

GLOSSARY

Pronunciation Key

ă	pat	ĭ	pit	ôr	core	ŭ	cut
ā	pay	ī	bite	oi	boy	ûr	urge
âr	care	îr	pier	ou	out	th	thin
ä	father	ŏ	pot	ŏŏ	took	*th*	*th*is
ě	pet	ō	toe	ŏŏr	lure	zh	vision
ē	be	ô	paw	ōō	boot	ə	about

accompany (ə kŭm′ pə nē) *v.* go along with or happen together with. *José asked Sara to* **accompany** *him to the movies.* (p. 243)

accomplishment (ə kŏm′ plĭsh mənt) *n.* something completed successfully. *Noemi's good grades were a big* **accomplishment.** (p. 304)

ache (āk) *v.* hurt. *My muscles* **ache** *from exercising so much.* (p. 248)

achievement (ə chēv′ mənt) *n.* something great you gain by working hard; success; accomplishment. *My most important* **achievement** *was earning my diploma.* (p. 141)

acid (ăs′ ĭd) *n.* a liquid that can burn. *The boy's skin is burned and stained from the* **acid** *in grapes he picks.* (p. 249)

active (ăk′ tĭv) *adj.* showing action. *If you stay* **active,** *you will be healthy.* (p. 235)

active reading thinking about what you are reading as you read. Active readers mark, question, react, predict, visualize, and clarify as they read. (p. 50)

activist (ăk′ tə vĭst) *n.* someone who works to make changes in society. *An* **activist** *talked to my class about keeping our planet clean.* (p. 304)

adjective (ăj′ ĭk tĭv) *n.* a word that describes a noun. In the phrase *tall woman, tall* is an adjective for *woman.* (p. 106)

admire (ăd mīr′) *v.* have a high opinion of someone or something. *I* **admire** *Mirea because she is such a good dancer.* (p. 144)

adventure (ăd vĕn′ chər) *n.* an unusual or exciting experience. *When I travel to a new place, it is always a great* **adventure.** (p. 243)

advocate (ăd′ və kāt′) *v.* support; speak in favor of. *Dentists* **advocate** *brushing your teeth after every meal.* (p. 305)

agenda (ə jĕn′ də) *n.* a list of goals or things to be done. *I made an* **agenda** *of things to talk about at the meeting.* (p. 305)

agree (ə grē′) *v.* be the same in number. *When a verb and noun* **agree,** *they are both singular or both plural.* (p. 178)

alphabetical (ăl′ fə bĕt′ ĭ kəl) *adj.* arranged in the order of the letters of the alphabet. *The teacher called our names in* **alphabetical** *order.* (p. 225)

amputate (ăm′ pyŏŏ tāt′) *v.* cut off all or part of a body part. *The doctor's decision to* **amputate** *Enrique's leg probably saved his life.* (p. 294)

apostrophe (ə pŏs′ trə fē) *n.* a mark of punctuation (') used with possessive nouns and with contractions, such as *isn't.* (p. 124)

arrange (ə rānj′) *v.* put in a special order or relation. (p. 94)

arrive (ə rīv′) *v.* get there. ***Arrive*** *at the airport two hours before your flight leaves.* (p. 312)

assign (ə sīn′) *v.* give to. *My teacher did not* ***assign*** *us homework over the weekend.* (p. 250)

assignment (ə sīn′ mənt) *n.* the work to do. *Our homework* ***assignment*** *was to write a paper about what we did last summer.* (p. 212)

astonishment (ə stŏn′ ĭsh mənt) *n.* wonder; surprise. *Annie looked at the flying squirrel in* ***astonishment***. (p. 188)

attempt (ə tĕmpt′) *n.* an effort or try. *The magician made an* ***attempt*** *to pull a rabbit out of his hat.* (p. 261)

audience (ô′ dē əns) *n.* the people who will read or hear what is written or spoken. (p. 38)

author (ô′ thər) *n.* a person who writes a book or other type of text. *The* ***author*** *of the book I'm reading wrote some very funny things.* (p. 140)

auxiliary (ôg zĭl′ yə rē) *adj.* something that helps or gives support to. *The* ***auxiliary*** *club is having a fundraiser for flood victims.* (p. 233)

axis (ăk′ sĭs) *n.* a straight line in a chart that contains measurements. *James measured the distance by plotting points on the* ***axis***. (p. 153)

B

babble (băb′ əl) *v.* talk in a way that can't be understood. *The baby likes to* ***babble*** *when she plays.* (p. 132)

baptize (băp tīz′) *v.* give a new beginning or rebirth to. *Esperanza wants to* ***baptize*** *herself and start over with a new name.* (p. 75)

bibliography (bĭb′ lē ŏg′ rə fē) *n.* a list of sources that a writer used to write a book or report. *The* ***bibliography*** *shows the author got some of her information from a TV show.* (p. 218)

bonfire (bŏn′ fīr′) *n.* a fire built outside for a celebration. *The students celebrated the end of the school year with a big* ***bonfire***. (p. 131)

boring (bôr′ ĭng) *adj.* dull, not interesting. *We left the movie early because it was* ***boring***. (p. 222)

bout (bout) *n.* a fight or contest. *Each fight or match is a bout. If James wins the next* ***bout***, *our wrestling team will win the tournament.* (p. 96)

boycott (boi′ kŏt′) *n.* a refusal to use or buy something as an act of protest. (p. 304)

bracero *n.* Spanish for "Mexican migrant worker." *She looked across the field at another* ***bracero*** *picking fruit with her.* (p. 242)

brag (brăg) *v.* talk about how good something is. *Andre wanted to* ***brag*** *to his friends about his new car.* (p. 282)

brain (brān) *n.* the part of the head that is used for thinking. *Even though Einstein was a genius, his* ***brain*** *was an average size.* (p. 52)

brainstorm (brān′ stôrm′) *v.* think of many possible ideas. *Before you write a paper,* ***brainstorm*** *some topics.* (p. 40)

broad (brôd) *adj.* large in width; wide. *The river was* ***broad*** *enough for the large ship.* (p. 40)

Brooklyn (brŏŏk′ lĭn) *n.* a section of New York City. (p. 296)

bumper (bŭm′ pər) *n.* a safety bar attached to the front or rear of a car. *The* ***bumper*** *was the only thing damaged in the car accident.* (p. 244)

C

capitalization (kăp′ ĭ tl ĭ zā′ shən) *n.* the use of capital letters. *Use* ***capitalization*** *at the beginning of a sentence.* (p. 44)

case (kās) *n.* the way a word functions or is used in a sentence. *Possessive is one case.* (p. 348)

casual banter light, playful talk or conversation. *Iris and her new friend sat on the porch enjoying* ***casual banter***. (p. 133)

cause (kôz) **1.** *n.* someone or something that makes something else happen. *Pushing the door is the* ***cause*** *for why it opens.* (p. 101) **2.** *n.* an idea or goal that many people want to see happen. *A worthy* ***cause*** *is fighting for the rights of others.* (p. 324)

chain-link fence a fence of metal rings. *The* ***chain-link fence*** *keeps the dog in the yard.* (p. 296)

challenge (chăl′ ənj) *v.* make you work hard; require special effort. *I knew my new math class would **challenge** me, so I studied twice as hard.* (p. 209)

challenge the system point out the wrongs in business and government and fight to change them. *Ursula ran for U.S. Senate to **challenge the system**.* (p. 305)

champion (chăm′ pē ən) *n.* a winner ahead of or above all others. *Whoever wins will be the **champion**.* (p. 98)

chandelier (shăn′ də lîr′) *n.* a light that hangs from the ceiling. *The hotel lobby has a large **chandelier**.* (p. 75)

chapter (chăp′ tər) *n.* a main division of a text. (p. 194)

character trait a quality a person has; a special part of a person's personality. *Shyness is her most noticeable **character trait**.* (p. 141)

characteristic (kăr′ ək tə rĭs′ tĭk) *n.* a quality or trait that makes something what it is. *A **characteristic** that all cats share is the ability to see in the dark.* (p. 282)

characterization (kăr′ ək tər ĭ zā′ shən) *n.* the way writers tell about the characters in a story, often through description and dialogue, that makes them seem real. *The **characterization** of the woman in the story made her seem brave.* (p. 280)

chronological order the order in which events happen. (p. 268)

cicada (sĭ kā′ də) *n.* an insect; the males make a high-pitched sound. *The **cicada** is an insect you hear during the summer.* (p. 133)

cite (sīt) *v.* make a reference to. ***Cite** your sources of information at the end of a paper.* (p. 218)

clarify (klăr′ ə fī′) *v.* make clear. *Ricky did not understand the instructions, so he asked his teacher to **clarify**.* (p. 50)

clause (klôz) *n.* a group of words within a sentence that has a subject and a verb. *Billy ran to the store is a clause in the sentence Billy ran to the store as fast as he could.* (p. 62)

cleats (klēts) *n.* metal pieces on the bottom of shoes used for sports. They keep players from slipping. *Because Sasha did not wear **cleats** during the game, she fell while running.* (p. 18)

climax (klī′ măks′) *n.* the turning point of a story, when the conflict is the greatest. *The **climax** of the story was when Derrick finally confronted the school bully.* (p. 261)

clue (kloō) *n.* a hint; a fact that helps solve a problem. *The sad look on my mother's face was my first **clue** that something was wrong.* (p. 259)

collect (kə lĕkt′) *v.* get, gather, or pull together. *Before you start the project, **collect** as much information as you can.* (p. 41)

college (kŏl′ ĭj) *n.* a school of higher learning after high school. *Laura was excited about going to **college** in the fall.* (p. 76)

common noun *n.* a word that names a person, place, thing, or idea. The words *baker, park,* and *peace* are common nouns. (p. 118)

communal (kə myoō′ nəl) *adj.* used by everyone in a community. *All the females in the college dorm shared a **communal** bathroom.* (p. 132)

comparative (kəm păr′ ə tĭv) *adj.* the form of an adjective or adverb that compares two things. (p. 292)

compare (kəm pâr′) *v.* show how things are the same. *In my paper, I **compare** two stories by the same author.* (p. 57)

complaint (kəm plānt′) *n.* a statement telling why one is unhappy. *Marcus made a **complaint** to his neighbors that they were being too loud.* (p. 325)

complicated (kŏm′ plĭ kā′ tĭd) *adj.* very hard and difficult. (p. 69)

conclusion (kən kloō′ zhən) *n.* an end result; an opinion formed after an experience or at the end of reading something; a judgment or decision made after careful thought. (p. 56)

conflict (kŏn′ flĭkt′) *n.* a problem or struggle between two things or people. *There is always a **conflict** between Jerry and his sister about who does the dishes after dinner.* (p. 261)

conjunction (kən jŭngk′ shən) *n.* a word that connects words or groups of words in a sentence or that connects sentences. The word *and* is a conjunction. (p. 352)

connect (kə nĕkt′) **1.** *v.* link, join, or be a part of. *Your hand and your arm* **connect** *at the wrist.* **2.** *v.* think about how you feel and what you have in common with something. *I really* **connect** *with the girl in the story because we have similar lives.* (p. 32)

context clue a word or a phrase that surrounds a word and helps you know what the word means. (p. 315)

contrast (kən trăst′) *v.* show how things are different. (p. 57)

corrido *n.* Spanish for a song that tells a story. *My grandfather sang me a* **corrido** *about a war that was fought before I was born.* (p. 251)

corridor (kôr′ ĭ dər′) *n.* a long hallway with rooms opening off of it. *The hall in your school is a* **corridor.** (p. 100)

courage (kûr′ ĭj) *n.* bravery; not being afraid. *It takes a lot of* **courage** *to admit when you have done something wrong.* (p. 262)

crate (krāt) *n.* a box used for packing and shipping something. *Alejandra was excited to find out what was in the* **crate** *her uncle had sent for her birthday.* (p. 248)

crisis-packed *adj.* full of problems. *Yadira would have enjoyed her vacation a lot more if it had not been so* **crisis-packed.** (p. 305)

cruelty (kroo′ əl tē) *n.* something that causes pain or suffering. *Hitting an animal is* **cruelty.** (p. 210)

dangle (dăng′ gəl) *v.* hang and swing loosely. *Darcy took off her shoes to* **dangle** *her legs in the water.* (p. 273)

dart (därt) *v.* move quickly and suddenly. *The fish will* **dart** *away if you tap the water.* (p. 133)

decade (dĕk′ ād′) *n.* a period of 10 years. *The 1960s was a* **decade** *of change.* (p. 21)

decision (dĭ sĭzh′ ən) *n.* the act of making up one's mind. *I will wait for you to make a* **decision.** (p. 56)

demented (dĭ mĕn′ tĭd) *adj.* insane; crazy. *The criminal was so* **demented** *he kept singing during the trial.* (p. 133)

demonstrate (dĕm′ ən strāt′) *v.* show how to do something. *The coach will* **demonstrate** *the proper way to swing the bat.* (p. 273)

dents and nicks small holes and scratch marks. *The car was cheap because it had a lot of* **dents and nicks.** (p. 245)

depart (dĭ pärt′) *v.* leave. *The woman at the counter said my flight will* **depart** *from Gate C.* (p. 312)

dependent (dĭ pĕn′ dənt) *adj.* must rely on someone or something else. *Until you are an adult, you are* **dependent** *on your parents for most things.* (p. 65)

descriptive paragraph a paragraph that includes adjectives, details, and sensory images. (p. 106)

design (dĭ zīn′) *n.* a drawing, sketch, or pattern. *The* **design** *on my grandmother's wallpaper is really ugly!* (p. 247)

destiny (dĕs′ tə nē) *n.* future events that are already decided. *Prince Ahmed fulfilled his* **destiny** *and was crowned king.* (p. 304)

detail (dē′ tāl′) *n.* the small part of a whole; single item. *Leaving out one* **detail** *in a math problem will result in a wrong answer.* (p. 31)

disheveled (dĭ shĕv′ əld) *adj.* messy or untidy. *When I wake up in the morning, my hair is always* **disheveled.** (p. 188)

distant (dĭs′ tənt) *adj.* far away. *Pablo won the race, and Troy came in a* **distant** *second.* (p. 77)

draft (drăft) *n.* the first, quick try at writing a paper. *Writers usually write more than one* **draft** *before they are finished.* (p. 42)

drone (drōn) *n.* a humming sound. *When I am home alone, the* **drone** *of the refrigerator is a comforting sound.* (p. 247)

dwell (dwĕl) *v.* live. *Fish **dwell** in water.* (p. 133)

E

earthworm (ûrth′ wûrm′) *n.* a common creature only a few inches long that is soft, wiggles, and lives in soil. *The **earthworm** moved across the wet ground.* (p. 246)

ease (ēz) *n.* freedom from any problems. *She finished her homework with **ease**.* (p. 220)

edit (ĕd′ ĭt) *v.* change and correct to use the right words and complete, smooth sentences. *You will get a better grade if you **edit** your paper before turning it in.* (p. 44)

editorial (ĕd′ ĭ tôr′ ē əl) *n.* a newspaper or magazine article that expresses an opinion. *I wrote an **editorial** in the paper about the new law.* (p. 325)

effect (ĭ fĕkt′) *n.* something brought about by a cause. *Because Viktor did not sleep well the night before, it had a negative **effect** on his test score.* (p. 101)

Ellis Island an island near New York City where many immigrants first landed. *When my grandmother moved to this country, she had to stop at **Ellis Island**.* (p. 20)

email (ē′ māl′) *n.* a letter sent by computer over the Internet. *Carmen sent all her friends an **email** to tell them the news.* (p. 338)

embarrass (ĕm băr′ əs) *v.* make uncomfortable or ashamed. *My little brothers always **embarrass** me when they talk to my friends.* (p. 283)

empire (ĕm′ pīr′) *n.* a group of lands or countries under one government. *An **empire** can last several hundred years!* (p. 20)

encounter (ĕn koun′ tər) *n.* a meeting. *Talking to the president was an **encounter** I will never forget.* (p. 131)

enroll (ĕn rōl′) *v.* sign up for or become a member of a class. *After watching an action movie, Darnell decided to **enroll** in a karate class.* (p. 250)

enthusiastic (ĕn thoō′ zē ăs′ tĭk) *adj.* interested and excited. *Everyone seemed **enthusiastic** about my idea for the group project.* (p. 250)

es todo Spanish for "that's everything." (p. 245)

evaluate (ĭ văl′ yoō āt′) *v.* decide about the value or importance of something. *The boss will **evaluate** me at the end of the month.* (p. 156)

event (ĭ vĕnt′) *n.* something that happens. *The spring festival is the biggest **event** of the year.* (p. 140)

exaggerate (ĭg zăj′ ə rāt′) *v.* speak or write about something as if it were greater than it really is. *When I tell my mother I'm starving to death, she tells me not to **exaggerate**.* (p. 282)

example (ĭg zăm′ pəl) *n.* a detail used to prove a point or make something clear. *The **example** helped me to do the assignment.* (p. 86)

exchange a few words have a very short talk. *Dirk and his mother usually **exchange a few words** before he goes out for the evening.* (p. 245)

exclamation (ĕk′ sklə mā′ shən) *n.* a sudden, strong outcry. *When Carlos yelled "Help!" his **exclamation** was heard by everyone.* (p. 68)

expand (ĭk spănd′) *v.* increase in number or size; make larger. *Kia began reading the newspaper to **expand** her knowledge of world events.* (p. 156)

experience (ĭk spîr′ ē əns) *n.* something that happens to a person. *The birth of my baby sister is an **experience** I'll never forget.* (p. 167)

explain (ĭk splān′) *v.* make clear and easy to understand. (p. 162)

expository (ĭk spŏz′ ĭ tôr′ ē) *adj.* a type of writing that gives information, such as an explanation, directions, or how to do something. (p. 162)

F

fact (făkt) *n.* a thing that can be shown to be true. *It is a **fact** that the Earth is round.* (p. 86)

fact or recall question a test question that asks for a detail that can be found and proven true. (p. 206)

fame (fām) *n.* public popularity or respect. *Celebrities enjoy both **fame** and fortune.* (p. 57)

feature (fē′ chər) *n.* a part; something that is special or noticeable. *Yoshi has a **feature** on her cell phone that allows her to take pictures.* (p. 313)

feminine (fĕm′ ə nĭn) *adj.* relating to the female gender. (p. 346)

fiction (fĭk′shən) *n.* the genre of literature that includes made-up stories. (p. 256)

figure out solve or discover. *I always try to **figure out** where my mother hides my birthday present.* (p. 28)

fluency (floo′ ən sē) *n.* ease; smoothness; easy flow of ideas from one thing to the next. *Ben took Spanish in school but didn't achieve **fluency** until he moved to Mexico.* (p. 275)

forehead (fôr′ hĕd′) *n.* the part of the face above the eyes. *The boxer had a cut on his **forehead**.* (p. 245)

foreigner (fôr′ ə nər) *n.* a person from another country or place. *When Shalim first moved to France, he felt like a **foreigner**.* (p. 142)

foreman (fôr′ mən) *n.* someone in charge of a group of workers. *With hard work, Eugene hoped to be **foreman** one day.* (p. 245)

formal (fôr′məl) *adj.* proper; following the rules. (p. 334)

fragment (frăg′ mənt) *n.* a part or piece. *This project is only a **fragment** of the homework I have this weekend.* (p. 66)

France (frăns) *n.* a large country in Europe. (p. 76)

frisky (frĭs′ kē) *adj.* playful and full of energy. *My new puppy is **frisky**.* (p. 273)

frown (froun) *v.* look unhappy or upset. (p. 189)

function (fŭngk′ shən) *n.* a purpose, use, or duty. (p. 346)

galvanized (găl′ və nīz′ d) *adj.* coated to prevent rusting. (p. 244)

gender (jĕn′ dər) *n.* whether something is masculine, feminine, or neuter. *It is illegal not to give someone a job because of that person's **gender**.* (p. 346)

genre (zhän′rə) *n.* a type of literature, music, or art. (p. 256)

glamorous (glăm′ ər əs) *adj.* fascinating, wonderful. *The life of a rock star seems **glamorous**.* (p. 282)

glue (gloo) *v.* stick to something. *You can fix the broken dish if you **glue** the pieces together.* (p. 247)

goal (gōl) *n.* an aim, objective, or purpose. (p. 286)

grade (grād) *n.* a hill or rise in the ground. (p. 249)

grammar (grăm′ ər) *n.* the rules for using words and sentences in language. *It is important to use correct **grammar** when you write an English paper.* (p. 44)

graphic (grăf′ ĭk) *n.* information shown visually, such as graphs, maps, photographs, and charts. (p. 150)

grimy (grī′ mē) *adj.* covered with dirt. *Damian's tools were **grimy** because he had not cleaned them in a long time.* (p. 111)

Guadalajara (gwŏd′l ə hä′ rə) *n.* a city in western Mexico. (p. 101)

hallo, babee, hallo "Hello, baby, hello." (p. 18)

heading (hĕd′ ĭng) *n.* a title or subtitle put at the top of a page, chapter, or section of text. (p. 194)

helping verb *n.* a verb added to other verbs to make the meaning clear. In the sentence, *We will walk to the store, will* is a helping verb for the main verb *walk.* (p. 177)

hesitant (hĕz′ ĭ tənt) *adj.* slow to act or decide. *After Don crashed the car, his father was **hesitant** about letting him drive.* (p. 250)

highlight (hīʹ līt´) *v.* mark or call attention to something. *The teacher wanted us to* **highlight** *our favorite passage.* (p. 52)

horizon (hə rīʹ zən) *n.* the line where Earth and sky seem to meet. *Nothing is more beautiful than the sun setting over the* **horizon.** (p. 296)

husky (hŭsʹ kē) *adj.* big and strong. *If you play football, it is helpful to have a* **husky** *build.* (p. 245)

identity (ī dĕnʹ tĭ tē) *n.* who a person is; how one knows oneself and is known by others. *A big part of Kalil's* **identity** *is making people laugh.* (p. 142)

imaginary (ĭ măjʹ ə nĕrʹ ē) *adj.* made-up, not real. *My little sister has an* **imaginary** *friend named Bubbles.* (p. 258)

imperative (ĭm pĕrʹ ə tĭv) *n.* a command or request. *The kind of sentence that asks you to do something is an* **imperative.** (p. 68)

imply (ĭm plīʹ) *v.* say indirectly. An implied idea is suggested by the information given. *Alicia tried to* **imply** *she was tired by yawning.* (p. 87)

impression (ĭm prĕshʹ ən) *n.* a lasting thought or feeling about something. *Caitlyn wanted to make a good* **impression** *at her interview.* (p. 138)

incentive (ĭn sĕnʹ tĭv) *n.* something that makes a person want to do something or make a special effort. *My father offered me $10 as an* **incentive** *for getting good grades.* (p. 187)

independent (ĭnʹ dĭ pĕnʹ dənt) *adj.* not controlled by anything or anyone else; free. *America became an* **independent** *country after the Revolutionary War.* (p. 65)

inevitable (ĭn ĕvʹ ĭ tə bəl) *adj.* sure; certain. *When something is* **inevitable,** *it is impossible to stop it from happening.* (p. 305)

infer (ĭn fûrʹ) *v.* conclude; arrive at an idea by putting together clues or bits of information; figure it out. *You could* **infer** *that Eliza was nervous from the way she was shaking.* (p. 88)

inference (ĭnʹ fər əns) *n.* a conclusion made by putting together facts or ideas. (p. 89)

inform (ĭn fôrmʹ) *v.* tell about. (p. 162)

informal (ĭn fôrʹ məl) *adj.* not following all the rules; casual. *Wearing shorts and a T-shirt was too* **informal** *for the party.* (p. 334)

inherit (ĭn hĕrʹ ĭt) *v.* receive land, money, or other things from a person who has died. *When my grandmother dies, I will* **inherit** *her diamond ring.* (p. 75)

innumerable (ĭ nooʹ mər ə bəl) *adj.* too many to count. *The stars in the sky are* **innumerable.** (p. 131)

insect (ĭnʹ sĕktʹ) *n.* an animal with 6 legs, a body, and usually wings. *The ant is a very strong* **insect.** (p. 247)

instill (ĭn stĭlʹ) *v.* fill with. *It is important for a teacher to* **instill** *a love of learning in her students.* (p. 189)

instinct (ĭnʹ stĭngktʹ) *n.* an inner feeling or way of behaving. *When I don't know what to do, I try to act on my* **instinct.** (p. 250)

instinctive (ĭn stĭngkʹ tĭv) *adj.* done without thinking. (p. 247)

instruction (ĭn strŭkʹ shən) *n.* a step that explains how to do something. *Eric and Munira put the bicycle together without any* **instruction.** (p. 316)

intense (ĭn tĕnsʹ) *adj.* very strong. *The flavor of the food was so* **intense** *I couldn't eat it.* (p. 261)

interjection (ĭnʹ tər jĕkʹ shən) *n.* a part of speech that interrupts or shows emotion, like *Yikes!* or *Ouch!* (p. 353)

Internet (ĭnʹ tər nĕtʹ) *n.* the connection of computers that lets people all over the world share information. *Research has been much easier since the* **Internet** *was invented.* (p. 41)

interrogative sentence a sentence that is a question. *What movie should we see?* is an interrogative sentence. (p. 68)

irregular (ĭ rĕg′ yə lər) *adj.* not normal or following a pattern; strange or unusual. *The shirts are cheap because they are **irregular**.* (p. 122)

irregular verb *n.* a verb that does not change in ways you can predict. *Teach is an irregular verb because the past tense is taught.* (p. 230)

issue (ĭsh′ ōo) *n.* something that is discussed or argued about. *The economy is always an important **issue**.* (p. 341)

judgment (jŭj′ mənt) *n.* an opinion about what is good, bad, truthful, important, and so on. *I'll make my own **judgment** about what is right.* (p. 55)

justice (jŭs′ tĭs) *n.* fairness; getting what is deserved. *All people deserve to be treated with **justice**.* (p. 262)

kerosene (kĕr′ ə sēn′) *adj.* using oil as fuel. *When we go camping, we use a **kerosene** lamp.* (p. 246)

key (kē) *n.* a caption on a map or chart that explains symbols used in it. *The **key** on the map tells me what the red lines represent.* (p. 154)

key event something important that happens. (p. 138)

key word a very important word. *Key means important. When I told you, "We need to work on that," the **key word** was "we."* (p. 85)

label (lā′ bəl) *n.* text that names the main parts of something. (p. 310)

laden (lād′ n) *adj.* completely covered; loaded with. *The queen was **laden** with jewels.* (p. 131)

Lakota (lə kō′ tə) *n.* a group of Native Americans from the Sioux tribe. (p. 282)

legend (lĕj′ ənd) *n.* a caption on a map or chart that explains symbols used in it. (p. 154)

lightweight (līt′ wāt′) *n.* a boxer who weighs between 127 and 135 pounds. (p. 98)

linking verb *n.* a verb that joins the subject to a noun or adjective in the predicate. (p. 176)

listo adj. Spanish for "ready." (p. 244)

location (lō kā′ shən) *n.* a place where something is found. *The **location** of the party was written on the invitation.* (p. 100)

lump (lŭmp) *n.* a bump or piece of something. *The boy has a **lump** on his head from getting hit with a ball.* (p. 245)

lunge (lŭnj) *v.* move suddenly forward. *A snake will **lunge** at its prey.* (p. 109)

main character the most important character. *The book had a sad ending because the **main character** died.* (p. 258)

main idea what the writer is saying about the subject. *The **main idea** of the story is friendship.* (p. 82)

major (mā′ jər) *adj.* main; most important. *Test scores will make up the **major** part of our grade.* (p. 141)

make a plan form an idea in advance about how to do something. (p. 196)

Maryland planter an owner of a large farm, called a plantation, in the state of Maryland, where slaves worked. The planters owned the slaves. (p. 186)

masculine (măs′ kyə lĭn) *adj.* relating to the male gender. (p. 346)

material (mə tîr′ ē əl) *n.* the specific information covered. (p. 208)

mattress (măt′ rĭs) *n.* a pad of heavy cloth filled with soft material that is used on or for a bed. *I didn't sleep well because the **mattress** was too hard.* (p. 244)

maze (māz) *n.* a path that is hard to find the way through. *Sergio was lost in the* **maze.** (p. 296)

meadow (mĕd′ ō) *n.* grassy land or ground. *The grass in the* **meadow** *is tall and yellow.* (p. 20)

medallion (mĭ dăl′ yən) *n.* a large medal. *The winner of the spelling bee is awarded a* **medallion.** (p. 96)

memorable (mĕm′ ər ə bəl) *adj.* important or unforgettable. Something is memorable if it should be remembered. *Jumping out of an airplane is* **memorable.** (p. 270)

memorize (mĕm′ ə rīz′) *v.* learn well enough that you can remember. *Gareth had to* **memorize** *a poem for English class.* (p. 122)

menu (mĕn′ yōō) *n.* a list of food served or available for a meal. (p. 312)

mi olla Spanish for "my pot." (p. 245)

migrant (mī′ grənt) *adj.* traveling. **Migrant** *workers move from place to place to find work.* (p. 242)

migration (mī grā′ shən) *n.* a movement from one country or region to another. *The bird* **migration** *occurs every winter.* (p. 220)

military (mĭl′ ĭ tĕr′ ē) *n.* fighting forces such as the army, navy, and air force. (p. 168)

minor character a less important character. *The sister was only a* **minor character** *in the story.* (p. 258)

misery (mĭz′ ə rē) *n.* great pain or suffering. *War causes* **misery** *for many people.* (p. 273)

mixture (mĭks′ chər) *n.* a little of each; a combination. *Green is a* **mixture** *of yellow and blue.* (p. 133)

modifier (mŏd′ ə fī′ ər) *n.* a word that changes or limits the meaning of another word. (p. 351)

modify (mŏd′ ə fī′) *v.* limit or change the sense of. *Inez said she could* **modify** *her essay to make it better.* (p. 64)

moldy (mōl′ dē) *adj.* covered with a fuzzy, often greenish, growth. *I threw away the bread because it was* **moldy.** (p. 111)

narrative (năr′ ə tĭv) *n.* something that tells a story or describes an event. *We read a slave* **narrative** *that told the story of slaves living during the Civil War.* (p. 268)

narrator (năr′ āt′ ər) *n.* the person or character who tells a story. *The* **narrator** *made the story interesting because he was funny.* (p. 259)

narrow (năr′ ō) *v.* make smaller or limit. (p. 40)

native (nā′ tĭv) *adj.* belonging to a place by birth. *I live in the United States but my* **native** *country is Brazil.* (p. 21)

necktie (nĕk′ tī′) *n.* a piece of men's clothing worn with a business suit. *Antoine wore a* **necktie** *to his job interview.* (p. 244)

negotiation (nĭ gō shē ā′shən) *n.* a discussion to come to an agreement. *Instead of fighting, the countries held a* **negotiation** *to work out their differences.* (p. 305)

neither-nor not one or the other. *Tamara was* **neither** *excited* **nor** *nervous.* (p. 19)

nervous (nûr′ vəs) *adj.* anxious or fearful. *Yao was* **nervous** *about going to the doctor.* (p. 249)

neuter (nōō′ tər) *adj.* neither masculine nor feminine. *It is a neuter pronoun.* (p. 348)

noncount noun *n.* a word that names a thing you cannot count. It does not have a plural form. Some noncount nouns are *homework, grass, rice,* and *spinach.* (p. 123)

nonviolent (nŏn vī′ ə lənt) *adj.* using peaceful methods; not using force. *Gandhi believed in* **nonviolent** *protest.* (p. 304)

note card (nōt kärd) a card used to record and keep track of information. *Angel wrote the recipe on a* **note card.** (p. 220)

note-taking (nōt′ tāk′ ĭng) *n.* the writing down of notes to remember important information. (p. 194)

noun (noun) *n*. a word that names a person, place, thing, or idea. (p. 118)

number (nŭm′ bər) *n*. how many of something; singular or plural. *There was a large **number** of people at the party.* (p. 348)

objection (əb jĕk′ shən) *n*. a reason not to believe or support an opinion. *I have an **objection** to what you are saying.* (p. 327)

opinion (ə pĭn′ yən) *n*. a belief that is based on what someone thinks or feels. *I want your **opinion** about a poem I wrote.* (p. 55)

opposing (ə pōz′ ĭng) *adj*. against, or on the opposite side. *Her debate team argued the **opposing** view.* (p. 327)

order (ôr′ dər) *n*. an arrangement of parts. (p. 94)

organization (ôr′ gə nĭ zā′shən) *n*. the way something is put together or arranged. (p. 224)

organize (ôr′ gə nīz′) *v*. put together or arrange in an orderly way. *I want to **organize** my desk so it looks neater.* (p. 28)

original (ə rĭj′ ə nəl) *adj*. first; earliest. *I like the **original** version of the song better.* (p. 244)

outcome (out′ kŭm′) *n*. an event that happens as a result. *Success is often the **outcome** of hard work.* (p. 211)

outline (out′ līn′) *n*. an organized list that summarizes or gives the main points. *Before Fiona writes a paper, she likes to make an **outline**.* (p. 221)

ownership (ō′ nər shĭp′) *n*. being an owner; having something that is yours. (p. 124)

paragraph (păr′ə grăf′) *n*. a group of sentences about one idea. (p. 82)

paraphrase (păr′ ə frāz′) *v*. put in your own words. *I will **paraphrase** the article so I remember it.* (p. 220)

parrot (păr′ ət) *n*. a tropical bird with a hooked bill and brightly colored feathers. *Anita has a pet **parrot** that can say her name.* (p. 244)

participle (pär′ tĭ sĭp′ əl) *n*. a verb form, such as *worried* or *worrying*. (p. 234)

parts of speech *n. pl*. the ways words are used. These include nouns, verbs, adjectives, adverbs, pronouns, prepositions, conjunctions, and interjections. (p. 346)

passage (păs′ ĭj) *n*. a part of a text or reading. *The author read a **passage** from his new book.* (p. 210)

passenger (păs′ ən jər) *n*. a person riding in a car, train, ship, or plane. (p. 189)

passive (păs′ ĭv) *adj*. not active; allowing things to happen. *I was surprised that my dog was very **passive** with the new puppy.* (p. 235)

password (păs′ wûrd′) *n*. a secret word or phrase that a person uses to get into a place. *You can't check your email without the **password**.* (p. 188)

past tense tells about something that happened in the past. *Laughed is the past tense of laugh.* (p. 235)

pastel (pă stĕl′) *adj*. pale color. A soft yellow or pink is a pastel color. *Everything in the baby's room was **pastel**.* (p. 109)

pattern (păt′ ərn) *n*. something that is regular and that you can predict. *His behavior is following a dangerous **pattern**.* (p. 236)

pause and reflect stop and think about carefully. *When I read a book, I **pause and reflect** between each chapter.* (p. 33)

peak (pēk) *n*. the busiest point. *The **peak** for traffic is 5 P.M.* (p. 242)

perceive (pər sēv′) *v*. look at; see as. *People often **perceive** things differently.* (p. 133)

person (pûr′ sən) *n*. the form of the word used to show the person speaking; point of view. The phrase *I think* is from a first-person point of view, and *you think* is from a second-person point of view. (p. 348)

personality (pûr' sə năl' ĭ tē) *n.* how someone acts or behaves. (p. 286)

persuasive (pər swā' sĭv) *adj.* something that changes the way someone thinks or acts. (p. 322)

phrase (frāz) *n.* a group of words that has meaning but is not a complete sentence. *The phrase "neat and tidy" applies to my brother.* (p. 62)

physical appearance the way someone looks. (p. 286)

pinky (pĭng' kē) *n.* the little finger. *My uncle wears a diamond ring on his pinky.* (p. 111)

pivotal (pĭv' ə tl) *adj.* very important, central. *Lisa played a pivotal role in the play.* (p. 327)

plot (plŏt) *n.* the problem or conflict that develops in a story. (p. 280)

plural (ploŏr' əl) *adj.* naming more than one. *Windows is plural for window.* (p. 121)

plural noun *n.* a noun that names more than one thing. (p. 118)

point of view *n.* a way of looking at things. (p. 138)

polish (pŏl' ĭsh) *v.* make last changes in order to make something look better and shine. *I polish my shoes every morning.* (p. 224)

polite (pə līt') *adj.* respectful. *My mother told me to be polite to the guests.* (p. 250)

populate (pŏp' yə lāt') *v.* live in. *Eskimos populate areas of Alaska.* (p. 246)

population (pŏp' yə lā' shən) *n.* all the people in a place. (p. 153)

possessive noun *n.* a word that shows who or what owns something. *Anna's book, the dog's paw,* and *the girls' game* are examples of possessive nouns. (p. 124)

possibility (pŏs' ə bĭl' ĭ tē) *n.* an option or choice that may work. *Quitting is not a possibility.* (p. 40)

predicate (prĕd' ĭ kĭt) *n.* what the subject does or what happens. In the sentence, *He runs fast,* the simple predicate is *runs.* (p. 62)

prejudice (prĕj' ə dĭs) *n.* a strong feeling or opinion formed before knowing all the facts. *We often learn prejudice from people we know.* (p. 168)

preposition (prĕp' ə zĭsh' ən) *n.* a word that gives location, direction, or position. *On is a preposition in the sentence, Look on the table.* (p. 351)

prepositional phrase *n.* a group of words that includes a preposition, an object, and any modifiers. (p. 351)

present¹ (prĭ zĕnt') *v.* share or put in front of others for them to see and hear; display. *The mayor will present the winner with a trophy.* (p. 45)

present² (prĕz' ənt) *n.* right now, at this very moment. *The store is not hiring at the present.* (p. 234)

present perfect *n.* a verb form that describes an action that started in the past but continues or is completed in the present. *A storm has passed* means a storm started in the past and has ended. (p. 233)

preview (prē' vyoō') *n.* a look at ahead of time. *The preview made the movie look exciting.* (p. 29)

prewriting (prē' rīt ĭng) *n.* finding a subject, gathering information, and organizing it; the first step in the writing process. (p. 40)

principal (prĭn' sə pəl) *adj.* main. *The principal thing to remember in a fire is to stay calm.* (p. 234)

process (prŏs' ĕs') *n.* a series of steps or actions. *Part of the process for getting into college is to earn good grades.* (p. 26)

promised land a place described in a story in the Bible. It can also be used to mean "our goal." (p. 305)

promote a cause speak, write, or act in support of an idea or belief. *She went to the protest to promote a cause.* (p. 157)

pronoun (prō′ noun′) *n.* a word that takes the place of a noun. In the sentence, *She had a book and then lost it*, *she* and *it* are pronouns. (p. 294)

proofread (prŏof′ rēd′) *v.* read and mark corrections in spelling, capitalization, grammar, and punctuation. *You should always proofread your work for mistakes.* (p. 44)

proper noun *n.* a word that names a specific person, place, thing, or idea. (p. 118)

protest (prō′ tĕst′) *n.* an action, such as marching and carrying signs, to persuade people that something is wrong. *Many people went to the antiwar protest.* (p. 352)

publish (pŭb′ lĭsh) *v.* make public or put on display for others to read; also print. *It takes hard work and luck to publish a novel.* (p. 45)

punctuation (pŭngk′ chŏo ā′ shən) *n.* the use of periods, commas, and other marks to make the meaning of written material clear. (p. 44)

punt (pŭnt) *v.* kick the ball after dropping it and before it touches the ground. *Football is a game in which you punt the ball.* (p. 112)

purpose (pûr′ pəs) *n.* a reason for doing something. *My purpose for studying hard is to get into college.* (p. 26)

pursuit (pər sŏot′) *n.* the act of chasing after something. *The police are in pursuit of a criminal.* (p. 186)

quarantine (kwôr′ ən tēn′) *n.* being held apart from everyone else. It is a way of protecting people from getting disease. *I was put in quarantine when I had the measles.* (p. 20)

quince *n.* Spanish for 15. (p. 248)

quiz (kwĭz) *v.* test what someone knows by asking questions. *Ms. Sánchez will quiz the class.* (p. 208)

radical social change a large, sudden change in society. *The 1960s was a time of radical social change.* (p. 304)

raggedy as rats poor, worn out, dirty. *The stray puppies were raggedy as rats.* (p. 76)

ramble (răm′ bəl) *v.* talk without staying on topic. *The speech would have been better if the speaker didn't ramble so much.* (p. 273)

react (rē ăkt′) *v.* act in response to something. *She did not react well to the news.* (p. 50)

read with a purpose look for details and information as you read that help you answer the question "Why am I reading this?" (p. 197)

reading journal a notebook in which you write notes and thoughts about your reading. (p. 31)

realistic fiction the type of fiction that includes believable characters and events. (p. 256)

reason (rē′ zən) *n.* the cause or thing that makes you think, feel, or act in a certain way. *The reason I am happy is because I got an "A" on my test.* (p. 55)

recommendation (rĕk′ ə mĕn dā′ shən) *n.* a suggestion about what to do. (p. 340)

reference (rĕf′ rəns) *n.* something that gives information, such as a book, magazine, or encyclopedia. (p. 218)

refrigerator (rĭ frĭj′ ə rā′ tər) *n.* an appliance, usually in the kitchen, used to keep food cold. *Put the milk in the refrigerator.* (p. 77)

regular verb *n.* a verb that changes according to a set of rules. (p. 230)

reliable (rĭ lī′ ə bəl) *adj.* worthy of trust; dependable. *My information comes from a very reliable source.* (p. 154)

relief (rĭ lēf′) *n.* an easing of pain or worry. *It is a relief to know you are safe.* (p. 249)

remember (rĭ mĕm′ bər) *v.* bring back into your mind. *Did you remember Mom's birthday?* (p. 33)

report (rĭ pôrt′) *n.* words said or written to tell about something. *The assignment was to read the book and write a report.* (p. 220)

require (rĭ kwīr′) *v.* must have something; need. *The permission form will require your parent's signature.* (p. 179)

reread (rē rēd′) *v.* read again. *I had to reread the chapter to understand it.* (p. 33)

research (rē′ sûrch′) *n.* the work done to learn about a subject. Usually research is done by studying books about the subject at the library or by searching the Internet for information. *We learn a lot about diseases through research.* (p. 164)

respond (rĭ spŏnd′) *v.* act as a result, or because, of something. *The fire department took 5 minutes to respond to the phone call.* (p. 258)

reverend (rĕv′ ər ənd) *n.* someone with religious duties in a church. *The reverend preaches every Sunday and Wednesday.* (p. 304)

revise (rĭ vīz′) *v.* rethink and redo writing, changing sentences and ideas to make the writing clearer. *The teacher said we could get a better grade if we revise our papers.* (p. 38)

rhyme (rīm) *n.* words that have the same ending sounds. *Grow and slow is a rhyme.* (p. 208)

riser (rī′ zər) *n.* a step or platform on a stage. *You can see the performers better because they are standing on a riser.* (p. 109)

risky (rĭs′ kē) *adj.* dangerous. *It's risky to ride a bike without a helmet.* (p. 327)

run-on (rŭn′ ŏn) *n.* a sentence made by two or more sentences that are put together without correct punctuation. (p. 66)

S

sacrifice (săk′ rə fīs′) *n.* the giving up of something valuable for an important cause. *Manny's sacrifice was to give up his Sunday to volunteer at the homeless shelter.* (p. 304)

salsa music a popular kind of Latin-American music. (p. 99)

salutation (săl′ yə tā′ shən) *n.* a greeting; hello. *"Hello" is a common salutation in a friendly letter.* (p. 336)

samurai (săm′ ə rī′) *n.* a kind of Japanese soldier. (p. 132)

savor (sā′ vər) *v.* enjoy very much. *Eat slowly and savor every bite.* (p. 248)

scene (sēn) *n.* the place where something happens, including the details and action. *The first scene of the play took place in London.* (p. 109)

schedule (skĕj′ ōō əl) *n.* a list of arrival and departure times. *The schedule said my cousin's flight would arrive in 20 minutes.* (p. 312)

scratch (skrăch) *v.* rub or scrape with one's fingernails. *Be nice to the cat or she may scratch you.* (p. 245)

segregation (sĕg′ rĭ gā′ shən) *n.* the system that kept African Americans apart from white Americans. (p. 122)

selection (sĭ lĕk′ shən) *n.* a story, article, poem, or chapter. *Read the selection by next week.* (p. 29)

selective (sĭ lĕk′ tĭv) *adj.* careful in choosing only what is important or necessary. *Maria was very selective about what she told me.* (p. 271)

self-conscious (sĕlf′ kŏn′ shəs) *adj.* shy; embarrassed in front of others. *The girls made her feel self-conscious by staring at her.* (p. 273)

selfless (sĕlf′ lĭs) *adj.* unselfish; thinking about others first. *It was a very selfless act to give Amelia your ticket.* (p. 304)

sensory image an image that helps the reader see, hear, feel, smell, or taste something. (p. 106)

sentence (sĕn′ təns) *n.* one or more words that express a complete thought. (p. 64)

series (sîr′ ēz) *n.* a number of similar things in a row or following one another; a sequence. *They conducted a series of tests.* (p. 143)

set your purpose ask yourself questions to make clear why you are reading. (p. 196)

sever (sĕv′ ər) *v.* cut off. *The lights will go out if you sever those wires.* (p. 294)

shack (shăk) *n.* a small, poorly built house, often with only one or two rooms. *My grandmother and her 4 sisters grew up in a shack.* (p. 243)

shadow (shăd′ ō) *n.* a dark image made when light is blocked. *The tree casts a shadow over the path.* (p. 130)

sharecropper (shâr′ krŏp′ ər) *n.* a farmer who gives part of his crops to the owner of the land in place of rent. *Many African Americans worked as sharecroppers after the Civil War.* (p. 242)

shower us with give us a lot of. *Our grandparents shower us with gifts every time they visit.* (p. 130)

shrine (shrīn) *n.* a place of worship. *They built a shrine to their god.* (p. 131)

signal (sĭg′ nəl) *v.* give a command or other information using signs or gestures. *Yell, "Surprise!" when I signal.* (p. 242)

signal word a word that points out or shows something. Examples are *first*, *next*, and *then*. (p. 99)

sincere (sĭn sîr′) *adj.* real, honest, or genuine. *I was being sincere when I apologized.* (p. 336)

singular (sĭng′ gyə lər) *adj.* naming one. (p. 121)

singular noun *n.* a word that names one person, place, thing, or idea. (p. 118)

skill (skĭl) *n.* something you get better at doing the more you practice it. *It is a skill to play a musical instrument well.* (p. 28)

skim (skĭm) *v.* read quickly, skipping over parts that aren't important. *I want to skim the instructions before we start.* (p. 210)

smooth (smōōth) *adj.* not rough; even. *I need a smooth surface to write on.* (p. 275)

sob (sŏb) *v.* cry with short, quick breaths. *Weddings always make my Aunt Rita sob.* (p. 74)

solve (sŏlv) *v.* find an answer to. *I think I can solve the puzzle.* (p. 261)

source (sôrs) *n.* someone or something that gives information; where information originally comes from, such as a book, magazine, website, or encyclopedia. *The source for my history paper was the encyclopedia.* (p. 152)

spar (spär) *v.* boxing for practice or training. *The two fighters spar in order to become better at fighting.* (p. 96)

specific (spĭ sĭf′ ĭk) *adj.* clearly stated; definite. *She gave me specific instructions.* (p. 120)

spelling (spĕl′ ĭng) *n.* the use of the correct letters to form a word. (p. 44)

spiral (spī′ rəl) *v.* move in a circling way; moving in the shape of a screw or coil. *The car will spiral out of control if you stop too suddenly in the rain.* (p. 112)

springy (sprĭng′ ē) *adj.* bouncy. *The bed is springy.* (p. 109)

stable (stā′ bəl) *n.* a building for horses and cattle. (p. 246)

statement (stāt′ mənt) *n.* something expressed in words. *He made a statement to the police about what happened.* (p. 68)

sticky note a small paper note that sticks to the page. *I put a sticky note in my book to mark my favorite page.* (p. 31)

strain (strān) *v.* try very hard. *The walls strain to support the ceiling because they aren't strong enough.* (p. 246)

strategy (străt′ ə jē) *n.* a plan to help you get from one step of a process to the next. (p. 26)

stun (stŭn) *v.* amaze, confuse, or shock. *The news will stun the world.* (p. 112)

subject (sŭb′ jĭkt) *n.* who or what a sentence, paragraph, or text is about. (p. 62)

success (sək sĕs′) *n.* getting what was wanted after working for it. *People often work their whole lives to achieve success.* (p. 262)

suffix (sŭf′ ĭks) *n.* a word ending. For example, *ing* is a suffix that can be added to the word *play* to make *playing*. (p. 234)

summarize (sŭm′ ə rīz′) *v.* tell the main points of something. *Tim was taking too long to tell the story, so I asked him to quickly summarize.* (p. 30)

superlative (soŏ pûr lə tĭv) *adj.* the form of an adjective or adverb that compares 3 or more things. (p. 292)

support (sə pôrt′) *v.* explain, give evidence to, or help make stronger. *Please support your answer.* (p. 55)

supporting detail an example or fact that explains a main idea. (p. 86)

surplus store a place where leftover items are sold to the public, often at cheap prices. *These pants were cheap because I got them at an Army surplus store.* (p. 245)

syllable (sĭl′ ə bəl) *n.* the part of a word that you hear separately. *You hear 4 syllables when you say the name "Es-per-an-za."* (p. 75)

symbol (sĭm′ bĕl) *n.* something that stands for or represents something else. *The Statue of Liberty is a symbol of freedom.* (p. 154)

T

table of contents the section of a book that lists the parts of the book, including chapters and headings. (p. 194)

take roll call the name of each student in a class or group. *Teachers know which students are absent when they take roll.* (p. 250)

temper (tĕm′ pər) *n.* a feeling or attitude. *He has a mean temper.* (p. 327)

tense (tĕns) *n.* a verb form. The tense of a verb tells when the action takes place. (p. 180)

termite (tûr′ mīt′) *n.* an insect that eats wood. *A termite can cause a lot of damage to a house.* (p. 246)

testimony (tĕs′ tə mō′ nē) *n.* a statement used as proof. *My testimony at the trial helped my brother win.* (p. 111)

text (tĕkst) *n.* written material. Poems, novels, and articles are texts. *This class will use one book as its main text.* (p. 30)

thorough (thûr′ ō) *adj.* very careful; complete. *The doctor gave me a very thorough examination and said I was healthy.* (p. 244)

tienen que tener cuidado Spanish for "you have to be careful." (p. 247)

tolerate (tŏl′ ə rāt′) *v.* allow or put up with. *I could hardly tolerate the heat.* (p. 131)

tombstone (toōm′ stōn′) *n.* a stone that marks a grave. *His tombstone said that he was a loving husband.* (p. 132)

tongue (tŭng) *n.* a language. *Kaya did not understand what they asked her because they were not speaking in her native tongue.* (p. 132)

topic (tŏp′ĭk) *n.* who or what a sentence, paragraph, or text is about. (p. 82)

topic sentence a sentence that states the main idea of a paragraph. (p. 86)

tortilla with "carne con chile" a cornmeal pancake with meat and peppers. (p. 248)

U

unconcealed (ŭn kən sēld′) *adj.* easily understood or seen. *She stood unconcealed in the middle of the yard.* (p. 188)

unison (yoō′ nĭ sən) *adj.* all together. *The class recited the poem in unison.* (p. 133)

upcoming (ŭp′ kŭm′ ĭng) *adj.* expected to happen in the future. *I did not study for the upcoming test.* (p. 208)

valuable (văl′ yōō ə bəl) *adj.* having great importance; worthy. *This CD is **valuable** because it's hard to find.* (p. 156)

vámonos Spanish for "let's go." (p. 248)

vanish (văn′ ĭsh) *v.* disappear suddenly. *My mother uses a cream to make her wrinkles **vanish**.* (p. 112)

varsity (vär′ sĭ tē) *adj.* the highest level team that represents a school in a sports competition. *Both my brother and I played on the **varsity** team.* (p. 112)

vein (vān) *n.* a tube in the body that carries blood. *The nurse stuck a needle in my **vein** to take some blood.* (p. 21)

veranda (və răn′ də) *n.* a porch or balcony that usually has a roof. *We had breakfast on the **veranda**.* (p. 132)

verb (vûrb) *n.* a word that shows action or state of being. In the sentence, *Anis sang a song*, the verb is *sang.* (p. 174)

vertical (vûr′ tĭ kəl) *adj.* straight up and down. *The new ride at the amusement park has a 200-foot **vertical** drop.* (p. 296)

view (vyōō) *n.* a belief; an opinion; a position about something. *Everyone seems to have a different **view** about what happened.* (p. 142)

viewpoint (vyōō′ point′) *n.* an opinion or something a person believes. *I want to hear your **viewpoint** on the situation.* (p. 326)

vineyard (vĭn′ yərd) *n.* the land where grapevines are grown, often to make wine. *There are many **vineyards** in Napa Valley, California.* (p. 246)

visionary (vĭzh′ ə nĕr′ ē) *n.* someone who has a dream and wants to make it real. *An inventor is a **visionary** who makes his or her dream come true.* (p. 304)

visualize (vĭzh′ ōō ə līz′) *v.* picture something in your mind. *Before Salvador paints a picture, he will **visualize** his subject.* (p. 17)

voice (vois) *n.* the way a person's writing reflects the writer. *The narrator's **voice** was sad but strong.* (p. 224)

volunteer (vŏl′ ən tîr′) *v.* help someone or do something for free. *Helga likes to **volunteer** her time at the animal shelter.* (p. 314)

walnut tree a tall tree with nuts you can eat. *My brother and I eat the nuts from the **walnut tree** in our backyard.* (p. 247)

water hose a long tube used to carry water. *I use the **water hose** to wash my car.* (p. 248)

weary (wîr′ ē) *adj.* tired. *I grew **weary** from working such long hours.* (p. 245)

weathering (wĕth′ ər ĭng) *n.* a change or hardening of something caused by the weather. ***Weathering** has caused the gate to rust.* (p. 111)

website (wĕb sīt) *n.* a place or address on the Internet where World Wide Web documents can be found. (p. 150)

wholly (hō′ lē) *adv.* totally; completely. (p. 187)

work out run, lift weights, and exercise. *I **work out** every morning to stay in shape.* (p. 98)

ya esora Spanish for "it's time." (p. 243)

yellow jacket *n.* a wasp; a yellow winged insect, like a bee, that stings. *Anthony was stung by a **yellow jacket**.* (p. 111)

INDEX

A

a/an, 91, 127
abbreviations, capitalizing, 119
action verbs, 107, 174, 176, 229, 232
active reading, 48–59
active voice, 175, 235
adjective(s), 106, 294–295, 345
   making comparisons with, 203, 298
   position in sentence, 115, 292
   strong, clear, 107, 111
adjective clauses with *that* and *which*, 227
adjective phrases, 296–297, 301
adverb(s), 295, 345
   making comparisons with, 299
   position in sentence, 293
   spelling, 301
adverb phrases, 296–297, 301
agreement, subject-verb, 147, 178–179
an/a, 91, 127
and, to combine sentences, 69, 71
apostrophes
   in forming contractions, 124
   in forming possessive nouns, 124
   to show missing letters or numbers, 124
Argument Chart, 354
arguments
   parts of, 326–327
   supportive, 328
audience for writing, 39
author's purpose, 303, 307
autobiographies, 129, 134, 136–147
   cause and effect in, 139, 141
   feelings about author, 144
   forming impression in, 145
   key events in, 140–143
   point of view in, 129, 138

B

bar graphs, 151–154
bibliographies, 218
   preparing, 225
biographies, 134, 138

C

boldface terms and headings, 194, 196
brainstorming, 40, 220
business letters, 339–341
but, to combine sentences, 69, 71

capital letters
   to begin a sentence, 47, 61, 65
   in letters, 334–335
   for proper nouns, 65, 118–119
cause-effect order, 95, 101, 139
   in autobiographies, 139, 141
   in expository paragraphs, 166–167
   signal words for, 101
Cause-Effect Organizer, 101, 141, 166, 170, 213
Chapter Notes, 199
chapters, 194, 196
characterization, 88, 280, 285
Character Map, 260
characters, 258, 262
   analyzing, 126
   developing, 260, 280–281, 286
Character Trait Web, 146
chronological order, 268–269
clauses, 62, 65
   adjective, 227
   dependent, 65, 69
   independent, 65, 69
climax, 257
close reading, 51
combining sentences, 63, 71, 293
commands, 68
commas, to set off dialogue, 190, 281, 289
common nouns, 118, 120
comparatives, 292, 298–299
comparing and contrasting, 51, 57, 94, 96–97, 202, 318
complaint letters, 325, 340
complete predicates, 64
complete subjects, 64
complex sentences, 69
compound sentences, 69
compound subjects, 103
   verb agreement with, 179
computer, using, for writing, 329
computer catalog, 225

D

conclusions, drawing, 50, 56, 83, 207
concrete nouns, 107
conflicts, 261
conjunctions, 345, 352
connecting words in combining sentences, 63, 69, 71, 352
connotations, 306
contractions, apostrophes in forming, 124
count nouns, 121, 331

days, capitalizing, 118
demonstrating, 238
denotations, 306
dependent clauses, 65, 69
descriptive paragraphs, 104–115
   adjectives in, strong and clear, 111
   details and images in, 109–110, 112–113
   main idea in, 108
   subject in, 108
   tips for writing, 106–107
details, 109–110, 112–113
   adding, 274
   organizing, 41, 271–272
   supporting, 326
Details and Statement Organizer, 70
dialogue, 190, 281, 289
direct objects, 349
Double-entry Journal, 27, 50, 58, 143
drafting, 38, 42, 222–223, 286
drama, 134

E

editing, 39, 44, 224, 274, 287
   peer, 227
editorials, 325
email, 338
end punctuation, 47, 61, 68
   with quotation marks, 190
essay questions, 212–213
essays, 134, 139
Evaluation Chart, 214
exaggeration, 323
exclamation marks, 68, 353
exclamations, 47, 68
exposition, 256

INDEX

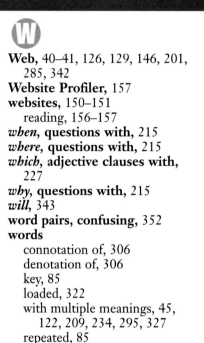

AUTHOR/TITLE INDEX

TERMS AND ELEMENTS OF LITERATURE

SKILLS AND FEATURES

Acknowledgments

TEXT CREDITS

18 (26, 27, 29, 30, 31, 32, 49, 50) "Immigrants" by Pat Mora is reprinted with permission from the publisher of *Borders* (Houston: Arte Público Press—University of Houston, 1986). **19** (50) "Saying Yes" copyright © by Diana Chang. Reprinted by permission of the author. **20** (21, 22, 51, 52, 54, 56, 58) "Ellis Island" from *The Remembered Earth*, edited by Geary Hobson, 1979. (Red Earth Press, Albuquerque). Reprinted by permission of Barbara S. Kouts Literary Agent. **57** "Fame is a Bee," reprinted by permission of the publishers and the Trustees of Amherst College from THE POEMS OF EMILY DICKINSON, Thomas H. Johnson, ed., Cambridge, Mass.: The Belknap Press of Harvard University Press, Copyright © 1951, 1955, 1979 by the President and Fellows of Harvard College. **61** Excerpt from LASTING ECHOES: AN ORAL HISTORY OF NATIVE AMERICAN PEOPLE. Copyright © 1997 by Joseph Bruchac, reprinted by permission of Harcourt, Inc. **74** (75, 76, 77, 78, 81, 84, 85, 86, 87, 91, 101) From THE HOUSE ON MANGO STREET. Copyright © 1984 by Sandra Cisneros. Published by Vintage Books, a division of Random House, Inc., and in hardcover by Alfred A. Knopf in 1994. Reprinted by permission of Susan Bergholz Literary Services, New York. All rights reserved. **96** (98, 99, 100) From *Stories from El Barrio*, by Piri Thomas. Reprinted by permission of the author. **105** (108, 109, 110, 111, 112) From MANIAC MAGEE by Jerry Spinelli. Copyright © 1990 by Jerry Spinelli. By permission of Little, Brown and Company, (Inc.) **117** From ROSA PARKS: MY STORY by Rosa Parks with Jim Haskins, copyright © 1992 by Rosa Parks. Used by permission of Dial Books for Young Readers, A Division of Penguin Young Readers Group, A Member of Penguin Group (USA) Inc., 345 Hudson Street, New York, NY 10014. All rights reserved. **119** Cover from TO BE A SLAVE by Julius Lester, illustrated by Tom Feelings, copyright © 1968 by Tom Feelings, illustrations. Used by permission of Puffin Books, A Division of Penguin Young Readers Group, A Member of Penguin Group (USA) Inc., 345 Hudson Street, New York, NY 10014. All rights reserved. **130** (131, 132, 133, 137, 138, 140, 142, 144, 166) THE INVISIBLE THREAD. Reprinted with permission of Simon & Schuster Books for Young Readers, an imprint of Simon & Schuster Children's Publishing Division from THE INVISIBLE THREAD by Yoshiko Uchida. Copyright © 1991 Yoshiko Uchida. **138** (186, 187, 188, 189, 190) *Harriet Tubman: Conductor on the Underground Railroad*. Reprinted by the permission of Russell & Volkening as agents for the author.

Copyright © 1955 by Ann Petry, renewed 1983 by Ann Petry. **139** USA TODAY. Copyright May 23–26, 2003. Reprinted with permission. **139** From *The Man Made of Words*. Copyright © 1997 by N. Scott Momaday. Reprinted by permission of St. Martin's Press, LLC. **149** (150, 151, 152, 153, 154, 156) U.S. Census Bureau. **150** Chicago Public Schools. Used by permission. **166** From THE BRACELET by Yoshiko Uchida, illustrated by Joanna Yardley, copyright © 1993 by Joanna Yardley, illustrations. Used by permission of Philomel Books, A Division of Penguin Young Readers Group, A Member of Penguin Group (USA) Inc., 345 Hudson Street, New York, NY 10014. All rights reserved. **166** University of Washington Press. Used by permission. **173** From TWO OR THREE THINGS I KNOW FOR SURE by Dorothy Allison, copyright © 1995 by Dorothy Allison. Used by permission of Dutton, a division of Penguin Group (USA) Inc. **193** (194, 195, 196) Excerpt from HARCOURT HORIZONS: UNITED STATES HISTORY: BEGINNINGS, copyright © 2003, reprinted by permission of Harcourt, Inc. **194** From AMERICA WILL BE in HOUGHTON MIFFLIN SOCIAL STUDIES by Armento, et al. Copyright © 1999 by Houghton Mifflin Company. Reprinted by permission of Houghton Mifflin Company. All rights reserved. **218** Chicago Public Library. **219** Google. **242** (243, 244, 245, 246, 247, 248, 249, 250, 251, 259) *The Circuit* by Francisco Jiménez. Used by permission of University of New Mexico Press. **267** (269, 273) "One Last Time," from *Living Up the Street* by Gary Soto. Used by permission of the author. **281** (282, 283, 284) From *Grandpa Was a Cowboy and an Indian and Other Stories* by Virginia Driving Hawk Sneve. Reprinted by permission of the University of Nebraska Press. © 2000 by Virginia Driving Hawk Sneve. **294** (296, 300) From ALMOST A WOMAN (HARD) by Esmeralda Santiago. © 1998 by Perseus Books Group. Reproduced with permission of Perseus Books Group in format Textbook via Copyright Clearance Center. **304** (305, 306, 307) "Lessons of Dr. Martin Luther King, Jr." by Cesar Chavez. TM/© 2004 the Cesar E. Chavez Foundation. www.chavezfoundation.org **309** Reprinted with permission from Pacific Cycle, LLC, owners of the Schwinn, Mongoose and GT trademarks. **311** Map © 2004 Chicago Transit Authority. All rights reserved. Used with permission. **314** Chicago Transit Authority. Used with permission. **316** Canon USA **321** (323, 327) From MALCOLM X: BY ANY MEANS NECESSARY by Walter Dean Myers. Copyright © 1993 by Walter Dean Myers. Reprinted by permission of Scholastic Inc. **356** Pronunciation Key, Copyright © 2003 by Houghton Mifflin Company. Reproduced by permission from The American Heritage Student Dictionary.

PHOTO CREDITS

4 *upper right* ©Royalty-Free/CORBIS **4** *lower right* ©Getty Images **5** *upper right* ©Getty Images **5** *lower right* ©Getty Images **6** *upper right* ©Eileen Ryan Photography **6** *bottom* ©Eileen Ryan Photography **7** *upper right* ©Bettmann/CORBIS **7** *lower left* ©Karen Huntt/ CORBIS **8** *upper right* ©Horace Bristol/CORBIS **8** *bottom* ©Index Stock Imagery, Inc., **9** *upper right* ©Alan Bailey/ RubberBall Productions/ PictureQuest **9** *bottom* ©Roger Ressmeyer/ CORBIS **10** *upper right* ©Courtesy of Library of Congress **10** *lower right* ©Jose Luis Pelaez, Inc./CORBIS **11** *upper right* ©Shepard Sherbell/CORBIS **11** *bottom* ©Getty Images **12** *upper right* ©Courtesy of Library of Congress **12–13** *bottom* ©Charles O'Rear/CORBIS **13** *upper right* ©Eileen Ryan Photography **14** *upper right* ©Bob Adelman/ Magnum Photos **14** *lower right* ©Getty Images **15** *upper right* ©Courtesy of Library of Congress **15** *bottom* ©Roger Ressmeyer/CORBIS **16** *center background* ©Bettmann/ CORBIS **16** *upper right* ©Najlah Feanny/ CORBIS SABA **16** *center left* ©Bettmann/ CORBIS **16** *lower right* ©Najlah Feanny/ CORBIS SABA **17** *upper right* ©SuperStock **17** *top* ©Tom Stewart/CORBIS **18** *center left* © Jerry Tobias/ CORBIS **18–19** *lower right* ©Bill Ross/ CORBIS **19** *upper right* © Tom Nebbia/ CORBIS **19** *center background* © Royalty-Free/ CORBIS **19** *lower left* © Gareth Brown/ CORBIS **20** *upper right* ©Royalty-Free/ CORBIS **20** *lower left* ©Bettmann/ CORBIS **21** *top* ©Bettmann/ CORBIS **21** *lower right* ©Bettmann/ CORBIS **22** *lower right* © Hulton-Deutsch Collection/ CORBIS **23** *top* © Cheron Bayna **23** *center left* © Gordon Robotham **23** *lower left* © Tom Stock **24** *upper left* ©John Schaefer, Director, Children's Media Workshop **24** *center* ©Getty Images **25** *upper left* © Jose Luis Pelaez, Inc./ CORBIS **25** *center*

upper left ©Dejan Patic/CORBIS **139** *bottom center* ©Time Inc./Time Life Pictures/ Getty Images **140** *upper left* ©Michael Freeman/CORBIS **141** *upper right* ©Historical Picture Archive/CORBIS **142** *lower left* ©Hulton/Getty Images **143** *center* ©Harry Gruyaert/ Magnum Photos **144** *upper left* ©Courtesy of the Bancroft Library, University of California, Berkeley **144** *lower left* ©Roger Ressmeyer/ CORBIS **145** *upper right* ©Eileen Ryan Photography **147** *lower right* ©John Schaefer, Director, Children's Media Workshop **148** *upper left* ©John Schaefer, Director, Children's Media Workshop **148** *center* ©Peter Guttman/CORBIS **150** *top* ©Getty Images **152** *upper left* ©Getty Images **155** *lower right* ©Steve McCurry/Magnum Photos **157** *upper right* ©Getty Images **158** *lower left* © Royalty-Free/CORBIS **159** *lower right* ©John Schaefer, Director, Children's Media Workshop **160** *upper left* ©John Schaefer, Director, Children's Media Workshop **160** *center* ©Courtesy of Library of Congress **161** *bottom* ©Courtesy of Library of Congress **162** *lower left* ©Courtesy of Library of Congress **162** *lower right* ©Michael S. Yamashita/ CORBIS **163** *lower left* ©AP Photo/ National Park Service **163** *lower right* ©Courtesy of the Bancroft Library, University of California, Berkeley **164** *lower right* ©Courtesy of the Bancroft Library, University of California, Berkeley **164** *upper left* ©Bill Aron/ Photo Edit **165** *lower left* ©Courtesy of the Bancroft Library, University of California, Berkeley **165** *lower right* ©Courtesy of the Bancroft Library, University of California, Berkeley **166** *upper left* ©Courtesy of the Bancroft Library, University of California, Berkeley **166** *lower left* ©Courtesy of the Bancroft Library, University of California, Berkeley **167** *upper right* ©Courtesy of Library of Congress **168** *upper left* ©Courtesy of Library of Congress **168** *center left* ©Courtesy of Library of Congress **168** *center right* ©Courtesy of Library of Congress **170** *lower left* ©Courtesy of Library of Congress **171** *lower right* ©John Schaefer, Director, Children's Media Workshop **172** *upper left* ©John Schaefer, Director, Children's Media Workshop **172** *center* ©Todd Powell/ Index Stock Imagery, Inc. **173** *lower left* ©Joseph Sohm; ChromoSohm Inc./CORBIS **173** *lower right* ©Getty Images **174** *upper left* ©2004 PunchStock **174** *upper right* ©2004 PunchStock **174** *lower left* ©Patrik Giardino/ CORBIS **174** *lower right* ©Royalty-Free/ CORBIS **175** *lower left* ©Alan Bailey/ RubberBall Productions/ PictureQuest **175** *lower right* ©Peter Poby/ CORBIS **176** *center left* ©Duomo/ CORBIS **177** *center* ©Reuters/ CORBIS **178** *left* ©Getty Images **179** *upper right* ©Michael S. Yamashita/ CORBIS **179** *lower right* ©Gabe Palmer/ CORBIS **180** *right* ©Lawrence Manning/ CORBIS **182** *lower left* ©Jim Cummins/ CORBIS **182** *bottom center* ©Getty Images **182** *lower right* ©Royalty-Free/CORBIS **183** *lower right* ©John Schaefer, Director, Children's Media Workshop **184** *upper right* ©DiMaggio/Kalish/ CORBIS **184** *bottom* ©CORBIS **185** *upper right* ©Courtesy of Library of Congress **186** *upper left* ©Smithsonian American Art Museum, Washington, DC/ Art Resource, NY **187** *center* ©renowned artist Paul Collins-collinsart.com **188** *center* © On to Liberty, 1867, Kaufmann, Theodor (1814–1887)/Private Collection, Christie's Images/Bridgeman Art Library **191** *lower left* ©From the Ann Petry Collection in The Howard Gotlieb Archival Research Center at Boston University **192** *upper left* ©John Schaefer, Director, Children's Media Workshop **192** *center* ©Mark Peterson/ CORBIS **194** *top center* ©Courtesy of Library of Congress **195** *upper right* ©Eileen Ryan Photography **195** *bottom, far left* ©The Charleston Museum, Charleston, South Carolina **195** *lower left* ©Scala / Art Resource, NY **196** *upper left* ©Royalty-Free/ CORBIS **196** *bottom center* ©The Charleston Museum, Charleston, South Carolina **196** *bottom right* ©Scala / Art Resource, NY **197** *bottom center* ©Eileen Ryan Photography **198** *bottom* ©Getty Images **199** *center right* ©North Wind Picture Archives **200** *bottom* ©2004 Gwendolyn Knight Lawrence/ Artists Rights Society (ARS), New York **201** *lower right* ©Eileen Ryan Photography **202** *lower right* ©Getty Images **203** *lower right* ©John Schaefer, Director, Children's Media Workshop **204** *upper left* ©John Schaefer, Director, Children's Media Workshop **204** *center* ©Getty Images **205** *upper right* © The Underground Railroad Aids with a Runaway Slave, Davies, Arthur Bowen (1862–1928)/Private Collection/ Bridgeman Art Library **205** *center right* ©Courtesy of Library of Congress **205** *lower left* ©Ariel Skelley/ CORBIS **206** *lower left* ©Eileen Ryan Photography **207** *upper left* ©Courtesy of Library of Congress **207** *upper right* ©Courtesy of Library of Congress **208** *upper left* ©Eileen Ryan Photography **209** *center left* ©Eileen Ryan Photography **209** *lower right* ©Jose Luis Pelaez, Inc./ CORBIS **210** *lower left* ©Bettmann/ CORBIS **211** *upper right* ©Courtesy of Library of Congress **212** *lower left* ©Courtesy of Library of Congress **214** *lower left* ©Courtesy of Library of Congress **215** *lower right* ©John Schaefer, Director, Children's Media Workshop **216** *upper left* ©John Schaefer, Director, Children's Media Workshop **216** *center* ©Courtesy of Library of Congress **217** *center* ©Getty Images **218** *upper left* ©2004 PunchStock **218** *lower left* ©Jose Luis Pelaez, Inc./ CORBIS **218** *lower right* ©Jose Luis Pelaez, Inc./ CORBIS **219** *lower left* ©Jose Luis Pelaez, Inc./ CORBIS **220** *bottom* ©Courtesy of Library of Congress **221** *center right* ©Schomburg Center/ Art Resource, NY **222** *upper left* ©Getty Images **222** *lower right* ©Courtesy of Library of Congress **223** *bottom* ©Getty Images **224** *lower left* ©Bob Krist/ CORBIS **227** *lower right* ©John Schaefer, Director, Children's Media Workshop **228** *upper left* ©John Schaefer, Director, Children's Media Workshop **228** *center* ©Bettmann/ CORBIS **229** *upper right* ©Bettmann/ CORBIS **229** *upper left* ©Bettmann/ CORBIS **229** *center right* ©Bettmann/ CORBIS **229** *lower left* ©Bettmann/ CORBIS **230** *lower left* ©John Van Hasselt/ CORBIS **231** *lower right* ©Courtesy of Library of Congress **232** *lower left* ©Bettmann/ CORBIS **233** *upper right* ©Courtesy of Library of Congress **233** *lower right* ©Courtesy of Library of Congress **234** *lower left* ©Nathan Benn/ CORBIS **235** *upper right* ©Shepard Sherbell/CORBIS **236** *lower right* ©Malcah Zeldis/Art Resource, NY **237** *lower right* ©Royalty-free/CORBIS **238** *lower left* ©Courtesy of Library of Congress **239** *lower right* ©John Schaefer, Director, Children's Media Workshop **240** *upper right* ©Courtesy of Library of Congress **240** *center* ©Bernd Obermann/ CORBIS **240** *lower left* ©Peter Turnley/CORBIS **241** *upper right* ©Bettmann/ CORBIS **242** *lower left* ©Courtesy of Library of Congress **243** *upper right* ©Sean O'Neill **243** *lower right* ©Stephanie Maze/ CORBIS **244** *upper left* ©Courtesy of Library of Congress **245** *lower right* ©Kevin R. Morris/ CORBIS **246** *center right* ©Royalty Free/CORBIS **246** *center left* ©CORBIS **247** *center right* ©Dale C. Spartas/ CORBIS **248** *lower left* ©Keith Dannemiller/CORBIS SABA **249** *center right* ©Courtesy of Library of Congress **250** *lower left* ©Bettmann/ CORBIS **251** *lower right* ©Courtesy of Library of Congress **252** *bottom* ©CORBIS **253** *bottom* ©Charles Barry, Santa Clara University **254** *upper left* ©John Schaefer, Director, Children's Media Workshop **254** *center* ©James A. Sugar/ CORBIS **255** *upper right* ©Charles O'Rear/ CORBIS **255** *center left* ©Courtesy of Library of Congress **255** *center right* ©Courtesy of Library of Congress **255** *bottom* ©Creatas **256** *lower left* ©Courtesy of Library of Congress **257** *upper right* ©Ken